Joseph Priestley

An appeal to the public, on the subject of the riots in Birmingham

Joseph Priestley

An appeal to the public, on the subject of the riots in Birmingham

ISBN/EAN: 9783337305352

Printed in Europe, USA, Canada, Australia, Japan

Cover: Foto ©ninafisch / pixelio.de

More available books at **www.hansebooks.com**

AN

APPEAL

TO

THE PUBLIC,

ON THE SUBJECT OF

The Riots in Birmingham.

TO WHICH ARE ADDED,

STRICTURES ON A PAMPHLET,

INTITLED

Thoughts on the late Riot at Birmingham.'

By *Joseph Priestley*, LL.D. F.R.S. &c.

QUIS NOVUS ISTE FUROR; QUO NUNC, QUO TENDITIS?
VIRGIL.

Birmingham,
PRINTED BY J. THOMPSON;
SOLD BY J. JOHNSON, NO. 72, ST. PAUL'S CHURCH YARD, LONDON.
MDCCXCL

THE DEDICATION.

To the People of England.

MY COUNTRYMEN,

I PRESENT myfelf before you in a fituation that ought to engage your attention, becaufe, in fact, it no lefs concerns yourfelves than me. It has hitherto been your great boaft, that you were poffeffed of the beft form of government in the world; that in England all men are fubject to the laws, from the king upon the throne to the meaneft perfon in the realm; that no man can be long confined, much lefs punifhed, without the fent-

ence

ence of law ; that whenever any man is accufed of a crime, opportunity is given him to make his defence, in the prefence of his accufers and of the witneffes ag iinft him ; and that in all cafes he muft be tried by his peers, by perfons in a fituation in all refpects fimilar to his own, fo that they them-felves may expect the fame treatment in the fame circumftances. Without this you are fenfible there can be no equal law, or equal liberty. It has alfo been the great pride of Englifh-men, that with us the prefs is free; fo that any opinion whatever, civil or religious, may be openly propofed, and difcuffed, without any apprehenfion of danger.

A jealoufy with refpect to law has ever diftinguifhed Englifhmen, fo that you have been content to fuffer the greateft pefts of fociety to efcape

punifhment,

punifhment, rather than the law fhould be violated in their perfons ; reafoning juftly, that it is better that one man, though ever fo criminal, fhould efcape punifhment, than that a precedent fhould be eftablifhed, in confequence of which thoufands of innocent perfons might be expofed to fuffering ; and this might be the cafe if any arbitrary mode of proceeding fhould be encouraged in courts of juftice. Should a perfon actually condemned to die for the greateft crime, be put to death otherwife than by the fentence of a judge, and by the direction of the fheriff, it would be deemed *murder* ; fo facred do you juftly efteem the regular execution of the laws, not bearing that any punifhment fhould be inflicted but fuch as the law directs, and in the precife manner directed by it. Need I then to fay what you ought to think of the mode of proceeding againft me

and

and my friends at Birmingham, when all that I am charged with is the freedom of my writings?

I was born an Englifhman as well any of you. Though labouring under civil difabilities, as a Diffenter, I have long contributed my fhare to the fupport of government, and fuppofed I had the protection of its conftitution and laws for my inheritance. But I have found myfelf greatly deceived; and fo may any of you, if, like me, you fhould, with or without caufe, be fo unfortunate as to incur popular odium. For then, as you have feen in my cafe, without any form of trial whatever, without any intimation of your crime, or of your danger, your houfes and all your property may be deftroyed, and you may not have the good fortune to efcape with life, as I have done. Other innocent

nocent perfons alfo may be involved in the fame calamities with yourfelves. What are the old French *Lettres de Cachet*, or the horrors of the late de-molifhed *Baftile*, compared to this? Make then my cafe, what it foon may be, your own, and you will not rate the advantages of the Britifh conftitution fo high as you have generally done. For in what part of the world could a peaceable citizen have had lefs protection of law, or enjoy lefs *fecurity*, which is the great end of all civil go-vernment?

If we offend againft the laws, let us be tried according to law, and fuf-fer the penalty denounced by it. I do not flee my country, and am at all times amenable to the laws of it. But as you would not allow me to judge in my own cafe, and take my revenge upon any perfon whom I might have conceived

conceived to have injured me, let not others wreak their vengeance upon me.

You will fay that fuch outrages as thefe cannot be prevented under any government, that they are like hurricanes or earthquakes; fo that to complain of them, is to complain of the order of nature and providence. But not to fay that fufficient provifion might eafily be made to prevent any diforder of this kind, our complaint is that the injury is not univerfally refented. The Country does not yet fufficiently feel the difgrace that has been done to it, and great numbers rather exult in our fufferings, fo that we are far from thinking ourfelves fecure from farther injuries. Many perfons not only exprefs no difapprobation of our fufferings, or of the illegal manner in which they were inflicted, but

but plainly enough threaten us with more outrages of the fame kind*.

Before you, therefore, I accufe my townfmen, and many others, whom I have defcribed, of the greateft in-juftice and cruelty; and not having had an opportunity *before* my pu-nifhment, I now *after* it, plead my caufe, and explain my whole conduct in this *Appeal*. Rather, the laws themfelves, the laws that have been violated in my cafe, complain that *they* have been infringed, and that a

---

* Among other circumftances which prove this, is the following extract from a printed paper, dated *Birmingham Conftitutional Tavern*, Oct. 17, 1791, fent to me by the poft from Birmingham. " But let them" (the Diffenters) " beware——The *arm of Loyalty* has been raifed againft " them—Their *prefent deportment* is in proof that it was " *needful*. The bolt, though fhot, is not *intirely fpent*, " and the people at large have too much affection for their " KING, and reverence for their prefent GOVERNMENT, " to fuffer either of them to be attacked with *impunity*, by " *the arts of the feditious*. The lion is too magnanimous " to trample upon the *fallen—Mifufe not* then his noble " nature, ye Diffenters—for if ye *again aroufe him*—Your " Commentator Mr. Keir may *explain* the *confequences*."

principle

principle which leads to all confufion, and the diffolution of all government, has ufurped their place. And no foreign enemy can be fo dangerous to you as this within yourfelves.

But we fuffer, it is faid, as Diffenters from the eftablifhed religion. On this account we have a double title to protection. A Diffenter is one of a minority, and the Unitarian Diffenters, with whom I clafs myfelf, are a fmall minority, though an increafing one. We therefore ftand in greater need of the protection of law; and it is the more inexcufable to treat us ill, becaufe you have nothing to fear from us. You are more obliged to Diffenters than to other members of the community, as, befides bearing the whole expence of our own religion, we contribute our fhare to the expence of yours. If we be not defective in

any

any civil duty, why fhould we be expofed to any civil punifhment? Leave
our religion to our confciences, and to
God, whom alone it concerns, and
confider how you would wifh to be
treated if you lived in a country where
any other religion than your own was
profeffed. We are excluded, and we
think unjuftly, from civil employments
and emoluments. If you think proper to continue this *negative* punifhment, do not add *pofitive* ones, and
leaft of all encourage fuch as are illegal, and which may introduce evils of
an unknown nature and extent, which
even your lateft pofterity may feel.
For fuch has been the cafe of perfecution in other countries, even when it
was carried on in a much more unexceptionable manner than it has been
at Birmingham.

As to the *French Revolution*, the
defence and commemoration of which
has

has been imputed to myself and others as so great a crime, you will soon see it in a different light. The enormous expences of all modern European governments have opened the eyes of men to the nature and uses of government in general ; and in confequence of this, the whole of the Gothic Feudal fyftem, embracing matters both of a civil and ecclefiaftical nature, is beginning to fhake to its foundation. This will neceffarily produce a convulfion that will be felt in every ftate in Europe. All nations muft ultimately be benefited by it, though they may fuffer by the temporary fhock. But be affured that thofe countries will fuffer the leaft in which great *revolutions* will be prevented by temperate and feafonable *reforms*. Then we, who have fuffered by the fury of a mifguided populace (who have committed their lawlefs devaftations in the name of *the church* and *the King*)

King) shall be confidered as the martyrs of your liberties; and in the firm belief of this we joyfully bear all their outrages.

As individuals we pretend not to deferve your notice; but our cafe is general, and we hope it will lead you to refpect, if not us, at leaft the law, yourfelves, and your pofterity.

Though an advocate for reformation, I am a friend to the general principles of our conftitution; and as a well-wifher to my country, and every defcription of men in it, I fubfcribe myfelf,

Your injured Countryman,

J. PRIESTLEY.

London, Nov. 1, 1791.

F EW perfons who have addreffed the Public have ever been in circumftances which made it fo difficult to give fatisfaction to their different readers as I now am in, owing to their different opinions and prepoffeffions with refpect to the fubject of this Appeal. Thofe who have already formed their opinion as to the facts, will conclude that every account which reprefents them as having been different from what they have conceived them to be, is certainly falfe, if not from defign, yet from mifapprehenfion. They who are agreed with refpect to the *facts* will draw different *conclufions* from them ; and even they who agree both with refpect to the facts and the conclufions, will think very differently of the *temper* and *manner* in which they fhould be fpoken of, efpecially by myfelf, who am fo much a party concerned.

b   With

With refpect to my enemies, do what I will, I fhall be equally cenfured. With them all my facts will be falfehoods, the language of juft indignation will be infolence, and that of chriftian meeknefs either meannefs or hypocrify. I fhall therefore make myfelf perfectly eafy as to what *they* may fay of me. Where there is nothing to lofe, there is nothing to fear.

My friends whofe feelings are as different as their conftitutions, will expect that, writing as it were in a common caufe, I fhould exprefs their precife fentiments and feelings. But this being evidently impoffible, I can only exculpate them, by declaring that both the fentiments and the language of this work are folely my own, and fuch as arofe from my feelings at the time of writing, which was prefently after my arrival in London, while the fcenes that I have defcribed were frefh in my mind, with a very few alterations and additions occafioned by fubfequent accounts.

I make no apology for the feverity with which I have occafionally condemned the conduct of my adverfaries. For what greater

crimes

crimes can men commit with refpect to fociety, than thofe which they either have committed, or intended, and in which they now exult? But this implies no malice, or ill-will towards them. I fincerely pray for them in the language of the liturgy, for which they pretend to have fo nobly exerted themfelves, that as "my enemies, perfecu- " tors, and flanderers, God would forgive " them, and turn their hearts." As to the doctrine of chriftian meeknefs, forgivenefs of injuries, and love of our enemies, it fhould be interpreted by our Saviour's own conduct. For it will not be faid that *he* felt otherwife than he ought to have done with refpect to *his* enemies; and certainly his language is invariably that of the ftrongeft indignation and reproof. The fame was that of Paul, and of all the apoftles, to- wards thofe who, in their opinion, cor- rupted the gofpel, and oppofed their mi- niftry.

A ftrong fenfe of the impropriety of men's fentiments and conduct naturally ex- preffes itfelf in indignant language, though, when coming from a chriftian, it will al- ways be accompanied with the moft fincere compaffion for the ftate of depravity into

which

which malignity of mind neceffarily finks men; and all that chriftianity can do, is earneftly to wifh and pray, that our adver-faries may be brought to a better ftate of mind, in order to their being entitled to our complacency, and forgivenefs in the proper fenfe of the word.

With refpect to the high church party in this country, I may be confidered as in a ftate of open war. I utterly diflike their prin-ciples and maxims, as they do mine; and I fcruple not to take any fair opportunity of expreffing this diflike in the moft unequivo-cal language. Let them do the fame with refpect to my principles; but let us obferve the rules of honourable war. If, however, they chufe to proceed as they have begun to do at Birmingham, I do not wifh to follow their example. They will find in time that to conquer in that manner is no victory. To conciliate thefe perfons I confider as a thing abfolutely impoffible, and therefore not worth attempting. Whatever tends moft completely to my juftification, will only irritate them the more; as was the cafe with my *Letter to the Inhabitants of Birmingham.* They are *parties* againft whom I plead; and thofe that I wifh to conciliate are our com-

mon

mon judges, our countrymen in general, the world at large, and efpecially pofterity.

Whatever has been my indignation againft my enemies, I have never forgotten, and I hope never fhall forget, that their conduct forms a part of the plan of a wife and juft providence; that they, as well as myfelf, have a proper place in the general fyftem, the great fcope of which is general and infinite good, of which they alfo, in due time, will partake; though I rejoice, and am truly thankful, that their place is not mine. On this occafion I fhall take the liberty to quote what I wrote long ago in the *Dedication* of my *Treatife on Philofo-phical Neceffity* to the late excellent Dr. Jebb.

" You and I, Sir, rejoice in the belief,
" that the whole human race are under the
" fame wholefome difcipline, and that they
" will all derive the moft valuable advan-
" tages from it, though in different degrees,
" in different ways, and at different periods;
" that even the perfecutors are only giving
" the precedence to the perfecuted, and ad-
" vancing them to a much higher degree of
" perfection and happinefs; and that they
" muft themfelves undergo a more fevere

b 3   " difcipline

" difcipline than that which they are the
" means of adminiftering to others."

" With this perfuafion we cannot but
" confider every *Being* and every *thing* in
" a favourable light. Every perfon with
" whom we have any connexion is a friend,
" and every event in life is a benefit, while
" God is equally the father, and the friend,
" of the whole creation."

Feeling myfelf to be a publicly *injured
perfon*, I cannot abandon the fenfe of dignity, peculiar to that character, or not
feel the fuperiority which it gives me over
my *injurers*, and which will neceffarily influence the language in which I fpeak of
them.

If I be afked whom I confider as my enemies, as holding principles moft oppofite to
mine (which has been the true caufe of their
animofity towards me) I anfwer without
hefitation, all thofe, of the clergy or laity,
who are the avowed advocates for every
thing continuing as it now is, in church
and ftate. Their genuine fentiments may
be feen in the late *Addrefs of the Town of
Birmingham to the King*, in which they fay
that

that " they will oppofe with their lives and " fortunes, every attempt at innovation."

Thofe who diflike this language, who are a great number, even among the clergy, I am far from confidering in the light of adverfaries. They are friends, engaged in the fame caufe, though occupying different pofts. We equally wifh that the world, and every thing in it, fhould improve. We think there are things both in church and ftate that require reformation, and that in every country pretending to freedom, there fhould be full liberty to point thefe out, and make them the fubjects of free dif-cuffion.

From the love that we bear to our country, and even to our enemies in it, we think it our duty to point out whatever we think to be defective in its conftitution ; and we fhall do it with the more freedom and energy, from confidering the dreadful evils which have lately arifen from thefe defects at Birmingham. What was there worfe than this that took place during the great revo-lution in France, which I and many others confider as having iffued in a moft glorious ftate of liberty and happinefs? Whereas, all

that

that we yet fee at Birmingham, is the mad triumph of bigotry, and fuch as was feldom exhibited even in ages of acknowledged bar-barifm*.

I truft, however, that though nothing but *evil* appears at prefent, much *good* will in due time arife from it, if not to this country, in which the fpectacle is exhibited, yet to Europe, and the world at large. To every reflecting mind the riots in Birmingham, muft fet in a peculiarly ftrong light the baneful nature of bigotry, and the evils to which men are expofed in a country deftitute of a good police. Even the laws of this country, whofe great boaft it has been that it is the only feat of *true liberty,*

---

* How different are the fpectacles that are now exhibited in France and in England? Here bigotry has been foftered, and has acquired new ftrength. There it is almoft extinct. Here the friends of the eftablifhment are burning the meeting-houfes of the Diffenters, with all the rage of Crufaders; while in Paris one of the churches has been procured by the Proteftants. It was opened by one of their minifters to a crouded audience, among whom were many Catholics, all in tears of joy for the happy change. The preacher's text was, *The night is far fpent, the day is at hand.* Here we muft rather preach from Ifaiah lx. 2. *Behold, darknefs fhall cover the land, and grofs darknefs the people.*

are

are in a great degree intolerant; but the
fpirit of the people, if not that of the government, appears to be much more fo, and
the world will foon fee to what this leads.

If it be to *good*, it will be a new thing in
this old world of ours, viz. that perfecution,
and that by a mob, legiflating, judging, and
punifhing, in the inftant, is favourable to
truth, and confequently to virtue and happinefs. But if, which is moft to be apprehended, this bufinefs, which certainly was
evil in itfelf, fhould lead to farther evil, it
will be another, and I wifh it may be the
laft, inftance of the baneful effects of intolerance, and will alfo fhow in a ftriking
light the evils that arife from a civil eftablifhment of chriftianity. If this be the
cafe, and the world fhould take warning by
it, I fhall not think our fufferings, great as
they have been, a fubject of lamentation;
confidering myfelf, and my fellow-fufferers,
as the inftructers, and benefactors of mankind.

Some parts of this Appeal, I am well
aware, will expofe me to the charge of
vanity, efpecially the *addreffes* which I have
thought proper to fubjoin to it. But they
were

were in a great meafure neceflary to the narrative part of the work, particularly thofe of my late congregation, and that of Leeds, as they will fhew that, notwith-ftanding my other purfuits, I did not, in their opinion, neglect the proper duties of my profeffion. The addrefs from the Academy of Sciences at Paris, will fhow in what light the riots at Birmingham are confidered by fcientifical perfons in a neighbouring and highly enlightened country; and that from Great Yarmouth, how they are thought of by Diffenters of different denominations at home*. I may likewife add in my juftification, that perfecution and calumny more than once extorted felf praife from an apoftle.

* As fome perfons may wifh to fee an account of all the addreffes I have hitherto received to this time, Nov. 1, 1791, I fhall briefly mention them with their dates.

From the Academy of Sciences at Paris, July 30, 1791.
From the Friends of the Conftitution at Lyons, Auguft 6.
From the Friends of the Conftitution at Nantz, Auguft 9.
From the Friends of the Conftitution at Marmande on the Garonne, Auguft 15.
From the Friends of the Conftitution at the Jacobins Rue St. Honoré, Paris, Auguft 16.
From the Friends of the Conftitution at Clermont, Auguft 20.
From the Friends of the Conftitution at Touloufe, September 21.

It will, however, be a gratification to my adverſaries to be informed, that, except

From the Miniſters and Members of the three denominations of Proteſtant Diſſenters in Great Yarmouth, July 29.

From the Miniſters and Members of the three denominations of Proteſtant Diſſenters in Maidſtone, Auguſt 8.

From the Society of the Old Meeting in Birmingham, Auguſt 21.

From the Proteſtant Diſſenters of Mill Hill Chapel, Leeds, Auguſt 24.

From the Committee of Proteſtant Diſſenting Laymen and Miniſters of the three denominations in the Weſt Riding of the county of York, September 1, at their quarterly meeting.

From the Proteſtant Diſſenting miniſters of the three denominations at Llechryd, South Wales, Auguſt 25.

From the Philoſophical Society at Derby, September 3.

From the Proteſtant Diſſenting Miniſters of Exeter, September 7, at their half yearly meeting.

From the Revolution Society at Norwich, September 8.

From the Conſtitutional Society at Mancheſter, September 13.

From the Students at the New College, Hackney, September 21.

From the Proteſtant Diſſenters belonging to ſeveral congregations in the Southern and Weſtern parts of the county of Somerſet, at their annual meeting, September 28.

From ſeveral Proteſtant Diſſenting miniſters in the neighbourhood of Bolton, Lancaſhire.

From the Proteſtant Diſſenters of the cities of Briſtol and Bath.

From the Revolution Society at London.

in one inftance, viz. the addrefs from the
Philofophical Society at Derby, I have received no addrefs from any fet of perfons in
this country who have not profeffedly feparated themfelves from the reft on the principle of civil or religious liberty. Indeed,
I fear there may be even literary focieties in
England, and much more the inhabitants
of whole towns, who, if they formed any
refolutions on the fubject, would make
them more favourable to the rioters, than
the fufferers at Birmingham; fo general, in
my prefent opinion, is the fpirit favourable
to church eftablifhments, and thofe high
maxims of government, by which the inftigators of the riots at Birmingham were
actuated. How long this will continue to
be the cafe, I do not fay.

Gratitude requires that I fhould fay I
have had very flattering profpects held out
to me if I would remove to France, where
both the laws, and the fpirit of the people,
would be much more favourable to me.
But there I fhould be in a manner ufelefs;
and as, according to the courfe of nature,
I have yet fome years of activity left, and I
can employ them to the moft advantage in
this country, I think it my duty to fpend
them

them in it. As to my perfonal fafety, I may furely hope that the horrid fcenes at Birmingham, which will long make it *a proverb and a bye word* in Europe, will not be repeated any where elfe. Or if they be, my life will always be at the difpofal of him that gave it.

If I were difpofed to boaft, it will be, like Paul, of my fufferings; and though his lift, no doubt, far exceeds mine, yet in one refpect I think I need not yield to him, or to any man whatever. I mean with re-fpect to *calumny*, which can hardly go deeper, or extend farther, than it has done with re-fpect to me. To fay nothing of old calum-nies, which are, however, now circulated with as much confidence as ever, fuch as my having declared that I would never reft till I had pulled down that impoftor Jefus Chrift; that I made a convert of Silas Deane to atheifm, &c. &c. &c. thoufands have been made to believe that I am not only a fpeculative republican, and an enemy to our prefent government by king, lords, and com-mons, but an advocate for abfolute anarchy or government by mobs, without any rule of proceeding whatever; that by mere mobs I ferioufly intended to fubvert the conftitution

tution in church and ſtate, and that Mr.
Ruſſell and myſelf had armed men in readi-
neſs to act under our orders for this purpoſe, ſo that there could not be a more
dangerous ſubject in any ſtate *.

* In a Song entitled *Old Mother Church*, deſcribing
the Diſſenters, are the two following ſtanzas.

> Sedition is their Creed,
> Feign'd ſheep, but wolves indeed,
>   How can we truſt?
> Gunpowder Prieſtley would,
> Deluge the throne with blood,
> And lay the great and good,
>   Low in the Duſt.

> Hiſt'ry thy page unfold.
> Did not their ſires of old,
>   Murder their king?
> And they would overthrow,
> King, lords, and biſhops too,
> And while they gave the blow,
>   Loyally ſing;

> O Lord our God ariſe,
> Scatter our enemies
>   And make them fall.
>   &c. &c. &c.

The following paragraph from p. 42, of an *Addreſs to
Unitarians*, by T. G. Hancock is ſo curious, that I ſhall
ſubjoin it to this note.

" Dr. Prieſtley at preſent ſeems a chaos in miniature,
not worth God's notice, has neither belief nor under-
ſtanding

With refpect to the fubject of this Appeal, the populace of Birmingham were made to believe that I not only dined at the Hotel on the fourteenth of July laft, but declared that, if no other perfon whatever would join me, I would dine there alone. At that dinner it was confidently faid, that I gave the toafts *No church, no king*, and *The king's head in a charger*. It was even afferted that I had conveyed gunpowder into one of the churches, and had contrived that it fhould explode during divine fervice, and fome pious ladies, I am well informed, actually forbore going to church under the apprehenfion of it. This report was ftrengthened by another, viz. that two barrels of gunpowder were certainly found in my houfe.

It has been advanced with equal confidence, and as little regard to truth, that no party fpirit exifted in Birmingham till my preaching and writing introduced it. It was

ftanding given him. For a careful analyfis proves his fpirit of the order of rebelling angels, his principles frothy and fiery, like fixed and inflammable air, mixed with gunpowder, his body a *terra damnata,* and the whole compound a *devil incarnate.* I hope Diffenters will be aware of his feduction, and take heed left they are deceived through philofophy.''

no wonder, they alſo ſaid, that I ſhould diſcover this turbulence here, when I had
ſhown the ſame ſpirit at Leeds, and had
been driven from that, and every other place
where I lived, in the ſame manner as I had
been from this. It was even ſaid that my
own congregation declared that I had miſled
them, and hoped, that I ſhould never be
permitted to return.

Nothing now remains but to charge me
with a robbery or houſe breaking; and then,
on ſuch evidence as that on which the preceding and many equally falſe allegations
gained credit, I may, by *a Warwickſhire
jury*, be legally convicted and executed;
the principal people of Birmingham not
interpoſing to procure me a pardon. If I
be ſo formidable an enemy to the church
and the ſtate as I have been repreſented, let
thoſe who call themſelves the friends of the
church and the king invent their lies, and
forge their letters for *this* purpoſe, and not
merely for the burning of my houſe, my
library, and laboratory. This was like
ſhaving the lion's beard, which will grow
again, when with the ſame razor, and with
much leſs trouble, they might have cut his
throat.

are

Let them, however, remember, if they believe any thing of the matter (for the moſt zealous friends of church eſtabliſhments, and the moſt unrelenting perſecutors of conſcientious men, are not always real believers in chriſtianity) that there is an *hereafter*, and other juries than thoſe of Worceſterſhire or Warwickſhire, before whom they muſt ſoon appear. To this judgment I appeal, and before it I cite my accuſers.

The reaſon why I have added *Strictures on the Pamphlet intitled* THOUGHTS ON THE LATE RIOTS AT BIRMINGHAM, which was publiſhed after the greater part of this Appeal was printed, was that, whether it came from any authority, as ſome have ſuppoſed, or not, it ſpeaks the genuine language of the high church party on the ſubject, ſuch as has appeared in a leſs concentrated ſtate in numberleſs paragraphs in the public newſpapers, and without ſuch authentic evidence, what has been ſaid of the low prejudice, the malignant ſpirit, and abſurd reaſoning of that party, would hardly be credible, eſpecially to my readers abroad. In any other view, this work would have been unworthy of any notice.

c   N. B. The

N. B. The Narrative part of this Appeal is in a manner confined to what I was witnefs to myfelf, and therefore chiefly relates to myfelf. For an account of the fufferings of others, I refer my readers to *An Authentic Account of the Riots in Birmingham*, printed by Mr. Belcher. And here I would obferve, that if, to the loffes that may be claimed in a court of juftice, be added thofe that were neceffarily occafioned by the riots, to many perfons who were driven from their houfes, obliged to remove their goods, and purchafe protection, &c. &c. the fum would be enormous. If the lofs of *peace of mind* could be eftimated by money, to what would it not amount? What then have not the pretended friends of the church and the king at Birmingham to anfwer for?

CONTENTS.

CONTENTS.

SECTION VI.

SECTION VII.

SECTION VIII.

SECTION IX.

SECTION X.

.............:.....

....

APPENDIX.

An

Copy

From

....

ADDENDA.

Errata et Corrigenda.

Preface, p. xxxii, l. 14, read *such a Warwickshire jury as the last*

P. 13, l. 5, dele *if any*

P. 23, l. 23, read *some persons*

P. 27, l. 5, add, I had also *Notes on all the Psalms*, which I had delivered from the pulpit

P. 47, l. 15, for *make*, read *have made*

P. 62, l. 12, for *No.* III. read *No.* V.

P. 70, l. 4, for *opinion*, read *opinions*

P. 83, l. 2, *(b)* for *the*, read *or the*

P. 84, l. 8, after *of me*, add, *and that without any truth*

P. 96, l. 12, read *many of them would*

P. 124, l. 18, for *to burn, viz.* read *viz. to burn*

P. 134, for *No.* V. read *No.* IV.

P. 142, l. 6, for *besiring*, read *desiring*

₊ *(b)* Signifies from the bottom of the page.

N. B. The first article of *the Reflections* is copied from the Preface to the *Letters to the Members of the New Jerusalem Church*, which was the first of my publications after the riots. That work will not fall into many hands, and if ever it be re-printed, that part of the Preface will be omitted.

AN APPEAL

THE PUBLIC,

THE LATE RIOTS IN BIRMINGHAM.

―――――

THERE is no tranfaction, efpecially one of a public nature, that will not be viewed by perfons of different difpofitions, or placed in different fituations, in different lights; and leaft of all can the diligent inquirer expect an impartial account from the perfons immediately concerned in it. All that he can do muft be to compare every account that he can collect, and then form his own judgment. In fome refpects one party, and in others another, will be the beft qualified to give him juft information, and among the reft, in all cafes of great calamity, he would certainly wifh to hear the fufferers themfelves, and not wholly depend on the accounts of thofe who either inflicted the fufferings,

or

or who rejoiced in them. I hope, therefore, it will not be thought improper in me, who am a principal fufferer by the late riots in Birmingham, to give *my* account of them, and my ideas of their caufes and probable confequences. I fhall endeavour to be as candid and impartial as I can, and the intelligent reader will eafily perceive whether I be fo, or not. I fhall divide the work into two parts, *Narrative,* and *Reflections.*

....

NARRATIVE.

I became an inhabitant of Birmingham in the year 1780, without any other view than as a proper fituation for attending to my philofophical purfuits, in which, having no original fortune of my own, I was affifted by a few liberal friends of fcience, who were pleafed to think favourably of me in that refpect. It was a plan fuggefted by the late Dr. Fothergill, and chearfully adopted by Sir George Saville, Sir Stephen Theodore Janffen, Mr. Conftable of Burton Conftable, and Dr. Price; all of them, it is fomething remarkable, of different religious perfuafions, but equally lovers of experimental philofophy and difinterefted promoters of it. Before, and fince their deaths, the fcheme was patronized by many other generous friends of fcience, whofe names, as they are ftill living, I forbear to mention. None of them, I believe, have feen any reafon to be diffatisfied with my conduct, as their operator.

In

In two adminiſtrations propoſals were made to aſſiſt me by a *penſion.* It was alleged that, ſince my ſtudies had been highly uſeful to the public, and very expenſive to myſelf, there was much more reaſon why I ſhould receive this aſſiſtance than almoſt any other perſon who ever had obtained it. But in both the caſes I declined the overture, chuſing rather to be obliged to generous individuals, notwithſtanding ſome unpleaſant circumſtances occaſionally attending this ſituation, than add to the burdens of my country.

My original and favourite profeſſion, however, was that of a chriſtian miniſter, in my opinion, the moſt important, uſeful, and honourable of all others; for which, though diſcontinued ſix years while I was tutor in the academy at Warrington, and ſeven years while I was with the Marquis of Lanſdown, I always had the ſtrongeſt predilection, and in which I never failed to officiate occaſionally, when I was out of the employment. But having been led, in the courſe of my theological ſtudies, which I never diſcontinued, to adopt opinions materially different from thoſe of the generality of Diſſenters, and in which I could not expect that any conſiderable ſociety of them would ſoon concur with me, I had no thought of ever being employed except as an occaſional preacher, in aſſiſting thoſe of my friends whoſe congregations might not diſlike my ſervices.

It was, therefore, with equal ſurprize and pleaſure that, on Mr. Hawkes's reſignation of his office

of

of minifter at the New Meeting in Birmingham, I had an almoft unanimous invitation to fucceed him. This, however, I accepted on the exprefs condition of the congregation having no claim upon me except on Sundays; the reft of the week being devoted to my philofophical and other purfuits. The other duties of the place were difcharged by my worthy colleague Mr. Blythe. To my philofophical purfuits I gave conftant attention, of which the public have feen the effects, and as a minifter I did nothing more than attend to what appeared to me to be the faithful difcharge of my duty, and I have reafon to think to the fatisfaction of my congregation.

Having, in every former fituation, been upon terms of intimacy with fome or other of the clergy of the church of England, men of liberal minds, and lovers of fcience, I fhould have been happy to have found thofe at Birmingham with whom I could have formed a fimilar connexion. But the fpirit of party, I faw with regret, ran higher there than in moft other places in the kingdom.

Such was the bigotry of the clergy of Birmingham, that long before I went thither, as well as during the whole time of my refiding there, they refufed to go into the fame coach with the diffenting minifters at funerals, or to walk with them in the proceffion. We had hoped that they had become afhamed of this abfurd inftance of clerical pride, which I had never heard of before, and
hoping

hoping better things of Mr. Curtis, who was of a diffenting family, Mr. Scholefield, the minifter of the Old Meeting, being invited to a funeral at which he officiated, fent to know whether he might be permitted to walk along with him. The anfwer was a civil but a peremptory refufal, and the propofal was never repeated. When I gave the late Bifhop of St. Afaph an account of this behaviour of the clergy of Birmingham, which was long before my controverfy with Mr. Madan, he expreffed much concern at it, and faid that he thought fuch bigotry had now exifted no where.

That I was not eager to engage in any controverfy with the clergy of the town, was evident from my making no reply whatever to two of their publications refpecting me, before the appearance of Mr. Madan's Sermon. One had the fignature of Luther, and the other that of M. S. The real names of the writers were well known; but I did not fo much as read either of them. The latter I flightly looked into at a bookfeller's fhop; and perceiving that it contained much general and virulent invective, I paid no farther attention to it. In order to invite purchafers, the profits of this publication were advertifed to go to the ufe of the General Infirmary. It was re-advertifed during my controverfy with Mr. Madan. The fame clergyman was fuppofed to be the author of one of the tracts in that controverfy, and of a virulent reply to my late *Letters to the Inhabitants of Birmingham.* But thefe alfo were unnoticed by me.

The

The fpirit of the high church party was confpicuous on the eftablifhment of Sunday fchools in
Birmingham; and this alfo was previous to my
controverfy with Mr. Madan. At firft perfons of
all religious perfuafions acted on this occafion in
concert, of which an example had been fet us in
London; and at a meeting of all the fubfcribers,
convened for the purpofe, it was agreed that the
children fhould go to whatever places of public
worfhip their parents fhould chufe. As there were
no children of Diffenters who wanted that inftruction, all the Sunday fcholars, without exception,
went to the eftablifhed church, and no complaint
was ever made of this by any Diffenter. But the
high church party, not being content with this, at
a meeting of the fubfcribers, the bufinefs of which
was not advertifed, the former rule was refcinded,
and the children were then abfolutely ordered to
do what they ever had done, and always might have
done, that is, attend the worfhip of the eftablifhed
church, *and no other.*

The Diffenters waited more than a year, to fee
whether the high church party would revert to
their former more liberal maxims, and continued
their fubfcriptions. But having waited fo long to
no purpofe, they opened their own feparate Sunday
fchools, with advantages, I will venture to fay, far
fuperior to thofe of the eftablifhment, but with
liberty to every parent to order his child to attend
whatever place of public worfhip he pleafed. Still,
however, feveral of the Diffenters continued their
fubfcriptions

subscriptions to the former Sunday schools, as well as to their own.

Such was the well known bigotry of the town in general, that when Mr. Newlin, a person of the most respectable character (who preceded Mr. Madan in the rectory of St. Philip's) came from Shrewsbury to Birmingham, though he had been, and continued to be, upon the best terms with the dissenting ministers in the former situation, he found he could have no intercourse with them in the latter; and yet I will venture to say there were not in all England three more respectable, or more peaceable dissenting ministers, and men who had less troubled the church of England in any way whatever, than those who served the two congregations of the Old and New Meetings at that time. Mr. Curtis himself, the Rector of St. Martin's, on his first coming to Birmingham, had the liberality to come and hear me preach a fast sermon at the Old Meeting, and brought his curate along with him. He even expressed himself much pleased with the service. But afterwards, I suppose, he perceived the true spirit of the place, and the necessity of conforming to it.

For a true representation of these facts I appeal to the town at large. With what truth, then, can it be said, as is now confidently done, that my coming to Birmingham, and my conduct there, was the sole cause of the animosity

between

between the church people and the Diffenters of that place ?*

Wifhing to difcover the caufe of this exceffive party fpirit, and to apply, if I fhould be able, fome remedy to it, I found the Diffenters were in poffeffion of all the civil power in the place, by having the nomination to all the offices; and though they conftantly gave the principal office, viz. that of *High Bailiff,* to a member of the church of England, they chofe to retain the power of nominating, of which they had long been in pof-feffion. This power, though I never heard of there being any complaint with refpect to the exercife of it) I took much pains, from the be-ginning of my refidence in Birmingham, to per-fuade the Diffenters to relinquifh; and I gradually brought over to my opinion fome of the principal

---

* A Letter lately addreffed to me and Mr. Ruffell has thefe words:
" It is notorious that the town of Birmingham had enjoyed an uninter-
" rupted fcene of peace and happinefs for more than fifty years.
" Every thing in it moved in perfect order and harmony, till you,
" like a noxious planet, approached towards it."

A Poem written fince the riots, in which I am reprefented as an enemy to God, and the government under which I live, concludes as follows :—

> Pure was the breeze that fans this " Seat of Arts,"
> 'Ere tainted by thy breath : in every ftreet
> The voice of labour fung away its cares ;
> The Church and Sectaries harmonious breath'd
> The genuine fpirit of fraternal love :
> But when thy puritanic *fcowl* appear'd,
> The heav'ns grew dark, and thy familiar fiend
> Flam'd in the pulpit, thunder'd from the prefs,
> 'Till all was uproar, and juft vengeance hurl'd
> Sedition's Temples fmoking to the ground.

could

of them. The objection to my propofal was that, fuch was the fpirit of party, that without this power every burdenfome office would be thrown upon the Diffenters. I always replied that I would willingly rifk *that*; thinking that no fet of men could make fo ungenerous a return for fuch generous conduct; but that I would even bear every kind of ill ufage, rather than that things fhould continue as they were.

I fpake both to quakers, and to fome of the more moderate members of the church of England on the fubject; and though one of the latter told me that he knew the temper of the people of Birmingham better than I did, and that he believed no good would come of the meafure, I perfifted, as is well known, in my firft opinion; and no objection was ever made to it by the Diffenters from any diflike of the meafure itfelf, but only from the apprehenfion of the ungenerous ufe that might be made of it.

There are two annual dinners given by the *Low Bailiff*, who has long been a Diffenter, and who has the nomination of that *Jury*, which appoints to all the offices in the town, and alfo the Low Bailiff for the enfuing year. Having, from the habits of a ftudious life, a diflike of all public entertainments, I never attended more than one of thefe feafts, the firft after my arrival; but I frequently faid that I would with pleafure attend the firft dinner of the kind that fhould be given by a member of the

church

church of England. This conduct of mine, of which I can produce abundant evidence, did not, furely, favour of much bigotry.

Till the application to parliament for the repeal of the Teft Act, I neither wrote, nor preached, any thing that had any particular relation to the principles of Diffenters, and I fent my fons to the public grammar fchool, which is conducted wholly by clergymen, and the head mafter of which, a man of candour, as well as an excellent claffical fcholar, occafionally vifited me.

When Mr. Burn came to Birmingham, having met him at a committee of the public library, I thought I perceived in him great marks of liberality, and on my invitation, he paid me two vifits. In Mr. Madan, whom I met at a committee for abolifhing the Slave Trade, and who was particularly civil to me there, I flattered myfelf I had found a clergyman entirely to my mind, and one with whom I might form a pleafing acquaintance. This I mentioned to a particular friend, requefting that he would endeavour to bring it about, as he is ready to witnefs if called upon. This, furely, did not favour of bigotry. Indeed, I have ever lived, and now live, in confiderable intimacy with perfons of every religious perfuafion in this country, the members of the church of England not excepted, though not thofe refiding in Birmingham. The greateft difference of opinion never led me to keep aloof from any man.

Before

Before I left Birmingham I was happy to have begun fome pleafing intercourfe with Dr. Parr, who had lately come to refide near Warwick. We had vifited each other, and I am confident that the continuance of the intercourfe would have been a pleafing circumftance to us both, though our religious principles are very different, and he was an avowed oppofer of the repeal of the Teft Act. When he dined with me, he was purpofely met by Mr. Berington, a catholic prieft, and Mr. Galton, a quaker. Mr. Porfon was alfo of the party. I have a peculiar pleafure in the fociety of perfons of different perfuafions, and more inftances of this are given in the *Preface to my Letters to Mr. Burn,* now publifhed together with my *Familiar Letters to the Inhabitants of Birmingham.* Dr. Parr, however, gave great offence to the clergy, and the high church party in Birmingham, by introducing fome praife of me into a fermon of his, preached at the new church before our acquaintance commenced.

The firft difference that I had with any of the clergy in Birmingham, arofe from four of them withdrawing from our public library becaufe my *Hiftory of the Corruptions of Chriftianity* had been voted into it; a meafure to which, it is well known, that I gave no countenance, but had always oppofed, on the idea that it would be better to omit purchafing any books of controverfy, till the library fhould be better ftocked with books of other kinds, and more generally interefting. Finding,

ing, however, the funds of the library sufficiently ample, and a disposition in many persons, members of the establishment, as well as Dissenters, to read on these, as well as on other subjects, without the obligation of purchasing the books for themselves, I at length concurred with them; but on the express condition that in every interesting controversy, books on both sides should be equally purchased; and I myself generally recommended such as were against my opinions. At length, however, the party opposed to me gained the ascendancy, which they still keep, in the conduct of the library, which was wholly new modelled by myself; and in this I quietly acquiesced, and withdrew from the committee, though I continued a member of the society. I appeal to my townsmen whether my whole conduct in this business was not uniformly open and generous. It had, however, an unfavourable effect in increasing the animosity against the Dissenters, who in this were joined by the more moderate churchmen.

But the great increase of party spirit in the town, and what, to all appearance, contributed most to the fatal catastrophe, the cause of which we are now investigating, arose from the application of the Dissenters for the repeal of the Corporation and Test Acts, the nature and tendency of which were strangely misapprehended by the great body of the clergy, and other zealous members of the church of England. For had the repeal taken place, without their opposition, and with the con-

currence

currence of the court, no difference whatever would have been perceived in our condition, and our interest as a dissenting body would probably have suffered by it, as indeed many of us were well aware.

As the case now is, few, if any, Dissenters are, in fact, excluded from any civil office which they wish to serve, so that the repeal would only have removed a mode of admission to them, highly disgraceful to religion in general, peculiar to this country, and which was not originally intended to affect Dissenters, many of whom were at that time in the habit of communicating with the church of England, though the practice has become less frequent since. And whatever tends to mix us with the world at large, is well known to lead us to think, and to act, as the world does, and consequently to lessen our zeal as Dissenters, and bring us to conformity with the established church.

On this principle great numbers of the most intelligent Dissenters were from the first more than indifferent to the measure, and sincerely wished that we might remain as we were in that respect; and I believe it was as much a regard to the honour of the nation, and of christianity, as for any positive advantage to themselves, that any Dissenters concerned themselves about it. The effect has shewn the truth of these apprehensions. The number of Dissenters had been evidently diminish-

ing

ing before the late application, and they are greatly increafed fince, both in Birmingham and in many other parts of the kingdom.

Alfo religion in general, with the peculiar tenets of it, having by this means been brought into notice, and more public difcuffion, the increafe of *unitarians*, whofe fentiments are the moft oppofite to thofe of the church of England, has been in much more than a ten fold proportion. Thefe converts to unitarianifm confift chiefly of the middle, and fome of the higher rank of perfons, men who are known to read, and to think for themfelves, and who of courfe have influence with others; fo that there is now a moral certainty of this doctrine continuing to prevail in this and other countries.

Before the late applications to Parliament, and the violent oppofition which the clergy made to them, the different claffes of Diffenters were hoftile to, and had little communication with, each other. But the oppofition then made to their claims, (claims which we think to be founded in natural juftice, on the clear principle that all who contribute to defray the expences of government fhould have equal accefs to its honours and emoluments, whatever be their religious faith) has brought us to feel a common intereft, and has united us as one body, from one end of the kingdom to the other; fo that we can act in concert, as we are now in the habit of doing. This happy
union

union ftrengthens every day, and in confequence of it religious bigotry in general is much decreafed among us. We now attend more to the great things in which we all agree, and lefs to thofe with refpect to which we differ from each other. On thefe accounts the ftrength of the Diffenters, has been greatly increafed by the clerical oppofition to our claims. So wretched has been the policy of our enemies, apprehending danger where there was even lefs than none, and having no apprehenfion at all of what is real.

In this bufinefs, however, whether there be merit or demerit in it, I had nothing to do. I did not fo much as hear of the intention of applying to Parliament for the repeal of the Teft and Corporation Acts till it was determined upon by the Diffenters in London.

Had I been confulted, I fhould rather have advifed an application for the repeal of that Act of King William which makes it eventually confifcation of goods, and imprifonment for life, to deny the doctrine of the trinity. This is a cafe of fimple toleration, as we fhould only have defired exemption from pofitive punifhment, for maintaining opinions which we deem important, contrary to thofe of the ftate, and we fhould have had the better plea, as it is the great, though vain boaft of this country, that here *toleration is complete*, whereas for thefe twenty years laft paft, I have walked at large only by the connivance of
my

my neighbours, and my opponents have not omitted to hold out to me the terror of this law which hangs over my head.

They who, in their speeches in Parliament, quoted my writings, as an authority with the Diffenters in general, were as ignorant of the Diffenters, as they were of the maxims of found policy. If I had had any weight with the body of Diffenters at that time, we should have joined the Catholics, who generoufly made the propofal, in applying for the repeal of all the penal laws in matters of religion. But that golden opportunity was fuffered to pafs by, and I fear will never more return.

When the meafure of applying for the repeal of the Acts above-mentioned (which affect the laity much more than minifters) was taken, I could not help wifhing well to it; but well knowing my unpopularity even among the Diffenters (which till of late was much greater than with the members of the eftablifhed church) I took no active part in promoting it, and what I did was altogether accidental.

Being in London at the time of the firft debate on the fubject, I heard Mr. Pitt (whom, juftly or unjuftly, we had been led to confider as friendly to our caufe) fpeak againft it; and perceiving, as I thought, his total mifapprehenfion of the fubject, I addreffed a *Letter* to him relating to the fituation of Diffenters, and on other collateral fubjects, efpecially

cially the ftate of the eftablifhed church, both here and in Ireland. This *Letter* gave great offence. But I appeal to the impartial public, whether, though written with fome degree of indignation, at recent, and as we thought, unjuft treatment, there be any thing in it unbecoming men and Englifhmen, unjuftly and ignominioufly treated. This *Letter* was written, and publifhed, while I was in London, and therefore had no particular reference to Birmingham. What I did there was as follows.

It being ufual on the 5th of November to give our congregations a difcourfe on fome fubject relating to *religious liberty*, I made choice of that of the Teft Act, and at the requeft of my hearers the difcourfe was publifhed. But I will venture to fay that it is one of the calmeft, and moft moderate, of all difcourfes that was ever written on a political fubject.

What, now, was the conduct of the clergy throughout England, and efpecially at Birmingham, on this occafion ? Endeavours were ufed to render the Diffenters the objects not only of exclufion from civil offices, but of general odium and punifhment. Dr. *Croft's Sermon*, and that of Mr. Madan, both delivered at Birmingham, are extant, and the fpirit of them was the fame with that of hundreds, I may fay thoufands, that were echoed from other pulpits, charging the Diffenters, in oppofition to all hiftory, and even to recent and exifting facts, with principles inimical to the government of the country, and to the prince upon the

C   throne;

throne; as pure republicans in their hearts, and who would scruple no means to overturn not the church only, but also the state.

Dr. Price and myself were particularly pointed out as seditious and dangerous persons, the very pests of society, and unworthy the protection of government. Such language as this is even held to this day, and in spite of the most explicit denial of what is thus laid to our charge, and of every possible species of evidence to the contrary, including the constant language of our serious writings, will, to all appearance, long continue to be held.

Being particularly pointed at by Mr. Madan, and both friends and enemies looking upon me as called upon to make some reply; I did it with great reluctance, as to a clergyman, whom, on other accounts, I truly respected, and whom, as living in the same town with me, I might occasionally meet; to say nothing of the farther acquaintance which I had once flattered myself I might make with him. This reply I made in a series of *Familiar Letters to the Inhabitants of Birmingham*, and I appeal to any person who has the least pretention to impartiality, whether they be not a mild and good-humoured reply to an unprovoked invective.

I there showed that the Dissenters were, and always had been, the best friends to the present government, that I had myself written much in

defence

defence and praise of it; and though, being a Diffenter, I, of courfe, could be no friend to the eftablifhed church, with refpect either to doctrine or
difcipline, I allowed others to judge and act, as I
did, for themfelves, and that I wifhed for no alterations but fuch as fhould have the general concurrence of the country, and thofe made in fuch a
manner, as that no perfon living fhould be injured
by them. This has been my conftant language on
the fubject of reformation in church or ftate. Mr.
Madan replied without retracting any part of his
charge. But notwithftanding this, I continued,
and concluded, my *Letters* with the fame good-
humour with which I began them.

Thefe Letters were much read both in Birmingham and the neighbourhood, and indeed
throughout England. But though they convinced
many perfons that the Diffenters had been ill ufed,
and that we had much more to fay for ourfelves
than they had imagined, they were far from con-
ciliating the clergy, or the more violent fticklers
for the eftablifhed church.

Other attempts, and fome of them of a very
infamous kind, were made to render my character
odious. Old calumnies were revived, and new
ones invented, concerning my being an enemy to
Chriftianity, and to religion in general; and a clergyman (as there is every reafon to think) publifhed
an account of my having converted Mr. Silas
Deane to atheifm, and his confeffion of it upon his

death-bed.

death-bed. This was reprefented in public prints, and the pamphlet containing the account was induftrioufly circulated by fome of the clergy in Birmingham and its neighbourhood. At firft I neglected the idle ftory, as fufficiently contradicted by my writings and my whole conduct. Afterwards, however, at the inftance of my friends, I publifhed the cleareft refutation of it. But even this did not appear to make any favourable impref-fion on my enemies in Birmingham. The offence given by my *Familiar Letters* was never forgiven.

Mr. Burn alfo publifhed a fet of *Letters to me,* in which he charged me with rejecting the tefti-mony of the Apoftles concerning the perfon of Chrift; and though I denied the charge, and fhewed the abfurdity of it, he replied withour re-tracting it. In the *Preface to my Letters to Mr. Burn,* I gave my opinion with great freedom con-cerning the ftate of the Diffenters, and the clergy of the eftablifhed church, warning them of the violence and folly of their conduct, and the pro-bable confequences of it. But the ufe they made of this *Preface* was to print *Extracts from it,* fo cur-tailed and arranged, as to reprefent me as a mover of fedition, and a dangerous member of fociety. This printed paper was fent to the bifhops, and to all the members of the houfe of Commons the day before the laft debate on the fubject of the Teft and Corporation Acts, fo that it was impoffible to counteract the effects of it; and being put into the hands of Mr. Burke, and declaimed upon by

him,

him, was of material differvice to our caufe. I
fhewed the unfairnefs of this proceeding in a *printed
letter* fent to the bifhops, and all the members of
the houfe of Commons, as theirs had been. But
to all appearance, this complete juftification only
tended to exafperate my enemies, and they fpared
no pains to exafperate others.

The effect of this controverfy upon the common people in Birmingham, who were made to
believe that, fome way or other, both the church
and the ftate were in danger, and that my object was the utter deftruction of both, was great
and vifible enough. On the walls of houfes, &c.
and efpecially where I ufually went, were to
be feen in large characters, MADAN FOR EVER,
DAMN PRIESTLEY, NO PRESBYTERIANS, DAMN
THE PRESBYTERIANS, &c. &c. At one time I was
followed by a number of boys, who left their play,
repeating what they had feen on the walls, and
fhouting out, *Damn Prieftley, damn him, damn him
for ever, for ever, for ever,* &c. &c. This was, no
doubt, a leffon which they had been taught by
their parents, and what thefe, I fear, had learned
from their fuperiors. Such things as thefe were
certainly unpleafant to me; but I was confcious I
had done nothing to deferve fuch treatment; and
defpifing mere *obloquy,* I was far from fufpecting
that it would ever lead to the outrages which have
fince taken place.

In

In the exultation of the high church party on the defeat of our laſt application to Parliament, perſonal danger was apprehended to myſelf, by ſome of my more zealous friends; and a number of young men of my congregation came to tell me, that myſelf and my houſe were threatened, but that if I chofe it, they would undertake to defend both me, and it, at the riſk of their lives. I replied that I did not apprehend any danger, and that if any violence was offered to me on that account, I ſhould make no reſiſtance. It has always been my maxim, as may be feen in my writings, and what I have always maintained in converſation, that it becomes chriſtians to bear every kind of inſult and violence when it is offered on the account of *religion*, and that nothing but our *civil rights* are to be defended by the ſword.

I took no notice of any of the particulars above-mentioned; and though I was told that ſome of the clergy of the town and neighbourhood were frequently preaching againſt the Diſſenters, and often againſt myſelf by name, or by deſcription, I never preached a ſingle ſermon on the ſubjeſt, or wrote any thing more than the pieces above-mentioned, which are before the public, and may be examined at the reader's leiſure, till the appearance of *Mr. Burke's Reflections on the French Revolution*, a work that has been more generally read than any publication in my time, and which has contributed more than any other to excite a ſpirit
of

of party; the clergy almoſt univerſally approving it, and the low church party and Diſſenters as generally condemning it.

My friends well know that I was far from having any intention of animadverting upon this performance, being at that time engaged in other purſuits, and having a real reſpect for the writer, till I was preſſed to undertake it by ſeveral of my friends, who were pleaſed to think me better qualified than moſt others to reply to what Mr. Burke had advanced on the ſubject of *Civil Eſtabliſhments of Chriſtianity.* At their ſolicitation I wrote my *Letters to Mr. Burke,* and this publication, though a very temperate one, provoked the clergy, and the zealous friends of the eſtabliſhment ſtill more; and in conſequence of this, their efforts to inflame the minds of the populace againſt the Diſſenters in general, and myſelf in particular, were redoubled, and the profane habit of drinking *Damnation and confuſion to the Preſbyterians,* at the convivial meetings of perſons of better faſhion, as well as thoſe of the lower order, was much increaſed.

So apparent were the marks of extreme bigotry, and the true ſpirit of perſecution at this time, that upon occaſion of preaching the *Hackney College Sermon,* in April laſt (and which my friends know that I long declined) I was led to ſay, " In another " reſpect, alſo, we are now in the ſituation of the " primitive chriſtians; as the friends of reformation

" have

" have nothing to expect from *power*, or *general*
" *favour*; but muſt look for every ſpecies of abuſe
" and perſecution that the ſpirit of the times will
" admit of.   If even burning alive was a ſight that
" the country would now bear, there exiſts a ſpirit
" which would inflict that horrid puniſhment, and
" with as much cool indifference, or ſavage ex-
" ultation, as in any preceding age of the world."
But though I ſaw this, and that the marks of
this ſpirit were apparent in various other parts of
England, I had no ſuſpicion of its breaking out on
the innocent, occaſion of celebrating the *French
Revolution*, and therefore was far from being prepared for any ſuch outrage.

The celebration of this great event by a public
dinner at Birmingham was no meaſure of mine. Indeed, I am well known to all my friends to be averſe
to public entertainments, and never enjoy myſelf at
them; my habits of life, too long confirmed to be
eaſily altered, being quite oppoſite to every thing
of this nature.   However, when the friends of that
Revolution propoſed it, and wiſhed to have my
company, I did not decline their invitation, and we
had a meeting or two, partly for *that* purpoſe, and
partly to ſettle the rules of a CONSTITUTIONAL
SOCIETY, ſuch as that which is eſtabliſhed at Mancheſter, the chief object of which was to promote
a more equal repreſentation of the people of this
country in Parliament, and we had printed two
copies of *general principles of government*, to be ſubſcribed by all the members, and one copy of *par-*
" *ticular*

ticular rules for our conduct, copied chiefly from those of Manchester; but we had not pleased ourselves with them, and nothing was absolutely settled.

Many persons in different parts of the kingdom, but more especially at Birmingham, thought the celebration of the French Revolution to be a right and a wise measure, in order to conciliate the French nation, and to promote a friendly and commercial intercourse with it. It is well known that the late *commercial treaty* is not popular in France, and it was thought to be impolitic to heighten the dislike of that nation to *this*, by refusing to partake of their joy, in what was known to give them the greatest satisfaction.

With the dinner itself I had, in a manner, nothing to do. I did not so much as suggest one of the proper and excellent *toasts* provided on the occasion, though it was natural for my friends to look to me for things of that kind, if I had interested myself much in it; and when opposition was talked of, and it was supposed that some insults would be offered to myself in particular, I yielded to the solicitations of my friends, and did not attend. Others, however, went on that very account; thinking it mean, and unbecoming Englishmen, to be deterred from a lawful and innocent act, by the fear of lawless insult; and accordingly they asembled, and dined, in number between eighty and ninety.

When

When the company met, a croud was affembled at the door, and fome of them hiffed, and fhewed other marks of difapprobation, but no material violence was offered to any body. Mr. Keir, a member of the church of England, took the chair; and when they had dined, drank their toafts, and fung the fongs which had been prepared for the occafion, they difperfed. This was about five o'clock, and the town remained quiet till about eight. It was evident, therefore, that the *dinner* was not the proper caufe of the riot which followed: but that the mifchief had been pre-concerted, and that this particular opportunity was laid hold of for the purpofe.

Some days before this meeting, a few copies of a printed *hand-bill* of an inflammatory nature, of which a copy is given in the *Appendix*, No. I. had been found in a public houfe in the town, and of this great ufe was made to inflame the minds of the people againft the Diffenters, to whom, though without any evidence whatever, it was confidently afcribed. The thing itfelf did not deferve any notice, and paragraphs of as feditious a nature frequently appear in the public newfpapers, and other publications, and (as would, no doubt, have been the cafe with this) are neglected and forgotten. But the magiftrates of Birmingham, and other known enemies of the Diffenters, were loud in their exclamations againft it, though perhaps fabricated for the ufe that was made of it; and a copy was officioufly fent to the fecretaries of ftate, who ordered a ftrict enquiry to be made

after

after the author, printer, or diftributor; and in confequence of this a reward of an hundred pounds was offered, for the difcovery of any of them.

In confequence of all this preparation, we were informed that, though the trade of Birmingham had never been more brifk, fo that hands could not be found to manufacture the goods that were ordered, many of the public-houfes were that day full of people, whofe horrid execrations againft the Diffenters were heard into the ftreets; and it has been afferted that fome of the mafter manufacturers had fhut up their work-fhops, and thereby left their men at full liberty for any mifchief.

It has fince appeared that befides the dinner at the Hotel, there were alfo dinners of the oppofite party on this fourteenth of July, and thofe not of the loweft clafs of the people, with whom the common ale-houfes were filled. Thefe did not rife from their entertainment fo early, or with fo much fobriety, as thofe who dined at the Hotel; and it was at the breaking up of *their* companies that the riots commenced. Let the impartial then judge to which of the dinners the riot that followed is to be afcribed.

Mr. Adam Walker, the ingenious and well known lecturer in natural Philofophy, was paffing through the town with his wife and family, and dined with me at my own houfe, for the laft time,

on

on that day. Before dinner, I had walked to the town with him, and they left me in the evening. Some time after this, three of my intimate friends, whofe houfes were fituated near the fame road, and farther from the town than mine, called upon me to congratulate me, and one another, on the dinner having paffed over fo well; and after chatting chearfully fome time on the fubject, they left me juft as it was beginning to be dark.

After fupper, when I was preparing to amufe myfelf, as I fometimes did, with a game of backgammon, we were alarmed by fome young men rapping violently at the door; and when they were admitted, they appeared to be almoft breathlefs with running. They faid that a great mob had affembled at the Hotel, where the company had dined; that after breaking the windows there, they were gone to the New Meeting, and were demolifhing the pulpit and pews, and that they threatened me and my houfe. That they fhould think of molefting *me* I thought fo improbable, that I could hardly give any credit to the ftory. However, imagining that perhaps fome of the mob might come to infult me, I was prevailed upon to leave the houfe, and meant to go to fome neighbour's at a greater diftance from the town; but having no apprehenfion for the houfe itfelf, or any thing in it, I only went up ftairs, and put fome papers and other things of value, where I thought that any perfons getting into the houfe would not eafily find

find them. My wife did the fame with fome things of hers. I then bade the fervants keep the doors faftened; if any body fhould come, to fay that I was gone, and if any ftones fhould be thrown at the windows, to keep themfelves out of danger, and that I did not doubt but they would go away again.

At this time, which was about half paft nine o'clock, Mr. S. Ryland, a friend of mine, came with a chaife, telling us there was no time to lofe, but that we muft immediately get into it, and drive off. Accordingly, we got in with nothing more than the clothes we happened to have on, and drove from the houfe. But hearing that the mob confifted only of people on foot, and concluding that when they found I was gone off in a chaife, they could not tell whither, they would never think of purfuing me, we went no farther than Mr. Ruffell's, a mile on the fame road, and there we continued feveral hours, Mr. Ruffell himfelf, and other perfons, being upon the road on horfeback to get intelligence of what was paffing. I alfo more than once walked about half way back to my own houfe for the fame purpofe; and then I faw the fires from the two meeting-houfes, which were burning down.

About twelve we were told that fome hundreds of the mob were breaking into my houfe, and that when they had demolifhed *it*, they would certainly proceed to Mr. Ruffell's. We were perfuaded, therefore,

therefore, to get into the chaife again, and drive off; but we went no farther than Mr. Thomas Hawkes's on Mofeley-Green, which is not more than half a mile farther from the town, and there we waited all the night.

It being remarkably calm, and clear moon-light, we could fee to a confiderable diftance, and being upon a rifing ground, we diftinctly heard all that paffed at the houfe, every fhout of the mob, and almoft every ftroke of the inftruments they had provided for breaking the doors and the furniture. For they could not get any fire, though one of them was heard to offer two guineas for a lighted candle; my fon, whom we left behind us, having taken the precaution to put out all the fires in the houfe, and others of my friends got all the neighbours to do the fame. I afterwards heard that much pains was taken, but without effect, to get fire from my large electrical machine, which ftood in the library.

About three o'clock in the morning the noifes ceafed, and Mr. Ruffell and my fon coming to us, faid that the mob was almoft difperfed, that not more than twenty of them remained, and thofe fo much intoxicated, that they might eafily be taken. We therefore returned with him, and about four o'clock were going to bed at his houfe. But when I was undreffing myfelf for that purpofe, news came that there was a frefh acceffion of fome hundreds more to the mob, and that they were

advancing

advancing towards Mr. Ruffell's. On this we got
into the chaife once more, and driving through a
part of the town diftant from the mob, we went to
Dudley, and thence to my fon-in-law's, Mr. Finch
at Heath-Forge, five miles farther, where we arrived
before breakfaft, and brought the firft news of our
difafter.

Here I thought myfelf perfectly fafe, and
imagining that when the mifchief was over (and I
had no idea of its going beyond my own houfe)
and fuppofing that, as the people in general would
be afhamed, and concerned, at what had happened,
I might return; thinking alfo that the area within
the walls of the meeting-houfe might foon be
cleared, I intended, if the weather would permit, to
preach there the Sunday following, and from this
text, *Father forgive them, for they know not what
they do.*

At noon, however, we had an exprefs from
Stourbridge, to acquaint us that the mob had traced
me to Dudley, and would purfue me to Heath.
To this I paid no attention, nor to another from
Dudley in the evening to inform us of the fame
thing; and being in want of fleep, I went to bed
foon after ten. But at eleven I was awaked, and
told that a third exprefs was juft arrived from
Dudley, to affure us that fome perfons were certainly in purfuit of me, and would be there that
night. All the family believing this, and urging
me to make my efcape, I dreffed myfelf, got on
horfeback,

horſeback, and with a ſervant rode to Bridgnorth, where I arrived about two in the morning.

After about two hours ſleep in this place, I got into a chaiſe, and went to Kidderminſter, on my way to London. Here I found myſelf among my friends, and, as I thought, far enough from the ſcene of danger, eſpecially as we continually heard news from Birmingham, and that the miſchief did not extend beyond the town. Hearing, particularly, that all was quiet at Dudley, I concluded that there could be no real cauſe of apprehenſion at Heath; and being unwilling to go farther than was neceſſary, I took a horſe, and arrived there in the evening.

There, however, I found the family in great conſternation at the ſight of me; and Mr. Finch juſt arriving from Dudley, and ſaying that they were in momentary expectation of a riot there, that the populace were even aſſembled in the ſtreet, and were heard to threaten the meeting-houſe, the houſe of the miniſter, and thoſe of other principal Diſſenters, and that all attempts to make them diſperſe had been in vain, I mounted my horſe again, though much fatigued, and greatly wanting ſleep.

My intention was to get to an inn about ſix miles on the road to Kidderminſter, where I might get a chaiſe, and in it proceed to that town. No chaiſe, however, was to be had; ſo that I was
under

under the neceffity of proceeding on horfeback, and neither the fervant nor myfelf diftinguifhing the road in the night, we loft our way, and at break of day found ourfelves on Bridgnorth race ground, having ridden nineteen miles, till we could hardly fit our horfes.

Arriving at this place a fecond time, about three o'clock in the morning, we with fome difficulty roufed the people at an indifferent inn, and I immediately got into bed, and flept a few hours. After breakfaft we mounted our horfes, and I got a fecond time to Kidderminfter. There, finding that if I immediately took a chaife, and drove faft, I might get to Worcefter time enough for the mail-coach, I did fo; and meeting with a young man of my own congregation, he accompanied me thither, which was a great fatisfaction to me, as he acquainted me with many particulars of the riot, of which I was before ignorant. At Worcefter I was juft time enough for the coach, and fortunately there was one place vacant. I took it, and travelling all night, I got to London on Monday morning, July 18.

Here I was in a place of fafety, and had leifure for reft and reflection. I can truly fay, however, that in all the hurry of my flight, and while the injuries I had received were frefh upon my mind, I had not one defponding, or unbenevolent thought. I really pitied the delufion of the poor incendiaries, and the infatuation of thofe who had deluded them,

D   and

and never doubted but that, though I could not tell *how*, or *when*, good would arife from this, as well as from every other evil. The magnanimity of my wife was never fhaken; and, as at other times, fhe then felt more for others than fhe did for herfelf. It was a diftreffing circumftance, that our daughter was expecting to be brought to bed in about a month, fo that fhe was full of alarm, and her mother could not leave her to accompany me. We were, however, as happy as we could be in this ftate of forced feparation, I with my old friends in London, and fhe either with our daughter, or with one of the moft friendly, gene- rous, and worthy families in the world, in the neighbourhood of Birmingham.

That there were inftigators, as well as perpe- trators, of thefe horrid fcenes, was fufficiently evi- dent. Moft of thofe who committed the devafta- tions appeared by their profanenefs, intoxication, and their difpofition to indifcriminate plunder, to have no fenfe of religion at all, and therefore could only adopt the cry of *church and king* as a pretence. In the midft of their devaftations there were always fome cool heads mixed with the drunken ones, who rejected all offers of money, and faid that they muft obey their orders. But the moft decifive cir- cumftance was that of *forged letters* being read, one at my houfe, in the name of Mr. Ruffell, and an- other at his, in the name of Mr. Jeffries of Lon- don, on purpofe to inflame the mob to greater outrages. Whoever be the real author of the

hand-bill,

hand-bill, certainly they who forged thefe letters were capable of writing it, for the ufe that was actually made of it. Indeed, there is nothing too atrocious for fuch perfons not to be capable of.

Being now at my leifure, I wrote my *Addrefs to the Inhabitants of Birmingham,* APPENDIX, No. II. and upon the more moderate it had fome influence, in counteracting the ftrange and mifchievous accounts that had been every where induftrioufly propagated, in order to throw the blame of the whole tranfaction upon the Diffenters in general, and myfelf in particular (See APPENDIX, No. III.) though on others it had a different effect.

In London I found by accident that Mr. W. Ruffell had juft arrived in town, who, next to myfelf, was the principal object of diflike to the high church party in Birmingham. He came to reprefent to the miniftry a true ftate of things relating to the riots, and to learn what fteps they would take with refpect to it. When this was fettled, he returned to Birmingham, but not before he had publifhed an account of what had paffed at the Revolution dinner, with the toafts that were given on that occafion. (See APPENDIX, No. IV.) On the fame day alfo, as it happened, Mr. Keir publifhed an account of the proceedings, for the Birmingham newfpaper (See APPENDIX, No. V.) and foon after a more particular account of the toafts, with obfervations, in explanation and vindication of them. Thefe gentlemen giving their

names,

names, their accounts fatisfied the impartial, that the behaviour of the Diffenters had not been liable to any juft cenfure, and that it was not the dinner, but a deep-rooted animofity againft the Diffenters, that was the true caufe of all the mifchief.

In this fituation, what I regretted moft was the lofs, as I then fuppofed, of all my *manufcript papers*, for which no reparation could be made. They confifted of the following particulars:

I. My *Diaries* from the year 1752, containing the particulars of almoft every day; and at the beginning of each of them I had given the ftate of my mind, of my affairs in general, and of my profpects, for that year; which it was often amufing, and alfo inftructive, to me, to look back upon.

II. Several large *Common-place Books*, containing the fruits of my reading almoft ever fince I could read with any degree of judgment.

III. The *Regifter of my Philofophical Experiments*, and hints for new ones.

IV. All my *Sermons*, *Prayers*, and *Forms for adminiftering the Lord's Supper*, &c. many of which I had with great expence got tranfcribed into a fair long hand.

V. *Notes and a Paraphrafe on the whole of the New Teftament*, excepting the book of *Revelation*.

The

The whole of it had been delivered from the pulpit, and in a preface to another work, I had promifed to publifh it. I was within five days (employing my amanuenfis three hours a day) of having the whole fairly tranfcribed for the prefs.

VI. A *New Tranflation of the Pfalms, Proverbs, and Ecclefiaftes*; having undertaken, in conjunction with feveral other Unitarians, to make a new Tranflation of both the Old and New Teftament.

VII. *A feries of Letters to the Members of the New Jerufalem Church*, which was lately opened in Birmingham. Thefe were fairly tranfcribed, and were to have gone to the prefs the Monday following; and being on the moft friendly terms with the minifter, and principal members of that church, I had made an appointment to meet them on the preceding Friday, to read the work to them from the manufcript, in order to be fatisfied that I had not miftated any of their doctrines, and that I might hear their objections to what I had written. A rough draft of a great part of thefe *Letters* happened to be preferved, in confequence of taking a copy of them by Meffrs. Boulton and Watt's machine, and from this I have lately publifhed them.

VIII. Memoirs of my own Life, to be publifhed after my death.

IX. A great

IX. A great number of *letters* from my friends and learned foreigners, with other papers.

X. A fhort account of all the perfons whofe names are introduced into my chart of Biography, which I intended to publifh, though not very foon.

XI. *Illuftrations of Hartley's doctrine of Affociation of Ideas*, and *farther Obfervations on the Human Mind*, the publication of which I had promifed in the Preface to my *Effay on Education.* This would perhaps have been the moft orignal, and nearly the laft, of my publications. The hints and loofe materials for it were written in feveral volumes, not one fcrap of which is yet recovered.

XII. Befides thefe, I had what had coft me much labour, though, as I did not mean to make any public ufe of them, I do not much regret their lofs, viz. A large courfe of *Lectures on the Conftitution and Laws of England*, and another on *the Hiftory of England*, which I had read when I was tutor at Warrington, and of which a fyllabus may be feen in the former editions of my *Effay on Education.* In the fame clafs of manufcripts, not much to be regretted, I place a great variety of mifcellaneous juvenile compofitions, and collections of which I occafionally made fome, though not much, ufe.

XIII My *laft Will, Receipts* and *Accounts.*

.

Let

Let any man of letters, arrived, as I am, to near the age of fixty, confider what muft have been my accumulation of curious papers of various kinds, from the variety and extent of my purfuits (greater unqueftionably than that of moft men now living) and think what I could not but have felt for their lofs, and their difperfion into fuch hands as they fell into, and who make, as I hear, the moft indecent and improper ufe of them. This makes the cafe much worfe than that of mere plunder, and the deftruction of books and papers by Goths and Vandals, who could not read any of them. It was, however, no fmall fatisfaction to me, to think that my enemies, having the freeft accefs to every paper I had, might be convinced that I had carried on no treafonable correfpondence, and that I had nothing to be concerned about befides the effects of their impertinent curiofity.

The deftruction of my library did not affect me fo much on account of the money I had expended upon it, as the choice of the books; having had particular objects of ftudy, and having collected them with great care, as opportunity ferved, in the courfe of many years. It had alfo been my cuftom to read almoft every book with a pencil in my hand, marking the paffages that I wifhed to look back to, and of which I propofed to make any particular ufe; and I frequently made an index to fuch paffages on a blank leaf at the end of the book. In confequence of this, other fets of the

D 4   fame

fame work would not, by any means, be of the fame value to me; for I have not only loft the books, but the chief fruit of my labour and judgment in reading them.

Alfo my laboratory not only contained a fet of the moft valuable and ufeful inftruments of every kind, and original fubftances for experiments, but other fubftances, the refults of numerous proceffes, referved for farther experiments; as every experienced chymift will fuppofe, and thefe cannot be replaced without repeating the proceffes of many years. No money can repair damages of this kind. Alfo, feveral of my inftruments were either wholly, or in part, of my own conftruction, and fuch as cannot be purchafed any where.

Notwithftanding this deftruction of my manuscripts, I do not know that fuch a calamity could have happened at a more convenient time, in the courfe of the laft ten years. Had it been during the compofition of my *Hiftory of early Opinions concerning Chrift*, my *Church Hiftory*, or the *New Edition of my Philofophical Works*, I could never have completed, or refumed them; nor without the books which I then had, could I have undertaken what I have done fince. Very happily alfo, I had finifhed a long courfe of experiments on the doctrine of *phlogifton*, and the *compofition of water*, and my laft paper on the fubject was juft printed for the *Philofophical Tranfactions*.

One

One of the moft mortifying circumftances in this calamity was the difperfion of a great number of *letters* from my private friends, from the earlieft period of my correfpondence, into the hands of perfons wholly deftitute of generofity or honour. Thefe letters I had carefully arranged, fo that I could immediately turn to any of them, when I wifhed to look back to them, as a memorial of former friendfhips, or for any other purpofe. But they were kept in a box which was ordered by my laft will to be burned without infpection. Now, however, letters which I did not wifh even my executors to fee, were expofed, without mercy or fhame, to all the world. No perfon of honour will even look into a letter not directed to himfelf. But mine have not only been expofed to every curious, impertinent eye, but, as I am informed, are eagerly perufed, commented upon, and their fenfe perverted, in order to find out fomething againft me.

Some of my private papers are faid to have been fent to the fecretary of ftate. But fecretaries of ftate, I prefume, are *gentlemen,* and confider themfelves as bound by the fame rules of juftice and honour that are acknowledged to bind other men, and therefore, if this be the cafe, thefe papers will certainly be returned to me.

Of this kind of ill ufage, I do not accufe the illiterate mob, who made the deveftation; for few of them, I fuppofe, could read, but thofe perfons
of

of better education into whofe hands the papers afterwards came. Had perfons of this clafs inter-pofed, and exerted themfelves, they might, no doubt, have faved the greateft part of *this*, to me moft valuable property, for the lofs of which (but more efpecially for the ungenerous ufe that was made of it) no compenfation can be made me.

My numerous correfpondents in different coun-tries of Europe, but more efpecially thofe who wrote to me in confidence in this country, will be as much affected by this cataftrophe as myfelf. I might, no doubt, have deftroyed thofe letters, and other private papers, myfelf. But I could not fore-fee that men would act the part of brutes, without the leaft regard to law, to common equity, huma-nity, or decency; and that an event fhould happen at the clofe of the eighteenth century, of which it will not be eafy to find a parallel for three centu-ries before. For the perfecutions of chriftians by heathens, and of proteftants by papifts, were gene-rally conducted by fome *rule*; and in matters of *policy* and *religion* fome decent regard was ftill paid to a man's *private concerns*, in which the ftate had no intereft. Not to feel fuch loffes as thefe, and fuch ufage as this, would be not to be a man. But I am a chriftian, and I hope I bear them as fuch, acknowledging the hand of God, as well as that of man, in all events

I was alfo much confoled by the *addreffes* I re-ceived, not only from particular perfons, but from
various

various bodies of men, who interested themselves in my sufferings.   Some, if not all of them, I shall insert in the *Appendix*; as they may serve to encourage other persons in the pursuit of truth and the practice of virtue, notwithstanding the utmost malice of their enemies.   I need not say that I received the greatest consolation from the addresses of my congregation, and especially those of the younger part of it, to whom I had given particular attention.

REFLECTIONS

REFLECTIONS.

AFTER the preceding detail of *facts*, I now proceed to lay before my readers a feries of *Reflections* to which they have given occafion, and I hope they are fuch as will not be without their ufe; and then, great as my lofs has been ftated to be, it will not be the fubject of any regret.

....

SECTION I.

Of the Power of Refentment to prevent Compaffion.

I CANNOT help obferving on this occafion, as on a thoufand others, how much the leaft caufe of refentment tends to ftifle every emotion of fympathy and compaffion.

Had any perfon whatever fpent a great part of his life in the merely innocent employment of collecting medals, watching with the utmoft anxiety every opportunity of completing his fuite; had another given the fame time to a collection of fhells, foffils, prints, or books of any particular clafs,

without

any farther view than that of amuſing himſelf and his friends; and any of his neighbours, who knew in what manner, and how long, he had been employed, have come, and deſtroyed the labours of his life in an hour, there are few perſons, I believe, who would not have felt for the injury. For every man's labours are of value to himſelf; and every man has a natural right to enjoy the fruit of his labours, provided they do not interfere with the enjoyments of others. An injury of this kind would be conſidered as an injury done to ſociety itſelf, which engages for the protection of every individual in the quiet enjoyment of his innocent gratifications and purſuits, whatever they be. Every perſon would make the caſe his own, and have conſidered what he himſelf would have felt, not after having ſpent his life in the ſame purſuits, becauſe for them he might have had no particular taſte, but in any purſuit equally pleaſing to him, and would have reſented the injury with the greateſt ſenſibility.

Had this perſon's purſuits been of acknowledged utility to the public, and in the eye of the world done credit to his country, and to his age; had they been the labours of a Boyle, a Newton, or a Franklin, or thoſe of a Pope, an Addiſon, or a Locke, that had been thus wantonly and maliciouſly deſtroyed, all the world in a manner, and his country in particular, would have taken fire at the injury, and have thought no puniſhment too great for it.

But

But let *politics*, or *religion*, be concerned; let the curious collector, the naturalist, the poet, or the philofopher, be fufpected to be of an unpopular party in either, and the very circumftance that would have filled his countrymen with compaffion for him, and with rage againft his plunderers, would make many rejoice in the mifchief; and without the leaft regard to the innocence, or public merit, of his purfuits, they would receive a gratifi- cation from the idea of their hereby having it in their power to give him and his friends the more fenfible pain. Nay, provided they conceived that any advantage would accrue from it to their party, they would take a favage pleafure in deftroying him, and his labours together.

Such has been the fcene exhibited at Birming- ham, and I wifh it may prove an inftructive leffon to mankind. I do not fay what I have been, or what I have done. But had I been a Boyle, a Newton, or a Franklin, or had I had ten times the merit of each, or of all of them, I am confident, from what I have heard and obferved, that this circumftance would only have been an excitement to my enemies to the mifchief they have done me. The higher I had ftood in the good opinion of my friends, or of the public, the greater pleafure would they have taken in pulling me down.

This has, moreover, been done by perfons who do not want private virtue, by perfons of honour, juftice, and feeling in common life; and

who

who, if I had not been obnoxious to them on account of my *opinions*, would have relieved me in diftrefs, and have done me any kindnefs in their power; nay who, if they had had any knowledge of literature, or fcience, might perhaps have been proud of having me for a townfman and acquaintance, and have taken a pleafure in fhewing ftrangers the place where I lived.

Had I been a clergyman of the church of England, of little or no reputation, and the injury been done by Diffenters, no punifhment would have been thought fufficient for the perpetrators of fo much wickednefs; and, in the eyes of the nation, the whole fect would have been thought deferving of extirpation. Like the death of Charles I. the guilt of it would have been entailed upon our lateft pofterity.

I was forcibly ftruck with this idea on feeing a moft ingenious imitation of plants in paper, cut and painted fo like to nature, that, at a very fmall diftance, no eye could have perceived the difference; and by this means they were capable of being preferved from the attacks of infects, fo as to be greatly preferable to any *hortus ficcus*. It appeared to me that weeks, and in fome cafes months, muft have been employed on fome fingle plants, fo exquifitely were they finifhed.

What would this ingenious and deferving young lady have felt, how would her family and friends,

how

how would all botanifts, though they fhould only have heard of the ingenious contrivance, and of the labour and time fhe had fpent upon her plants; nay, how would the country in general have been filled with indignation, had any envious female neighbour come by force, or ftealth, and thrown all her flowers into the fire, and thus deftroyed all the fruits of her ingenuity, and patient working for years, in a fingle moment. And yet all this, excellent as it was, might with certainty have been done again, and perhaps in an improved manner. If this particular lady had not had time, or inclination, to do the fame work over again, fhe might have inftructed others, and precautions might have been taken to prevent fuch a misfortune a fecond time.

But the havoc that was made in almoft as fhort a fpace of time in my library and laboratory, neither myfelf or any body elfe can repair; and yet thoufands, and ten thoufands, I have no doubt, are fo far from feeling any fympathy with me, or my friends, on the occafion, that they rejoice in it, and would rejoice the more in proportion as the irreparable mifchief had been greater *.

If the fame malicious female fhould not only have thrown this lady's flowers into the fire, but ranfacked her apartments, and, getting poffeffion of all her private letters, have amufed herfelf with

---

* So far am I from being confidered an *injured perfon* by many, that they fcruple not to confider me as the proper caufe of the death of thofe who were executed for the riots, in fhort, nothing lefs than a *murderer*. Such is the idea conveyed by the author of a ballad in imi-

E   tation

reading them, and publishing them in all the neighbourhood, in order to do her all the injury in
her power, would not the crime be thought
worthy of the severest punishment, as a violent
breach of all the bonds of society? And yet in my
case, this very outrage has been committed without any sense of guilt in the perpetrators, or the
by-standers of the same party. Such is the baneful
influence of party spirit.

SECTION II.

My coming to Birmingham not the Cause of the Party Spirit in the Place.

IT will be evident from the preceding
narrative that my coming to Birmingham was by
no means the cause, as is now asserted, of the party
spirit which so unhappily prevails in that place.
Every thing that I wrote respecting the established
church was occasioned by the writings of others
against the Dissenters. In no case whatever was I

---

tation of the song of *William* and *Margaret*, sent to me by the post
from Chester.

> This is the dark and fearful hour,
> 　When Ghosts their wrongs disclose.
> Now graves give up their dead, to haunt
> 　The guilty soul's repose.
> Bethink thee, Priestley, of thy fault,
> 　Thy love of civil strife;
> And give me back my honest fame,
> 　And give me back my life.

the

the aggreſſor; and I never troubled even my own congregation with a ſingle diſcourſe on the ſubject, though this had been done again and again by my predeceſſor Mr. Bourne; and I never heard that he was particularly complained of on that account.

The long controverſy I had on the ſubject of the *trinity*, which, however, had no particular reſpect to Birmingham, was the conſequence of the attack of Biſhop Horſley, and others of the clergy, on one part of my *Hiſtory of the Corruptions of Chriſtianity.* All my *Defences of Unitarianiſm*, written in the courſe of this controverſy, are before the Public, and I appeal to all impartial readers, if they be not calm replies to ſome of the moſt virulent modes of attack of which there are any examples in this, or in any other, country. The Biſhop's profeſſed object was to deſtroy my credit *in toto*, ſo that nothing that I ſhould ever write on the ſubject might be regarded.

Beſides, what did I do, urged as I was, in every poſſible method, more than propoſe my *opinions*, with the *reaſons* on which they were founded. · There was no *violence* in this. And cannot opinion be oppoſed by opinion, and argument by argument? I ſeriouſly think that the doctrine of the *divine unity*, as oppoſed to that of the *trinity*, is of the greateſt importance in chriſtianity; and it is likewiſe my opinion, that *civil eſtabliſhments of chriſtianity* are the bane of it, tending to increaſe, and to perpetuate, every abuſe that has been introduced

E 2 into

into it. But many other perfons have maintained the fame opinions, and have held the fame language, before me. I, therefore, think it a peculiar honour to my writings, that my adverfaries have at length found no method of replying to them fo effectual as deftroying my property, and attempting my life; inftigating a furious mob to commit fuch ravages on general literature, as the European world has not known fince the ages of acknowledged barbarifm.

SECTION III.

Of Diffenters meddling with Politics.

IT is faid by many that, if I had not meddled with *politics* the riots in Birmingham would not have taken place. But this alfo is an hypothefis not fupported by facts. If the indignation of the populace had been excited againft me as a politician, and not as a Diffenter, why did they begin with demolifhing the meeting-houfe, before they proceeded to my own houfe, or made any attempt upon my perfon? Why did they demolifh the Old Meeting, the minifters of which had never appeared in a political character? And what had Mr. Taylor and Mr. John Ryland ever done in a political capacity? The rioters evidently made no diftinction between political Diffenters

and

and others, but confined their outrages to thofe who are generally called the more liberal, or unitarian Diffenters, as conceiving them to be peculiarly hoftile to the church, and therefore to the ftate, as connected with the church.

But what have been my writings as a politician? They are very inconfiderable, and never, that I underftood, gave much offence. All the time that I was with the Marquis of Lanfdowne, which was feven years, in which I had no employment as a minifter, I never wrote a political pamphlet, or paragraph. My ftudies were then, as before, and fince, *theology, philofophy,* and *general literature.*

My *Effay on the Firft Principles of Government,* which, of all my writings, may be thought the moft offenfive to the friends of arbitrary power, was publifhed more than twenty years ago, and never proceeded farther than a fecond edition, which alfo has been on fale almoft twenty years; fo that it could not have given any recent provocation. The political part of my *Lectures on Hiftory and General Policy,* is much in favour of the civil part of our prefent conftitution, though not without hinting at fuch improvements in it, as many upright and enlightened perfons of all denominations, wifh for.

Suppofing, however, that I had written much more largely on politics, particular as well as general, is this a fubject that Diffenters muft not

touch?

touch? As equal citizens, have we not an equal
intereſt in the concerns of the ſtate; and does
it not behove us to watch over that intereſt, as
much as others, whoſe ſtake in it is not greater
than ours?

When the government was friendly to the Diſſenters, our rulers were glad enough to avail themſelves both of our pens and of our ſwords. Our
right to give our opinion in affairs of ſtate was not
then queſtioned; and what has happened to affect
that right ſince? It is plain that it is only our
exerciſe of that right that gives offence. No
complaint was ever made of the conduct of Mr.
Bradbury, who was continually preaching political
ſermons, and who had a great hand in promoting
the acceſſion of the houſe of Hanover, except by
the clergy, who were generally enemies of that
acceſſion.

Though no change has taken place in our general principles, our opinions are now ſuppoſed to
be unfavourable to the maxims of thoſe who have
the conduct of adminiſtration; and hence the new
language, that Diſſenters, and particularly diſſenting miniſters, ought to confine themſelves to matters of religion; and that, content with our toleration, we ought not even to reflect on the eſtabliſhed church, which is now conſidered as an
eſſential part of the ſtate. I was never complained
of for having meddled with *philoſophy*, which is as
foreign to my proper profeſſion as *politics*.

But

But in what fenfe can this be called a *free country*, if every citizen be not at full liberty to deliver his opinion, in fpeaking or writing, on any fubject whatever, without the dread of civil penalties, legally or illegally inflicted? And how is our religion even *tolerated*, if we be debarred the privilege of writing in its defence, and freely advancing whatever we may deem of importance for that purpofe?

If umbrage be taken at Diffenters writing on any particular fubject, let us, at leaft, be prohibited by *law*, and let not any man be punifhed for doing what no known law makes to be a crime, and which in itfelf may be highly meritorious. Let an Act of Parliament be made to declare it felony, or treafon, for any Diffenter (or if that be thought too much, for any diffenting minifter) to write a political pamphlet, finding fault with the conftitution, or arraigning the conduct of adminiftration, and we fhall then confider what is to be done in thefe new circumftances,

Some weak politicians, and high churchmen, as an excufe for not appearing difpleafed at the riots in Birmingham, which did not affect the Calviniftic Diffenters, allege that the Diffenters of this day are a very different fet of perfons from thofe of former times, for whom the Act of Toleration was provided. This, no doubt, is true. All bodies of men have changed in a courfe of time, and the Diffenters among the reft. The clergy of the

E 4 eftablifhed

eftablifhed church are by no means the fame that they were at the Revolution; for they were then generally the enemies of the prefent reigning family, though they now make fo great a boaft of their being the friends of it. With refpect to their religious fentiments, they are greatly changed indeed fince the time of Queen Elizabeth, being, from Predeftinarians, become almoft univerfally Arminians, and till of late the more learned of their body are well known to have been Arians. There has alfo been a great change in the general fentiments of many of the Roman Catholics. But, to a politician, the only queftion is whether any of thefe changes of opinion give them lefs right to the protection of civil government.

The principal change in the Diffenters is fimilar to that which has taken place among the members of the church of England. They have receded farther from the fyftem of Calvinifm. Many of them became Arians, and many are now Unitarians, heretofore more generally called Socinians. But what has this to do with civil government? Can it be pretended that the man who confines his adoration to *one God*, and who calls this one God *the God and Father of Jefus Chrift*, is a worfe fubject of civil government than he who, in addition to the worfhip of this one God, pays equal divine honours to Jefus Chrift, and alfo to another divine perfon called *the Holy Ghoft*, or than he who adds to all thefe the worfhip of the Virgin Mary, and of all the faints and angels in the Popifh calendar?

The

The queſtion is ſurely too ridiculous to be diſcuſſed. Why then ſhould unitarian Diſſenters be more expoſed to lawleſs violence, and left out of the protection of the ſtate, than trinitarian Diſſenters, or than the Roman Catholics, to whom the favour of government has of late been very juſtly extended.

It is true alſo, that many of the Diſſenters are of late become enemies to all civil eſtabliſhments of religion. But ſo alſo are many Catholics, and even many members of the church of England itſelf. And in what ſenſe are they enemies, and how are they to be dreaded, and guarded againſt, as ſuch? They are only enemies in point of *argument.* They think it would be better for all ſtates not to trouble themſelves about religion, or at leaſt not to give any preference to one form of it more than to another. But this is not an opinion for which they will diſturb the peace of any ſtate. They wiſh to have *this,* as well as every other great queſtion, intereſting to man and to ſociety, to be freely diſcuſſed. But what is the proper uſe and termination of *diſcuſſion,* beſides the prevalence of *truth* and of *general happineſs?* No man who does not perſiſt in ſupporting what he himſelf believes to be falſe and miſchievous, will ever ſay the contrary. Why then ſhould not Diſſenters, and all other perſons, be tolerated in maintaining *this,* as well as any other opinion, though it has a remote relation to practice, as, indeed, every opinion of much importance neceſſarily has.

Whatever

Whatever were my political fentiments, though
I fhould be an avowed republican, and, as a
perfon high in office, but, in this refpect, of little
information, lately faid of me, " ready to de-
" ftroy the king, the houfe of Lords, and houfe
" of Commons too*," as this mifchief, unlefs I
were the dragon of Wantley, could only be effected
by *argument*, by convincing the people, that fuch
defcriptions of men were ufelefs, or mifchievous, to
them, it would be no juftifiable reafon for inflicting
on me what I have fuffered.

If my publications, be they what they will, be
not contrary to law, but merely fophiftical, let
them be anfwered.   My enemies will hardly fay
that my abilities as a writer are fuch, that, even
without the advantage of *truth*, I can out-write all
my opponents, and, in fpite of all their efforts, get
the great body of the people on my fide.   And till
this be done the ftate is in no manner of danger
from me.   If by writing, or acting, I expofe myfelf to the cenfure of the law, let it have its courfe;
but let not perfons, under the pretence of fupporting *government*, encourage lawlefs violence, fubverfive of all government whatever.

If by our writings any perfon be injured in
his private character, or affairs, Diffenters are pu-

---

* Such language as this may be faid to have been unintentionally
the caufe of the riots in Birmingham, with as much probability as the
fpeech of king Henry II. was that of the murder of Becket.   The
known, or the fuppofed, wifhes of men in power do not always require
to be accompanied with pofitive orders.   They fhould, therefore, be
particularly cautious what they fay.

nifhable

nifhable by law, like other citizens. But public meafures, and public characters, have always been, and it is to be hoped, always will be, open to public animadverfion in this country. Otherwife, there is an end of all true liberty; or if from this liberty the Diffenters alone are excluded, it is no free country for *us*, whatever it may be for others. Whenever I find myfelf debarred the exercife of the invaluable privilege of perfect freedom of fpeech and writing, I fhall confider it as a fignal for my departure to fome other part of the world, where it can be enjoyed without moleftation.

SECTION IV.

The Bigotry of the High Church Party the true Caufe of the Riots.

THAT the true fource of the late riots in Birmingham was *religious bigotry*, and the animofity of the high church party againft the Diffenters, and efpecially againft the Prefbyterians and Unitarians, and not the commemoration of the French Revolution, is evident from all that has paffed *before*, *at*, and *after*, the day.

In the public houfes where the people were inflaming themfelves with liquor, all that day, and fome time before, there were heard execrations of

the

the moft horrid kind againft *the Prefbyterians* One
perfon was heard not only to wifh *damnation* to
them, but that " God Almighty would make a
" week's holiday for the purpofe of damning them."
The mob did not arrive at the Hotel till more
than two hours after the company had left it, and
there they demanded only *myfelf,* who had not been
there. No part of their vengeance fell upon any
churchman, whether at the dinner or not. After
demolifhing the two meeting-houfes, and every
thing belong to *me,* their next objects were the
houfes of Mr. Taylor and Mr. John Ryland, who
were well known to have been much averfe to the
fcheme of the dinner; and during the whole courfe
of the outrages, the conftant cry was CHURCH AND
KING, and DOWN WITH THE PRESBYTERIANS.

That the celebration of the French Revolution
was not the true caufe of the riots, has indeed
fufficiently appeared from the narrative part of this
work. That the plan was laid fome time before,
and that proper perfons were provided to conduct
it, is probable from this circumftance, that thofe in
the mob who directed the reft, who were evidently not of the loweft clafs, and who were fometimes called their *leaders,* were not known to hundreds of all defcriptions of the inhabitants of the
town, who obferved them attentively; fo that perfons who were no Diffenters, concluded that they
came from a diftance, and probably from London.
The proper Birmingham mob were often perfuaded
to defift from their attempts, till they were joined
by

by thefe men, who both inftigated them to mifchief, and directed them how to proceed in the fhorteft and moft effectual manner.

If there be any foundation for this fuppofition, the plan of the riots muft have been laid fome time before, and of courfe, have been entirely inde-pendent both of the *hand-bill* and of the *Revolution dinner*, any farther than the latter directed to the proper time for the execution of the fcheme, as thefe directors muft have been engaged before hand. Time, it is hoped, will throw fome light on this dark bufinefs. It was probably intended to humble and intimidate the Diffenters, by fome perfons who thought it more prudent to do it by a mob, than by legal methods.

That the ftorm was directed folely againft thofe that are commonly called the more liberal Dif-fenters, and not the Calviniftic ones, was evident from the whole courfe of it, in which the houfes and meeting-houfes of the latter were fpared. The only exception was the houfe of Mr. Hutton who attends public worfhip at Carr's Lane, but whofe fon and daughter belong to the New Meeting. It is alfo thought that he was obnoxious to the lower claffes of the people on account of the ftrict and exemplary difcharge of his duty in the Court of Requefts. Let us now fee what paffed fubfequent to the event.

The

The exultation of the high church party, not only in Birmingham, but through the kingdom in general, on the fuccefs of this crufade, was undifguifed and boundlefs. All the newfpapers both in town and country, in the conduct of which they had particular influence, were full of the groffeft abufe of the Diffenters, and efpecially of myfelf; and fuch narratives of the proceedings were publifhed as cannot be accounted for from miftake, or mifapprehenfion, but muft have been wilfully fabricated for the worft of purpofes. Of this I have, in the APPENDIX, No. III. given one example from the paper called THE TIMES.

There were many of the high church party who did not hefitate to fay that, if the mifchief had terminated with the deftruction of my houfe, and every thing belonging to *me*, all had been well. Some openly lamented that the mob had not feized me, or that I had not perifhed in the conflagration. One clergyman in a public affize fermon, called our fufferings *wholefome correction*; and another declared that, if all my writings were put together, and myfelf were placed on the top of them, he fhould rejoice to fet fire to the pile.

Many of the high church party were fo far from lamenting my fufferings, or complaining of the illegal manner in which the mifchief was done, that they fcrupled not to juftify it, on the pretence, though abfolutely groundlefs, that my writings were

were hoftile to the *ftate*, if not directly, yet indi-
rectly fo, as being hoftile to the *church*.   One inftance of this, and one of the moft moderate of its
kind, I fhall give in the APPENDIX, No. VI. on
account of the fingular circumftance of its being
printed together with my own *Letter to the Inhabitants of Birmingham*, and thrown into many houfes
in London, with the title of SELF-MURDER, or
the DOCTOR TRIED AND CONVICTED ON HIS OWN
EVIDENCE.

The ftrange violence of the fame party fpirit
alfo appeared by a *hand-bill*, which was diftributed
in London the day after my arrival there, of which
a copy is given, APPENDIX, No. VII.   This could
only be intended to point me out as a proper
object of deftruction, by fome perfon who wanted
the courage, though not the will, to difpatch me
himfelf.

At the fame time I received an anonymous
letter, from a perfon who faid " he was concerned
" for my misfortunes and my folly," advifing me
to " have a ftrict guard on my future conduct;"
adding, " Depend upon it, if you proceed to
" foment difturbances in this place, nobody can
" anfwer for your fafety.   I can affure you the
" people of this country will not fee their happy
" conftitution infulted by any man."

The fame fpirit was but too apparent during
the trials; the moft notorious of the rioters being
acquitted

acquitted by the jury, againſt the cleareſt evidence, to the aſtoniſhment of the judge, and all the court, and their acquittal was received with the loudeſt applauſe by the ſurrounding audience. Nor was this indecent exultation confined to thoſe of the lower claſs, who were heard to wiſh " that the Bir- " mingham coin might circulate through the king- dom." Two perſons of better condition, as I was informed, meeting in the Town Hall at Warwick, immediately after the acquittal of two of the prin- cipal rioters, one of them obſerved to the other, that they " had ſucceeded beyond their expec- " tations, and that ſince thoſe two *hearty cocks*" (as " he called them) were ſafe, he did not much care " for the reſt." The poor wretches who were left to be hanged, it is preſumed, were ſuch as knew no ſecrets. This very much reſembles the caſe of *Demareé*, who was condemned for burning a Meeting-houſe in the time of Queen Ann, but was afterwards pardoned, and in the report of the trial, by judge Foſter, is called " one of Dr. Sacheverell's " ableſt advocates."

We ſtill have confidence in the juſtice of our country with reſpect to our *damages.* As to *lives*, we never wiſhed to take any more than might be deemed neceſſary for our own future ſecurity, and the peace of the country. We ſhall ſtill be ſuf- ferers in common with others, and much more than they, with reſpect to things for which no in- demnification can be made us.

They

The fame high church fpirit prevailed through moft parts of England, and in places where I had nothing to do. Similar outrages were threatened, and apprehended, at Manchefter; and it is thought they would have taken place there, as well as at Birmingham, if fome foldiers had not been ftationed in that town. Many are of opinion that if Dr. Price had been living, the ftorm would have fallen at Hackney in preference to Birmingham. A friend of mine at Exeter, who had invited me to fpend a few weeks with him this fummer, faid that he durft not now receive me. The Diffenters were alfo threatened by the high church party at Briftol, at Taunton, at Maidftone, and other places very diftant from each other. However, things wore a better afpect in the northern, and in fome of the eaftern parts of the kingdom. I had friends who offered me an afylum at Leeds, Norwich, and Ipfwich.

It will not be eafy to produce an example of treatment fo mercilefs and fhameful as mine has been; and yet the high church party are perpetually faying, that, though the proceeding has been *irregular*, I have not, in fact, received more than I *deferved*. As to my *manufcripts*, they fay that the lofs of one part of them, viz. the philofophical ones, is fufficiently compenfated for by the lofs of the other, viz. the *theological* ones; fo that I have my deferts, and the public is on the whole no lofer. This, however, is a virtual acknowledgment that, in their apprehenfions, there was fome-

F · ` · thing,

thing peculiarly formidable in my theological writings and that they found it eafier to difpofe of them in any other way than by anfwering them. This conduct is as weak as their arguments have always been; fince, as was the cafe with the books of the Sybils, the deftruction of fome of my writings increafes the value of thofe that are preferved; and by this moft convincing proof of the fuccefs of *my* writings, other perfons will be excited to write, though I fhould be fo overwhelmed by my misfortunes, as to be incapacitated from writing any more.

Never fhall *I* be heard to rejoice in the deftruction of any of the performances of my opponents. On the contrary, I have always wifhed, as my writings will evidence, that they had been more numerous, in order that their futility might more clearly appear. But my adverfaries muft have found that this conduct would not fo well fuit *them*, and therefore that their wifdom was not to produce any books of their own, but to deftroy mine.

On this occafion,* which would have called forth the commiferation of generous adverfaries,

---

* In an anonymous manufcript ballad, intitled *The Ghoft and the Doctor*, fent me by the poft from Chefter, one of the perfons lately executed for the riots, reprefented as a man of " honeft fame" and a " fimple zealot," appears to me, and reproaches me as the " profefled prieft of fedition," whofe object it has been to preach the deftruction of all order, as the caufe of his death, which in juftice I ought to fuffer. After this I am made to rife "raving from my bed," and to " burn my pen," with a refolution never to write again. To this is added *quod fit omnes boni piique ex imis pectoribus precantur.*
But

there have appeared ftronger marks of virulence
againft the Diffenters than have been known for
many years before. Not a grain of merit has been
allowed to us, as a compenfation for the crimes of
which we are accufed; and we are particularly
charged with the greateft ingratitude againft the
government under which we live.

Dr. Tatham of Oxford, exulting over us on
this occafion, fpeaks of the Diffenters as *gracioufly
indulged.* But whether is it *our* fyftem of religion,
or *his,* that is moft gracioufly indulged, and which
of them is beft entitled to this indulgence? Will
a mere parliamentary fanction give any form of religion a preference in the eye of God and of reafon; and if this fhould be a cafe in which the
judgment of man fhall be found to differ from
that of God, it will by no means be the firft of the
kind. The time is approaching when every thing
of this nature will be weighed in a jufter balance
than they ufually are at prefent, and while we are
all waiting for this final decifion, let us be humble
and forbearing.

But though many of the clergy expreffed the
moft rancorous fentiments againft us, there have
appeared on this occafion among them men of

But the zealots of Birmingham, and this martyr to the church of
England among the reft, took a much more natural method to filence
me than this ballad maker (probably a clergyman) of Chefter. What
he and his friends only *prayed for,* they ufed the proper means to fecure. That they were difappointed in their fcheme was not their
fault. They may fucceed better in a fecond atempt.

the

the moſt liberal minds and principles, who expreſſed the greateſt abhorrence of the conduct and
ſentiments of the reſt of their body, and who, together with ſome generous minded laity of the
eſtabliſhment, were among the firſt to afford me
the moſt ſubſtantial aſſiſtance.

SECTION V.

*Of the Pretence that Government was adverſe to the
Diſſenters and favoured the Rioters.*

IT was unfortunately a very general
opinion that *Government* favoured the violent proceedings againſt the Diſſenters at Birmingham. It
was the conſtant cry of the rioters, in the courſe
of their ravages, " We have nothing to fear. The
" juſtices are for us, Government is for us;" and
when they were told the troops were coming, they
ſaid the ſoldiers were on their ſide. When the
king's proclamation, offering the reward of an
hundred pounds for the diſcovery and conviction
of any perſon concerned in the riot was publiſhed,
ſome of the people were heard to cry, " Is he then
" turned Preſbyterian, and are we to be hanged for
this?" Similar language was held by ſome who
ought to have known better.

This

This is a circumftance which it greatly concerns the governors of a country to attend to, if they wifh to preferve the peace of it, and extend their protection alike to all the fubjects. For if any fmall part of the community, and efpecially fuch members of it as are leaft difpofed to violence, be held out, or imagined to be held out, to the reft of the community, as *unworthy of protection*, they will be confidered as in a ftate of *profcription*, and proper objects of perfecution, expofed to every infult; and they will have no refource but in temporary felf defence, and final emigration. And furely the experience of the laft century muft have fhewn this country the impolicy, if not the wickednefs, of fuch irritation.

The Diffenters have no mob to oppofe to fuch abandoned wretches as commited the outrages at Birmingham; and yet it is now pretended that if the high church party had not deftroyed our houfes, and places of public worfhip, we fhould have deftroyed theirs. But admitting that the Diffenters are *knaves*, they are not *fools*, or rather *madmen*, as they muft have been to have attempted violence in their fituation, unlefs every one of them had been confcious to himfelf of having the ftrength of Samfon, and that he was a match for a thoufand of his enemies.

But when did Diffenters attempt any thing of the kind? There are inftances enow upon record of fimilar outrages being committed *upon* the Diffenters, senters, in various parts of the kingdom; but no example of any being committed *by* them. They are universally a sober and orderly people; and whatever they may think of other people's opinions, they have no idea of promoting their cause by *force.* Not one Independent, Baptist, or Methodist, I am confident, had any hand in the riot at Birmingham, but only those members of the church of England (if they can be said to be the members of any church) who are in fact destitute of all sense of religion; and of such consists a very great proportion of the inhabitants of Birmingham, and all other large manufacturing towns. In the height of the riot they were addressed by the magistrates, and other respectable members of the church of England, who then thought they had done mischief enough, and wished them to proceed no farther, by the appellation of *Friends and Fellow-churchmen.* See APPENDIX, No. VIII.

It cannot be denied that a crime has been committed, and of the greatest enormity in a civilized country. Immense property has been destroyed, houses burned, lives endangered, and the peace of many families interrupted, by an illegal insurrection, in defiance of all law and good order, and that these violences were committed on the pretence of supporting *the church and the king.* It certainly, therefore, behoves both the church and the government, to exculpate themselves, and to make every satisfaction to the sufferers that the nature of the case will admit of.

The

The violences were committed by the lower orders of the people, but if the friends of the church and of the king in the higher ranks had been earneft to fupprefs the riot, it might, no doubt, have been effected before any mifchief had been done. If the magiftrates, and other principal inhabitants of the town, belonging to the church, of England, on the firft hearing of the rioters going to the New Meeting, had interpofed, by repairing to the place, and earneftly protefting againft the violence, even that meeting-houfe would not have fuffered. Had there not been time for *this* (which, however, there certainly was) their interpofition might have prevented the deftruction of the fecond meeting-houfe. At leaft, with the affiftance of a few men with fire-arms, which they could eafily have commanded, they might have prevented all the mifchief at my houfe, with every thing that followed. There was, therefore, at leaft a criminal remiffnefs in the friends of the church and the king. But the cleareft facts fhew that there was more than remiffnefs on the part of many perfons of better condition, and nothing that they ever did fhewed a real difapprobation of the conduct of the mob previous to the demolition of my houfe, but only a wifh that they fhould proceed no farther than that; and this on no other account than that of the *expence* it would be to themfelves. This is evident from the hand-bills laft referred to.

Making every allowance for the perpetrators and abettors of thefe horrid fcenes at the moment,

there

there has been time for reflection and compunction fince; and the eyes of the nation, and of all Europe, are open to fee what part both the town and neighbourhood, and above all the government of the country, will take in the cafe. On the part of the town and neighbourhood nothing favourable to juftice has appeared as yet.

Out of feveral thoufand rioters evidence has been procured againft no more than fifty-two. Of thefe not fo many as twenty have been apprehended, and of thefe only five have been condemned, and three executed*. Inftead of promoting an inquiry concerning the inftigators of this mob, and cenfuring the manifeft remiffnefs of the magiftrates, a town's meeting has voted the latter thanks and rewards for the part they acted; and an *Addrefs to the King* reflecting more on the Diffenters, as friends to innovation, than on the rioters†. The whole town and neighbourhood, therefore, muft

---

* On occafion of the riots in London, in which it is probable that fewer perfons were concerned than in thofe of Birmingham, one hundred and thirty-five were tried, fifty-nine convicted, and twenty-fix executed ; and I believe merely for what they did in the riots. Whereas it is remarkable that of the very few who were convicted on occafion of the riots in Birmingham, all who were executed were men of notorious bad character in other refpects. And certainly the execution of men who were univerfally confidered as the pelts of fociety, is no punifhment for this particular offence, and therefore no warning againft the commiffion of the like; fince it will be concluded, that if men be chargeable with nothing but deftroying the property of the Diffenters, they have no punifhment to fear. For either the jury will not find them guilty, or the cafe will be fo reprefented to the king that a pardon will certainly be procured.

† This addrefs, and alfo that of the Diffenters, I fhall infert in the APPENDIX, No. IX. that the abject fpirit of the one may be compared with the liberal and manly fpirit of the other.

fall

fall under the fufpicion of fcreening the criminals, and therefore partaking in the guilt.

The clergy, if they had wifhed to wafh their hands of this crime, and difclaim the conduct of thofe who call themfelves *their friends*, fhould have been the firft to reprobate their proceedings, and to preach moderation and peace. Inftead of this, they have been the firft to calumniate us, and reprefent the conduct of the mob in the moft favourable light. Since two meeting-houfes were deftroyed on pretence of fupporting the *church*, the leaft that they could have done, and the moft natural compenfation for the time, would have been to allow the Diffenters the ufe of their churches, till the meeting-houfes could have been rebuilt.

This would only have been doing, as a compenfation for an injury committed by churchmen, what the Diffenters at Banbury are at this very time doing in favour of the church of England, while the parifh church of that place is rebuilding, though they had no hand in pulling it down. There are feveral places in Germany in which the Catholics and Proteftants conftantly make ufe of the fame place of public worfhip. Such an offer on the part of the clergy, or the bifhop of the diocefe, would have done them the greateft credit, and have contributed very much towards exculpating them from having any fhare in the outrage. But this natural and eafy method, which would have coft them nothing, not having been done, they remain without that exculpation. The clergy alfo, and
other

other principal inhabitants of the town, if they had been properly fenfible of the injury done to myfelf in particular, might have joined in inviting me back again, and doing every thing in their power to make my re-eftablifhment fafe and eafy.

On the contrary, I am informed from various quarters, that the inveteracy againft me through the town in general, owing to the moft atrocious calumnies, and mifreprefentations, is rather increafed than diminifhed, andthat my return would both be hazardous to myfelf, and augment their hoftility*.

It is evident, therefore, that we have now nothing to expect either from the clergy or laity of the town and neighbourhood of Birmingham, but muft look to the general government of the country; and we hope it will be found that thence we do not look for juftice, activity, or energy, in vain.

Had the bifhop of the diocefe fent a proper *paftoral letter* to the clergy of Birmingham, lamenting the effects of party fpirit, and efpecially that any attempts fhould have been made to fupport a *chriftian church* by fuch unchriftian means as had been employed on that pretence; had he advifed an immediate reparation of the wrongs of the Diffenters, and the doing every thing that was in the power of the members of the church of England to reftore

---

* In order to fee the different fpirit that actuates diffenting minifters, and the generality of the clergy, with refpect to the late riots, I would refer my reader to Mr. Scholefield's truly chriftian *Difcourfe on loving our Enemies*, and his fpirited and excellent *Preface* to it.

the

the peace of the town, the inftigators of the riot would before this time have been made afhamed of their conduct, and greater harmony than ever might have taken place between the members of the eftablifhed church and the Diffenters. But though many of his flock have behaved like wolves, their conduct has not been reproved by their paftor, at leaft in that public manner which the nature of the cafe required. Confidering the part that many of the lower clergy have acted in this bufinefs, the eyes of the country are now upon the bifhops; and their filence will be conftrued into approbation; efpecially fince much of the bigotry of the prefent times is by many afcribed to their frequent and inflammatory charges againft the Diffenters, and efpecially the Unitarians, not without plain allufions to myfelf in particular.

In the reigns of king William and queen Ann, the bigotry of the inferior clergy was conftantly checked by the greater liberality of the bifhops; the lower houfe of convocation being controlled by the upper houfe. But in this reign the high church fpirit has defcended from the fuperior to the inferior clergy.

If the fpirit of perfecution proceed as it has begun, unchecked by the fuperior clergy of the church of England, I fhall not fcruple to fay of it, as of myftical Babylon in the Revelation (xviii. 4.) *Come out of her my people, left ye be partakers of her fins, and that ye receive not of her plagues.* But I hope, and I know better things of many of them,

and

and I have great expectations from their interference,

Of the two parties in whofe names the outrages
at Birmingham were committed, viz. *the church*
and *the king*, the latter has, in a great meafure,
exculpated himfelf, by his proclamation to apprehend and punifh the rioters. But the former, the
boafted *ally* of the ftate (and which, like Cardinal
Wolfey, always names herfelf before her king) has
not hitherto done any thing in concurrence with
her ally, but has taken another coadjutor. Henceforth, therefore, the cry fhould be not *church and
king*, but *church and mob*.

SECTION VI.

Of the principal Ufe of an eftablifhed Religion.

I CANNOT help obferving on this
occafion, that if the ftate be at the expence of pro-
viding the country with *religion*, it fhould be chiefly
for the benefit of thofe who ftand in the moft need
of it, and who would not provide any for themfelves.
The *better fort* of people, as we call them, will behave orderly and peaceably, which is the great end
of civil government, without it. But with us the
lower claffes of the community are nearly in the
fame condition as if there was no eftablifhed religion at all. If the inefficacy of an eftablifhed religion to correct the diforders of the lower orders
of the people, as manifefted in the riots at Birmingham,

ningham, does not open the eyes of this country to the true nature of church eftablifhments, it will be difficult to fay what will, and fo great and ferious a leffon will have been given us in vain.

In confequence of the too general neglect of the lower claffes of people by the minifters of the eftablifhed church, their profanenefs, brutality, and licentioufnefs, exceed that of the fame clafs of people in any other country whatever, civilized or uncivilized. For thofe whom we call *favages* have infinitely more regard to decency, equity, and civility, in their conduct, than the untaught vulgar with us. What thefe learn from a ftate of fociety are the vices to which it gives occafion, and they are fuch as have no place in what we call the *uncivilized* part of the world, becaufe, in their circumftances, there is no temptation to them.

If therefore, there muft be a *ftate religion,* and the object of this religion be not the emolument of the teachers of it, or the power of the governors in difpofing of thofe emoluments, but to infpire the people with a fenfe of their obligations to God and man, the moft exprefs provifion fhould be made for the inftruction of the lower orders of the people, in preference to that of all others. The clergy fhould know them all, and inftruct them all. But with us too little of this kind is done, nor does there appear much difpofition towards it.

The greateft part of the real advantage which this country derives from the religion of the lower orders

orders of the people cofts it nothing at all, being
that which accrues to it from the labours of the
Diſſenters and Methodiſts, who have been the
means of civilizing and chriſtianizing ſome of thoſe
for whoſe inſtruction principally the eſtabliſhed
clergy are paid, but who are too generally neglected by them, and are as ſheep without a
ſhepherd. The country will ſooner or later conſider the *cui bono* of this eſtabliſhment, as well as
of every thing elſe in the ſyſtem for which it furniſhes the expence.

The only thing that has of late years been done
in favour of this greatly neglected part of the community, is the inſtitution of *Sunday Schools,* which
was the happy thought of Mr. Raikes of Glouceſter,
a member of the church of England, and which
was immediately patronized by the clergy, and the
members of the church of England in general.
But becauſe many of the Diſſenters took them up
with more zeal than they, and made better proviſion
for inſtructing and rewarding Sunday ſcholars (ſo
that their ſchools came into greater repute than thoſe
of the eſtabliſhment) ſeveral of the clergy have
taken umbrage at them. Some of them have endeavoured to compel the Diſſenters to drop, or
reduce, their Sunday Schools, and others who pretend to more ſagacity than the reſt, now ſay that
they never approved of the ſcheme, becauſe they
foreſaw that it would be the means of adding to
the number of the Diſſenters, a thing which they
evidently conſider as a greater evil than that ſhame-
ful ignorance and profligacy of the poor, which this
excellent

excellent fcheme is calculated to remove. See *Dr.*
Tatham's Letters.

In this cafe it fhould be confidered out of what
clafs of the community is the addition to the Diffenters made. Is it not out of that which, previous
to this meafure, had no religion at all? The clergy
in general are far from adopting this unchriftian
maxim, and in fome places they act in concert with
the Diffenters, in a fcheme the object of which is
common chriftianity, and common utility.

When an account fhall be taken of the advantages and difadvantages of civil eftablifhments of
religion, every injury done by *perfecution* fhould be
placed on the *per contra* fide. For the different fects
of Diffenters in this country, where there is an eftablifhment, and the different religious denominations
in North America, where there is none, never mo-
left one another, but live in good neighbourhood
and friendfhip. It is when one fect enjoys temporal
advantages from which the reft are excluded, that
a bone of contention is thrown among them; and
then the envy of the depreffed party, but much
more the jealoufy and fpirit of domination, the
natural offspring of *power*, in the party that is favoured, may do infinite mifchief. For the fpirit of
church eftablifhments, which is ever jealous and
vindictive, is not peculiar to *them*. It is the fpirit
not of religion in particular, but of all *monopolies*.
Nor are the clergy fo much to be complained of.
Men in general are the fame. They are *fyftems* and
inftitutions, that corrupt mankind.

In all thofe who have poffeffion of power, there too eafily arifes the idea, that what cannot be accomplifhed by *argument* in favour of their fyftem, may be effected with much more eafe and certainty by external *force*. Hence, inftead of an-fwering our books, the members of the church of England at Birmingham, have burned them, to-gether with our houfes and places of public wor-fhip. If fuch a proceeding as this either breaks the fpirit, or leffens the number, of Diffenters, it will be the firft experiment of the kind that has fucceeded. But the heroic actors in this bufinefs probably never heard that any fuch experiment had ever been tried before.

I fhall conclude this article with obferving, that .it is ufual to praife every exifting reign, as great and glorious, and to afcribe every thing that the age produces to the prince upon the throne. But whatever other advantages have accrued to this country during the prefent reign, I will venture to fay that, if the defpicable fpirit of bigotry and into-lerance continue to prevail, unchecked by govern-ment, as it has done of late years, it will (confider-ing the increafing light of the age in every other country in Europe) be one of the moft difgrace-ful in the annals of Britain. There was fome-thing plaufible in the perfecution of chriftians by heathens, and in that of Proteftants by Catholics, becaufe they introduced great innovations, and great and unknown confequences were dreaded from them. They were religions of yefterday

overturning

overturning eſtabliſhments of the remoteſt anti-
quity. But the perſecution of one ſect of Proteſtants by another, all equally *novelties*, and very
much reſembling one another, is nothing better
than the mutual perſecution of the *Sonnites* and
Shütes in Mahomedan countries, or than that of
the *Littleendians* of Lilliput by the *Bigendians*.

A great number of the clergy, however, are
men of other minds. They are ſenſible of the
abuſes of their ſyſtem, and earneſtly wiſh for a
reform. They reſpect the Diſſenters, and are always ready to act in concert with them, wherever
humanity or common chriſtianity is concerned.
Theſe are generally called *low churchmen*, while
thoſe of the *high church party*, which is certainly
greatly encreaſed of late years, are ſtrenuous advocates for continuing every thing as it is, and op-
poſing all *innovation*, that is, every *reform*. They
hate, and they dread, all Diſſenters, except the
quieteſt among them, who neither ſpeak nor write
any thing on the ſubject of their diſſent, and
who, like all other Diſſenters, generally pay them
better, and more chearfully, than their other pa-
riſhioners. Such Diſſenters as theſe they might
not be very ſorry to ſee increaſe.

G

SECTION VII.

*Of the Importance of a good Police in a well con-
stituted State.*

WE may learn from the late riots
in Birmingham, as well as from those in London
in 1780, the necessity of having a force always
ready to repel an undisciplined mob.   On either
of these occasions, twenty men armed with muf-
quets, and only a general knowledge of the use of
them, would at any time have dispersed the rioters.
And how easy would it be to have many times
this small force in constant readiness in every town
and parish in the kingdom, without having re-
course to a *standing army*, at the command of the
crown only, which is the bane of all free states.
Let all the reputable inhabitants of any town, or
parish, be provided with fire arms, and exercised
in the use of them, and no riots would ever be
attempted.

What objection any wise and just government
can have to this measure, I do not see; and without a provision of this kind, we are disappointed
with respect to the principal advantage that a state
of society and government holds out to us, which
is protection from lawless violence, and the benefit
of a fair trial for any offences of which we are
accused.

accufed. While men offend againſt no law, they ſhould enjoy the protection of the law, and if they do offend, they ſhould be tried and puniſhed according to law. This is the firſt rule in all civil fociety, and yet in this country there is at this moment a too general exultation, that this rule has been violated in the cafe of the Diſſenters in general, and of myſelf in particular, though we have done no injury to fociety whatever.

It is fomething extraordinary that perfons uſed to a ſtate of law and government ſhould not be ſtruck with the impropriety of making a mob both the judges, and executioners, of law, and that in a ſtate of intoxication, when they are not capable of hearing any reafon. In the prefent cafe, on the ſimple aſſertion of fome malicious perfon, that I drank *no church no king*, and *the king's head in a charger*, at a place where I was not prefent, and that I was the author of a *hand-bill* which I had barely heard of, I am inſtantly, without examination of myſelf, or my accufer, expofed to fuffer infinitely more than I ſhould have done if I had been actually guilty of all thefe offences, and the whole charge had been proved in a court of law. For *that* could only have amounted to *fine and imprifonment.* It would not have involved the innocent labours of my paſt life. The fentence of the law would not have been the burning of my houfe, without giving me an opportunity of removing any thing out of it, the deſtruction of my library, apparatus, and manufcripts.

G 2 Suppofing

Suppofing the Diffenters fhould have had recourfe to fimilar methods of revenge, which would have been more juftifiable, as not having been the *aggreffors*, and have burned church for church, houfe for houfe, library for library, &c. &c. into what a ftate of anarchy, worfe than civil war, would the whole country have been thrown. The worft that my enemies can fay of me is that I wifh to fet up a republican form of government; but this is at leaft *fome* form of government, whereas thofe who planned, and directed, the proceedings at Birmingham, went by no fort of government at all; having adopted the very meafures which all governments whatever were intended to guard againft *.

Since the Diffenters are clearly innocent of what has been fo generally laid to their charge, and for which they have fuffered fo feverely, we may apply to their cafe the proverb ufed on a

---

* Some, however, take it for granted, that by a republican form of government, is meant no government at all, but to leave all people at liberty to act as they pleafed, from the impulfe of the moment. Thus the Ghoft in the poem from Chefter is made to fay,

" How couldft thou preach that mobs might rule."

A writer in the Gentleman's Magazine for September, 1791, p. 191, whofe fignature is OEDIPUS, fays of me, " His own engine *the mob*, " which he vainly imagined he could wield with ability, and with " which he has in the prefent inftance threatened the eftablifhment of " his country, has at laft recoiled upon him with ten-fold violence. " That Dr. Prieftley has done all in his power to ftir up the people " in oppofition to government, is a fact eafily proved." That Mr. Nichols, a man who has fome pretentions to literature, fhould fuffer this publication, which goes into the hands of moft men of letters, to be the hackneyed vehicle of fuch impudent and malicious falfehoods, againft a perfon in my fituation, will to many appear extraordinary. But he ranks with high churchmen, and on fuch, in the cafe of Diffenters, juftice and humanity feem to have no claim.

fimilar

fimilar occafion by our Saviour (who, however, was not punifhed without the form of *law*, and the authority of the chief magiftrate) *If thefe things be done in the green tree, what fhall be done in the dry.* If the innocent fuffer thus much, what have the guilty to expect?

It was a blind and furious zeal for *the law*, the eftablifhed religion of the country, a religion appointed by God himfelf, and the lawlefs violences to which their zeal led thofe of the Jews who were termed *zealots*, that preceded, and brought on, the deftruction of Jerufalem; and thofe zealots were not more blind and furious than the friends of the church of England at Birmingham, and in many other parts of this country. Let thofe of them who are able, read Jofephus, and take warning.

The number of fuch defperate and profligate wretches in this country as were inftigated to lawlefs havoc and plunder, on the pretence of fupporting the church and ftate, at Birmingham, and who will be equally ready to plunder on any other pretence, almoft exceeds belief, and we have more to dread from them than from all our other evils put together. Indeed, they all point to this.

Whenever the difficulties of this country fhall encreafe, fo that thefe people can neither be employed, nor fed, (and from more caufes than one we draw nearer to this fituation every day) every great town in England, if no provifion be made
againft

againſt it, may be expected to exhibit ſuch ſcenes as Birmingham has lately done, and as London did in the year 1780; when the labour of ages may be ſwept away in a day, and this whole country, at preſent the pride of the world, may become a ſcene of general deſolation. It has within itſelf the ample ſeeds of ſuch calamity, in the prodigious number of the ignorant, the profligate, and the profane part of the lower orders of the community, whom the impolicy of our *poor laws* chiefly, has rendered utterly averſe to labour and economy, to a degree far below that of any of the brute creation. Our common ſoldiers are chiefly of this claſs, and caſes may ariſe, in which little dependence can be placed upon *them*, for preſerving the peace and good order of the kingdom.

The eſtabliſhed clergy give little attention to the morals of this moſt depraved part of the community; nor indeed is it in their power to do much. But the caſe requires the immediate attention of government, if our ſtateſmen mean to do any thing more than put off the evil day from their own times, contenting themſelves with temporary expedients, inſtead of ſubſtantial remedies.

If our lives and properties are to be at the mercy of the mob, which may riſe, and commit its premeditated ravages, without giving us any warning; and if there be no redreſs but in a military force, and that frequently at a conſiderable diſtance; if this redreſs depend on the arbitrary will of the

crown;

crown; let any perfon fay in what our condition differs from that of perfect *defpotifm*; our imperfect fecurity from the greateft injuries arifing not from *law*, and *regular government*, but from *arbitrary will.* It would be a government in the ftricteft fenfe of the word *military*, and much worfe than that which is ufually fo called; becaufe in it there is at leaft fome known mode of proceeding.

Such, however, is the prefent fituation of this country, that there appears to be no effectual remedy for this great evil, but in voluntary affo-ciations for felf-defence; and this is little lefs than fuperadding a new government, at a great expence, to fupply the defects of an old one, which is already the moft expenfive in the world. It is fo far from being improper, or illegal, for men to defend themfelves, and their property, from lawlefs vio-lence, by any fufficient means, fire-arms not ex-cepted, that it is highly commendable to do it. See Sir William Jones's excellent tract on *The legal Method of fuppreffing Riots.*

In the riots at Birmingham relief was fent as foon as poffible, the expedition of the troops was extraordinary; and thanks were certainly due to thofe who actually faved the town, and efpecially the Diffenters in it, from total deftruction. But had government been remifs, or the troops tardy; nay, had the expreffes been delayed, as they might

might have been, by accident: and if, from any of thefe caufes, the fury of the mob had continued un-reftrained a fingle day longer (in which cafe it is the general opinion that the town would have been on fire) where could have been the remedy, when fuch a town as Birmingham, and the manufactures of it, had been loft to the kingdom? Should the fafety of a wife nation depend upon refources fo precarious as thefe?

Let thofe who are not difpleafed with mobs when they think that they only execute fummary juftice on thofe whom the laws cannot reach, con-fider how hazardous a weapon they wifh to employ, and how difficult it is to direct it. None of thofe who promoted the riots in Birmingham had, I am perfuaded, any intention that the mifchief fhould have proceeded fo far as it did; and I fhould not wonder if the time come when the fame lawlefs rabble, who lately fhouted *Church and king,* fhould take up the cry of *No church, no king,* or at leaft that of *No game laws, no tythes, no excife.* Nothing is wanting but an artful leader.

Who does not recollect how the tide of popular favour has turned both with refpect to our prefent fovereign, and the prefent king of France. No princes ever came to their crowns with more ge-neral popularity. But in a few years the cafe was fo much the reverfe in this country, that the king
conftantly

conftantly went abroad, if not amidft the hiffes (which was fometimes the cafe) yet with the moft marked and difrefpectful filence, of the people in general*. The cafe is now happily reverfed, and the prefent reign is likely to clofe with as much popularity as it began,

Who was ever more idolized than the prefent king of France, and yet what was not thought, and openly faid of him, on his late return to Paris? And he is now likely to be more, and more juftly, popular than ever. Both thefe princes, however, are, no doubt, the very fame that they ever were. The change has been in the people, and in their ideas of them.

The late king of France was almoft idolized at the time of his illnefs at Rheims. Had he been literally the father of every family in the nation, they could not have appeared to feel more for him than they did. Yet though there was little change in his principles or conduct, into what univerfal contempt did he fink before he died. Wife men

---

* I never faw a greater croud on any occafion than on the king's once going through St. James's park to the houfe of Peers, at the beginning of the American war, and becaufe one man, probably from the country, pulled off his hat as the coach paffed clofe to him, he was very near being knocked down for it by thofe who were next to him. It was the conftant cuftom for years to let the king's chair pafs without any notice, at the fame time that every perfon put off his hat in the moft refpectful manner to the queen. When, as by a kind of irrefiftible impulfe, I was at one time going to pull off mine to the king, the perfon I was walking with, perceiving that I was putting up my hand for that purpofe, checked me, by faying that if I did, I fhould certainly be infulted.

will

will reflect on thefe things, and the caufes of them; and from the changes that have taken place, they will not be furprized at any others of the fame kind, as great, and as fudden.

─────

SECTION VIII.

The Impolicy of checking the natural Expreffion of Men's Sentiments.

So many leffons as hiftory holds out to us of the kind, I cannot help expreffing fome furprize, that the pretended friends of our government fhould endeavour to fupprefs the natural ebullition of men's minds by fpeaking, writing, or public entertainments. No attempts of this kind can prevent men's *thinking*. Nay, thefe meafures have never failed to make men think the more, and the fooner to have recourfe to other methods of expreffing their fentiments, infinitely more hazardous to the public peace.

What did the late government of France gain by the moft rigorous meafures of this kind, reftraining all liberty of the prefs, and preventing, as far as *power* could do it, all the ufual modes of expreffing men's fentiments? In thefe circumftances, *prohibited books* did infinitely more mifchief,

as

as it would be called, than any that could have been published; and private converfation, in this ftate of reftraint, did more mifchief than any books whatever. For the Revolution, as is evident, found the whole nation, thofe who could not read, as well as thofe who could, fully ripe for the change; while to thofe who were unacquainted with the natural progrefs of things, there feemed to be an inftantaneous, and almoft miraculous, tranfition, from idolizing their kings, to a contempt and deteftation of kingly government, till, on farther reflection, they acquiefced in the prefent medium.

On the other hand, Englifhmen, being ufed to write and to fpeak freely, and to have convivial meetings whenever they pleafed, are generally content with giving vent to their fentiments in thefe ways, and never think of any thing farther. But if this outlet to their natural feelings be fhut, they will certainly find fome other, much more alarming, than dinners, toafts, and fongs. It may be like the ftopping the mouth of a volcano, the confequence of which would be the convulfion of all the country. If there is to be a revolution in this country, fimilar to that which has taken place in France (though our fituation is fuch as by no means to require it) attempts to deter men by illegal violence from doing what the law does not forbid, will, I am confident, bring it on in half the time. Men, who do not like to be infulted, will at length be prepared to refift violence by violence; and from fuch accidental and inconfiderate fparks as
thefe

thefe, a civil war may be lighted up, and confequences may follow which the wifeft among us
cannot forefee,

They who take any ferious umbrage at fuch
meetings as thofe for the celebration of the French
Revolution, throw the greateft reflection on the
prefent reign, and moft endanger the prefent happy
tranquility of it. For it is to reprefent it as no
better than the reign of Tiberius, a reign of univerfal fufpicion, and of real dangers arifing from
imaginary ones. That government muft be confcious of its extreme weaknefs, or be actuated by
the moft wanton cruelty, that can ferioufly refent
fuch trifling infults as thefe, admitting, what is by
no means true, that they were *intended* for infults.

The wifeft, and in all refpects the beft method,
is to indulge men in the freeft expreffion of their
natural fentiments, and even to encourage the fulleft
difcuffion of all topics, of a civil as well as of a religious nature, in order that one opinion and one
reafon may combat another, and that all truth,
religious, philofophical, or political, may prevail,
and eftablifh itfelf, without obftruction. By this
gentle and generous proceeding, no convulfion will
ever happen in any ftate. The public opinion will
thus be formed gradually, and have its natural and
eafy operation, producing changes as they are
wanted; and grievances will not be permitted to
accumulate, till the mafs fhall be fo great, as to
force its way through all oppofition.

This

This maxim is equally true with refpect to the church, or the ftate. If the clergy made no oppo-fition to the encreafing light of the age, but would themfelves fpeculate freely on every fubject relating to their own fituation, and that of the country, no-thing would ever hurt any individual of them. Should the confequence of this free difcuffion, and gradual change in the public mind, be the abolition of tythes, they would not be lofers by it; becaufe, if they themfelves fhould heartily concur in the meafure, fome better, and no lefs ample, provifion would be made for them. Should they allow a revifion of the public creeds, articles, and liturgy, the prefent fubfcription might be dropped, and any other alteration made, without affecting their reve-nues, or the general fyftem.

Should the clergy proceed a ftep farther, and acknowledge that the feat of the bifhops in the houfe of Lords (which had no other origin than the now antiquated feudal fyftem) was unfuitable to their fpiritual character; and of their own accord withdraw themfelves from Parliament, it would be with a dignity which would eftablifh them in the good-will of the people, and preferve their rank in other refpects, for ages.

But by proceeding on their prefent plan of a dread of all *innovation*, and altering nothing, not-withftanding the increafing light of the age, they lead many perfons to conclude, that they are deter-mined to hear no reafon, and that, from a regard

to

to their temporal honours and emoluments only, they wilfully ſhut their ears to the cleareſt voice of truth.

By this means the whole ſyſtem of the civil eſtabliſhment of chriſtianity will be ſuſpected to be irreconcilable to the cauſe of religious truth, and civil liberty; and on the firſt great change in the ſtate of public affairs, there will be ſome hazard of the country rejecting it as a nuiſance, without ſub-ſtituting any thing in its place.

It is eaſy to make ſimiliar remarks with reſpect to the ſyſtem of civil government. A more equal repreſentation of the commons in Parliament is moſt evidently wanted; and if this, and other ne-ceſſary reforms, be long withheld, the whole ſyſtem will be endangered, though it is not eaſy to foreſee in what manner the danger will come, or how far the evil attending a ſudden change of ſyſtem, in a ſituation ſo critical and complicated as ours, will extend.

SECTION

SECTION IX.

*Confiderations relating to Perfecution, and the Con-
fequences of it.*

MANY of the *friends of the church*,
as they are called, freely indulge themfelves in rejoicing at the calamities of the diffenting fufferers
at Birmingham, without having any idea of their
being actuated by a fpirit of *perfecution*. This fpirit,
it is fomething remarkable, all who have ever perfecuted have difclaimed; thinking their conduct
abundantly juftified by the difpofition, and behaviour,
of the fufferers; and it has almoft always been pretended, that thefe have been punifhed not for their
opinions, but for *difturbing the ftate*.

This was conftantly alleged by all the heathen
perfecutors. Though the Chriftians were the moft
innocent and peaceable of men, they were confidered as enemies of the Roman government, and
punifhed as for civil offences. The Catholics alfo,
at the time of the reformation, treated *herefy* as
a thing that was dangerous to the civil power,
and thus were influenced by political, as well
as religious confiderations. Both Philip II. and
Lewis XIV. thought Proteftants to be *bad fubjects*,
whofe aim it was to make difturbance in the ftate,
and this is precifely the character under which
the

the zealots of the church of England are continually exhibiting the Diffenters. Though it is unqueftionable, that the Diffenters in the late reigns were the beft friends of the family on the throne, and the clergy in general difaffected to it, wifhing, and not very fecretly, for the re-eftablifhment of the Stuarts, they now have the affurance to charge *us* with difaffection. And with the idea, however abfurd, that what they do is purely *defenfive*, and merely to prevent injury to themfelves (who they muft know are placed far beyond the reach of our *power*, if it was our *wifh*, to hurt them) would without remorfe be guilty of every outrage upon our property, and our perfons too, that the heathens and Catholics ever gave into.

Our Saviour apprized his difciples that *they who killed them would think they did God fervice.* Paul thought that he did right in perfecuting the chriftians, even unto death, and the bigoted Jews in general perfecuted through *ignorance.* But were they, therefore, innocent? And did not the juft judgments of God overtake that infatuated nation on this very account? There is a kind of ignorance that is highly criminal, arifing not only from neglect of making enquiry, which itfelf arifes from criminal prejudice, but from a fecret malignity of temper, which conceals itfelf under the notion of zeal for religion.

That perfons frequently miftake the real motives of their own conduct, and thereby form a

wrong

wrong judgment of their own characters, is notorious. What man ever thought himself to be covetous, though all the world saw him to be so in the extreme? Or what man ever thought himself proud, and yet pride is certainly not banished from the world? Nay, did ever any man, except in reflecting on his conduct afterwards, think himself a bad husband, a bad father, or a bad master? And yet there certainly are such characters. Men always find excuses for their own conduct.

Can we wonder then, that no man ever thought himself to be a persecutor? And is it not, therefore, very possible, that the church of England may be in a high degree intolerant and persecuting, without acknowledging, or even seeing it. But the question is, whether, notwithstanding this good opinion of herself, she be not truly so, and whether she be not liable to the just judgments of God on that account. Let the members of this church examine themselves on this head; and for this purpose I shall take the liberty to furnish them with a few queries, arising from the present circumstances of things.

Did they not, previous to the riots in Birmingham, wish myself, and other opposers of the doctrine of the trinity, to be silenced by other means than by *argument*? Several of those who engaged in public controversy with me on this subject gave sufficient intimation of their wish for the interposition of the civil power, and I doubt not lamented that the circumstances of the times

H   were

were unfavourable to fuch a mode of filencing us. And what is perfecution, but the application of *force* in the place of *argument* ?

Did thofe who exclaimed the moft againft us fo much as read our writings ? It is well known that, when the queftion has been put to many of them, they have not only anfwered in the nega- tive, but have even expreffed a kind of horror at the propofal, and have ftrongly diffuaded others from reading. Now what is this but a proof of extreme *bigotry* ? And is not bigotry the natural parent of intolerance and perfecution ?

Did not great numbers of the clergy exprefs a real fatisfaction in the riots, when they heard that the meeting-houfes, and every thing belonging to *myfelf*, were deftroyed ; and would they have been forry if I had perifhed too, manifeftly illegal and unjuft as this method of obtaining their end was ? The cleigyman who openly expreffed the fatisfac- tion he fhould have in burning me alive was, I am informed, one of the weaker of his brethren, but I doubt not, he expreffed the real fentiments of many others*. Now every perfon who was not dif- pleafed with the act, is, in the eye of reafon and of

---

* How far the ideas of fome perfons went on this occafion may be feen in the following paper written in a large print-hand, and found at Beaconsfield. " It is confidently reported from Birmingham and " London, that fhould the Diffenters attempt any thing farther againft " the king, church, or ftate, they will provoke the true patriot-re- " fentment, and nothing lefs will difpenfe or fatisfy them, but the ex- " tirpation of the whole race of Diffenters from this kingdom, or total " deftruction to a man."

God,

God, an abettor of it, and a partaker of the guilt. I therefore leave it to the confciences of the clergy in general, and at leaft thofe who clafs with the high church party, whether this was not their cafe, and confequently whether they ought not to clafs with perfecutors. Little do many of the clergy know *what fpirit they are* really *of*, or to what degrees of violence their principles, or tempers, would lead them. It is not neceffary, in order to be perfecutors, that they themfelves commit acts of violence. They fhould be forry for them, and endeavour to prevent them.

Perfecution affumes a variety of forms, and is generally progreffive. The edict of Nantes was not revoked without many previous fteps, and the clergy and the court of France fhewed their ill-will to the Proteftants by thwarting them, and harraffing them, in many indirect ways, before they threw off the mafk, and perfecuted openly. Still, they did not allow themfelves to be *perfecutors*, becaufe proteftantifm was always tolerated in France, though on hard conditions, and Proteftants were never by law excluded from civil employments, at the appointment of the crown, as Diffenters are in this country. But perfecution takes one form in one place, and a different one in another.

In the unqueftionably perfecuting reigns of Elizabeth, and the Stuarts, the Puritans were not put to death. But they were fo much harraffed in

H 2 various

various ways, that they were glad to take refuge in
the then inhofpitable climes of America, a country
worfe than defert. But they preferred the neighbourhood of the natural favages of America, to that
of the artificial, but more cruel, favages of Europe.
By perfeverance they conquered all their difficulties, and when the hand of oppreffion was
ftretched towards them in our own times, they
nobly refifted, and conquered again in another way.
The liberty of America was the proper parent of
that of France; and thus, in the wonderful order
of Divine Providence, has oppreffion, civil and religious, been the caufe of a greater extenfion of
liberty than the world had ever known before.

A lefs degree of perfecution will now induce
the defcendants of thofe Puritans to join their brethren in America, or the common fons of liberty
nearer home; either of whom would receive them
with open arms. Let the governors of the country
attend to this confideration, before the evil be fo
far advanced, as that nothing can prevent its farther progrefs. And rich as this country is boafted
to be, in refources of all kinds, it is not, I apprehend, in fo very flourifhing a condition, as to venture upon fuch an experiment as that of the expulfion of the Diffenters from England (which
would have much more ferious confequences than
that of the Morifco's from Spain) without greater
rifk than its moft fanguine friends would chufe. The
American war had a flighter commencement than
the

the riots in Birmingham, and the animofity againſt the Diſſenters is now more general, and more inveterate, than it ever was againſt the Americans. *Verbum Sapienti. Principiis obſta.*

I well know that our enemies would rejoice in our emigration*, without ever reflecting that preceding emigrations on ſimilar accounts have never diminiſhed the ſource from which they ſprung. Though the revocation of the edict of Nantz drove immenſe numbers of Proteſtants from France, the number within the country was not leſſened. To extirpate ſectaries is not ſo eaſy a buſineſs as to extirpate offenſive plants, or animals ; becauſe a man who is not a ſectary to-day may become one to-morrow. With care, the whole ſpecies of aſhes, or elms, for example, might be extirpated ; eſpecially in an iſland. But it would ſoon be found to be labour in vain, if oaks, beeches, and all other trees, ſhould be converted into aſhes or elms. In fact, to extirpate Unitarians, may come to be the ſame thing as to extirpate the human race.

A trinitarian, in conſequence of reading and thinking, may become an unitarian, as was the caſe with myſelf. It is poſſible that even a biſhop, and that biſhop he who now occupies the ſee of St. David's, may become an unitarian. For though he ſome time ago declared that he had not read my

---

* This appears from ſeveral publications of the high church party ſince the riots.

Hiſtory

Hiſtory of early Opinions concerning Chriſt, he ſtill may read it, and may be convinced by it. It is alſo within the ſphere of *poſſibility*, that an unitarian biſhop may, as he ought to do, declare himſelf one, and become a Diſſenter. The ſame may be the caſe with thoſe of the learned laity who have written in defence of the preſent church eſtabliſhment*; and the converſion of ſuch men as theſe may ſoon draw others after them.

To thoſe who are at all acquainted with hiſtory, I need not obſerve that the perſecution of the Proteſtants in France proved highly injurious to that kingdom. Men of property and of enterterprize were the firſt to emigrate, and they ſoon drew others after them, and in a few years formed eſtabliſhments in foreign countries, which rivalled, and afterwards eclipſed, thoſe which they had left.

Birmingham will not forget how much it owes to the ingenuity and ſpirit of one man, and that man a Diſſenter, the father of one of thoſe whoſe property has been ſo wantonly deſtroyed. The difference between Birmingham and the neighbouring towns is almoſt entirely owing to the ſpirited example of the late Mr. Taylor. Had he been

---

* This may be the caſe with Mr. Burke himſelf. He is not deſtitute of candour, any more than of good ſenſe, and therefore may come to ſee, and acknowledge, that *one* cannot be *three*, or *three*, *one*, which is our great argument ; and though it may be too much to expect of *him* to read my *Hiſtory of early Opinions*, or my *Defences of Unitarianiſm*, he may read my *Appeal to the ſerious Profeſſors of Chriſtianity*, or my *General View of Arguments againſt the Divinity or Pre-exiſtence of Chriſt*, the peruſal of which would not take an hour.

treated

treated as his fon has been, and carried his enterprizing fpirit into France, fome town in that country might have been what Birmingham now is.

I fhall juft mention three other men now living, and all of them Diffenters, whofe fpirit has fo much improved, that they may be almoft faid to have *created*, their feveral manufactures, from which this country already derives the greateft honour and advantage, Mr. Wedgwood, Mr. Wilkinfon, and Mr. Parker. Such men as thefe are the *makers of countries*; and yet fuch men as thefe, if not thefe men themfelves, would the mad bigotry of this country exult in feeing depart for France, America, or Ireland; and many would think themfelves happy in being quit of them. But what will their pofterity fay, or perhaps themfelves, a few years hence?

The French want nothing but the example of the Englifh method, and fpirit, in trade, to rival us in all refpects. They are not inferior in ingenuity, or induftry; and feeing the wonderful effects of large capitals employed in manufactures and commerce, and efpecially the ability which it affords of giving credit, they will from this time employ the money they get in trade to better purpofes than the purchafe of places, and titles. Having no *court* to look up to, and depend upon, they will immediately adopt our maxims, and the removal of a few Englifh manufacturers and merchants may inftantly decide

cide

cide the difference in their favour.   And what a figure will this country then make, with its encreafing debts, and enormoufly expenfive government, without any fuperiority with refpect to manufactures and commerce ?   Will pulling down diffenting meeting - houfes, and dwelling - houfes, with the deftruction of libraries, and philofophical inftruments, and drinking damnation to Prefbyterians, reftore the balance in favour of England? This conduct has already, in the eyes of all Europe, covered the country with' fhame, and may be followed by ruin; and then repentance, which has not come yet, will come too late.

Confidering the great number of Diffenters in all the trading towns of the kingdom, and the number of wealthy families who are continually going from the Diffenters into the church, it may not much exceed the truth, if we fuppofe that one half of the wealth of the nation has been the acquifition of Diffenters.   It is the opinion of many, that envy of the profperity of Diffenters was one confiderable ftimulus to the mifchief that was done to them at Birmingham.   But the wanton deftruction of wealth acquired by honeft induftry, is not the way to make a nation flourifh, and enable it to bear its burdens.

The only effectual remedy of the evil, which has fhewn itfelf at Birmingham, and which threatens the kingdom at large, is fuch as the fpirit of the . clergy at prefent will very ill brook.   It is nothing
lefs

lefs than making religious *toleration complete*, which it can never be faid to be, fo long as any man fhall be a fufferer in his civil capacity on account of his religion. And fince exclufion from places of truft and emolument is no lefs a punifhment than fine and imprifonment, and is a ftate of ignominy, which may be felt by fome in the moft fenfible manner; to make the toleration complete, the *Teft Act* muft be repealed, as well as all other penal ftatutes in matters of religion. All this might be done, and yet the church be left in the full poffeffion of her creeds, her fubfcriptions, her revenues; the feat of the bifhops in Parliament, and even the public univerfities, with every thing elfe that can be deemed neceffary to the moft complete *eftablifhment* of any fyftem of religion.

But the church of England is not content to enjoy her proper prerogatives. She is, like moft other eftablifhments, intolerant, and will not be fatisfied without the degradation at leaft, of thofe who diffent from her. Dr. Johnfon faid, " the " Diffenters muft not be admitted into the uni- " verfities, becaufe that would be to furnifh " their enemies with arms." But without having accefs to the univerfities, the church of England has found that we are in no want of fuch arms, offenfive or defenfive; and this jealous exclufion of us from the univerfities, and from other advan- tages which ought to be common to all citizens, is the circumftance which gives our weapons their keeneft edge.

This

This completion of the toleration muft, in the present ftate of this country, be the work of admi- niftration, checking the blind and impolitic bigotry of the clergy, which it is in the power of our go- vernors to do effectually, whenever they pleafe. But if they go on to thwart the Diffenters, and fup- port the high churchmen againft them, the fpirit of party will neceffarily increafe, till perfecution, legal or illegal, will become extreme. However, any farther application to Parliament for this purpofe by the Diffenters would only inflame matters more than ever; as the clergy are far from fhewing any difpofition to relent in our favour; and without the leaft regard to the political intereft of the country, many of them would proceed to any extremity. The advantage which the country derives from this this church in *fpirituals* ought to be very great, to counterbalance what it may fuffer by it in *temporals*.

If the ftate of the church of England with re- fpect to the whole of the Britifh empire be con- fidered by the members of it, they will fee the greateft reafon for moderation, and how impolitic it muft be to indulge that fpirit of perfecution which has broke out at Birmingham, and has manifefted itfelf in many other places. The Britifh empire, befides England, embraces Scotland, Ire- land, and Canada, in all which countries but a fmall number of the inhabitants are of her com- munion. Were thefe added to the Diffenters in England, and joined to thofe within the pale of the church who difapprove of its fyftem, but have not

the

the courage to break their connection with it, there is little doubt, but they would make a majority of the subjects.

Besides, all who are not Diffenters must not, therefore, be numbered among the proper adherents of the established church. Because the great mass of them have no preference for it, but because it *is* the established church; and no observing person can doubt, but that if Mr. Lindsey's Unitarian Liturgy should be patronized by government, and a few of the more zealous of the clergy should not found the alarm, not one person in a hundred would make any complaint of it.

Still less can those who attend no public worship at all, who abound in the highest and lowest classes of the community, be fairly reckoned to belong to any church; and in all large manufacturing and commercial towns, in which consist the great resources of the nation, they who attend public worship of any kind bear but a small proportion to the rest. In Birmingham, at least sixty thousand out of seventy are of this class; and of the remainder more persons attend public worship *out* of the parish churches than *in* them. In many parts of South Wales, and especially in the diocese of St. David's, I am informed that the parish churches are almost deserted, while the meeting-houses are numerous and full.

In fact, therefore, the true interest of the church of England, in the whole empire, is not great. It
has

has but little hold on the minds of the people; and is fupported by other means than a cordial appro-bation of it, and attachment to it. Her dependance is not upon *herfelf*, but upon the mere will and power of the crown, which may change to-morrow. It, therefore, certainly does not become her to be infolent.

In this ftate of things, alfo, it is certainly the beft policy in the crown to favour toleration, rather than perfecution, and to convince every part of the empire, divided as the inhabitants of it are with re-fpect to religion, that no difference of *this* kind will have any influence in *civil matters*. But at prefent, this country, which ufed to pride itfelf, and with reafon, on its pre-eminence with refpect to *liberty*, is far behind many other nations of Europe, to fay nothing of America, and difcovers a difpofition to recede, rather than to advance, with refpect to liberty, civil or religious.

SECTION

SECTION X.

The Conclusion, containing Reflections on the Power of Religion in general.

I SHALL clofe thefe Reflections with fome relating to *religion* properly fo called, as it has its feat in the mind, and influences the temper and conduct; and with thefe I particularly wifh to imprefs my chriftian readers. Other perfons do not need to proceed any farther, as what follows will to them be like fomething in an unknown tongue.

Having had a religious education, and originally a delicate conftitution, I had from my early years a thoughtful and ferious turn of mind. I have alfo ever been particularly attentive to hiftories of perfecution, and the ftate of men's minds in thofe trying circumftances. This will appear from my publications. Several of my printed *Difcourfes* relate to this fubject, much of my *Church Hiftory* (much more than is ufual in works of that extent) is appropriated to narratives of that kind, and I made a feparate re-publication, with a large Preface, of *An Account of the Sufferings of two eminent French Proteftants, Monfieur Marolles and Lewis le Fevre.*

Having myfelf experienced fomething that may be called *perfecution,* on account of the freedom of
my

my religious principles, in my firſt ſettlement, and having ſince that time had much experience in religious controverſy, mere *reproach*, however atrocious, never affected me much; much leſs, I believe, than it does moſt other perſons; and of late years, I can truly ſay that it is as nearly as poſſible a matter of perfect indifference to me, from whatever quarter it has come. Of ſufferings of this kind it is probable that few men have ever had a greater ſhare, almoſt every poſſible kind of evil having been *ſaid of me*, though *falſely*. But the reproach of enemies has been more than compenſated by the warm approbation and attachment of friends, of which alſo I have had my full ſhare, enough to encourage any man to perſevere in well doing, and even to bear any ſufferings on that account.

But though I had read and reflected much on the feelings of chriſtians in a ſtate of perſecution, and never doubted but that, in ordinary caſes, their joys far exeeded their ſorrows, I could not *know* that they did ſo to the *degree* in which I can truly, and I hope without much vanity (for in this I mean nothing but the inſtruction and encouragement of my readers) ſay that I have lately found it. It is only in trying ſituations that the full force of religious principle is felt, and that its real energy can ſhow itſelf. And firmly believing, from the doctrine of *philoſophical neceſſity*, that the hand of God is in all events, that in all caſes men are only his inſtruments; that under his ſure guidance all *evil* will terminate in *good*, and that nothing ſo effec-

tually

tually promotes any good caufe, by drawing men's attention to it, as the perfecution of its advocates, all that I have fuffered, and all that I can fuffer, has, in many feafons of the calmeft reflection upon it, appeared as *nothing, and lefs than nothing*.

I confider this perfecution (for fo I fhall call it, though my enemies will, of courfe, confider it as the punifhment of my evil deeds, and even much lefs than I deferve) let it be carried to what extent it will, as a certain prognoftic of the prevalence of every great truth for which I have contended; and this profpect, together with the idea of my being an inftrument in the hand of providence of promoting the fpread of important truth, by *fuffering* as well as by *acting*, has given me at times fuch exalted feelings of devotion (mixed, as fentiments of devotion ever will be, with the pureft good-will towards all men, my bittereft enemies not excepted) as I had but an imperfect idea of before. If the future peace of the country, and the fafety of my friends did not re-quire it, I would not have a fingle facrifice made to public juftice. Both the inftigators of the late violences, and their blind agents in them, fhould go without any other punifhment, than what, if they ever come to a juft fenfe of things, they will fufficiently inflict upon themfelves.

Admitting that our perfecutors really imagined that they were doing right, and promoting the caufe of truth, in their late outrages, yet the feel-ings of the man who *does* an injury, with whatever
view,

view, cannot be without a mixture of malevolence, in confequence of his rejoicing in that injury; a fentiment unworthy of a chriftian, and by which he will feel his mind debafed. Whereas the fentiments of the pureft benevolence eafily mix with thofe of devotion in the mind of the man who unjuftly *fuffers* the injury, and who is fatisfied that he is promoting the caufe of truth, and confequently the beft interefts of mankind, by his fufferings. When, fince my late difafter, I have given fcope to fuch reflections as thefe, I have had fenfations of joy and exultation which I fhould in vain attempt to defcribe; and in general they have immediately fucceeded the moft lively fenfe that I ever had of the injury done to me.

What I have fuffered in my perfon is in a manner nothing, and with refpect to all the common wants of nature, I have had fuch refources in my friends, and in thofe whom I did not before know to be my friends, as few perfons in my fituation could have found. But corporeal fufferings are not thofe which give men the greateft anguifh. Mental uneafinefs is much more dreadful than bodily pain; and the defpondency of fome friends, the fufferings to which others of them may be expofed, and the marks of prejudice in fome whom I had not confidered as enemies, have fometimes given me feelings peculiarly unpleafant. Alfo, the idea of my not being able, at my time of life, to replace my papers, library, and apparatus; the interruption of all my purfuits, and the uncertainty of my future profpects, prospects, cannot but some times be painful to me. But notwithstanding this, when I have attended to the considerations before mentioned, I have even been able to rejoice that I had so much to lose; since without some sacrifice of this nature, I should not, in reality, have sustained any loss at all, and consequently should have had nothing to boast of. This, I own, is a sentiment that is not of the most exalted nature, but I hope it is innocent; and as part of my *real feelings*, not improper to be mentioned, among my other sources of consolation.

So fully am I persuaded that more good than evil will result from what has happened to me, that, were it in my power, I would not be restored to my former situation. Had the late events not happened, I should, of course, have wished, and prayed, for continuing as I was. For no man, I believe, ever thought himself more happily situated than I did. But Providence having now declared itself, I acquiesce, and even rejoice in the decision.

As to the theological works which I had in view, one of which was to trace the origin, and ascertain the nature, of *Antient Idolatry*, in order to demonstrate the value of revelation, another to continue my *Church History*, to the present times; a third to publish my *Notes and Paraphrase on the New Testament*, and a fourth, to complete what I had undertaken of the *New Translation of the Scriptures*, I conclude, either that these works were not wanted, or that they will be better done by other hands.

I   If

If life, and the proper means, be continued to me, I shall refume, at leaft, fome of them, as well as my philofophical experiments; and if not, I shall confole myfelf with this verfe of Milton;

" They alfo ferve, who only ftand and wait."

I am ready and willing to labour, and to the utmoft of my ability, whenever my tafk fhall be given me.

I hope alfo that I fhall not be much condemned for deriving fome confolation from the thought, that though my library and apparatus be deftroyed, I made fome confiderable ufe of them while I had them, and therefore that I have not lived in vain. Of this confolation my enemies cannot deprive me; nor, if my life be continued, and my affairs be in any meafure re-eftablifhed, will any thing that I have yet fuffered, damp my ardour in frefh purfuits; and having the advantage of years and experience, I may yet live to ferve, not my country in particular, but mankind, and the world, of which I am now become more a citizen at large.

As to continuance of life, I was never very anxious about it. My writings fhew that I do not confider *death* in itfelf as any great evil; and a violent death, which is all that men can inflict, is not, in general, fo much to be dreaded as many difeafes. Perfecution is not to be courted by any chriftian. Death is never to be fought, but to be avoided; and no man can tell how he fhall behave in any very new and trying fituation. But I truft that the
same

fame principles which have fupported me hitherto will carry me through any trials that may yet remain for me.

I have often amufed myfelf, and my friends, with recounting my feveral migrations, which, though never of my own feeking, have been more numerous than thofe of any of my acquaintance; when I always faid that, having now obtained a happier fituation in all refpeéts, than I ever had before, I hoped I fhould never remove any more, and that I did not even wifh to be, in any refpeét, happier than I was, in this world. In every change of fituation, I ufed to fay, the difficulty of my removing had been increafed by the accumulation of my books and philofophical inftruments; but that, at Birmingham, my library and apparatus were become fo confiderable, that it was abfolutely impoffible for me ever to remove to any other place. But now I am light enough, and can move with more eafe than ever, ready, at a moment's warning, to go wherever it fhall pleafe divine providence to call me.

In general, the mind of man foon recovers its ufual level, whatever it has been; fcenes of profperity or adverfity only making a temporary impreffion upon it. Since, therefore, I have hitherto enjoyed a good fhare of uniform chearful fpirits, without being fubjeét to the extremes of elevation or depreffion, I have little doubt but that the fame

happy

happy ftate of mind will accompany me through whatever may yet remain of life.

Moreover, the fame good providence which has accompanied *me*, will, I doubt not, accompany my children, who, being educated in good principles, will, I truft, have no lefs ardour of mind than I have had in every laudable purfuit that fhall be within their reach. In this cafe I fhall not be forry to have been their parent, though they fhould be expofed to greater fufferings than I have been called to endure, in an equally good caufe; and they will not be afhamed of their father, who has fet them the example of it. Laftly, having acted a worthy and generous part in life, in the purfuit of truth and the practice of virtue, I fhall hope to meet them, and my other chriftian friends, in a better world, where we fhall have nothing to fear from open violence, any more than from fecret theft.

STRICTURES.

INTITLED,

Thoughts on the late Riot at Birmingam.

[Printed for John Sewell, Cornhill.]

——————

SINCE the preceding *Appeal* was fent to the prefs, there has appeared a pamphlet intitled *Thoughts on the late Riot at Birmingham,* written evidently by a high churchman (though in an *Advertifment* prefixed to it, he fays he has " no party " views, or intolerant fpirit) which abundantly juf-tifies all that I have advanced concerning perfons of that defcription. It is, in fact, nothing lefs than a declaration of war againft all Diffenters, who fhall prefume to write any thing againft the eftablifhed church, threatening us with utterdeftruction. With us writing is turbulence, and fuch turbulence as will authorize open hoftility of every kind. Such is the unavoidable inference from the following paffage, p. 52.

" It is not too late for the Diffenters to recover " the character of peaceable citizens, which they " have loft by their late political interference. It was " thought that many of them finned againft the peace " of the public through inadvertency, and that they

I 3　　　　　　　　" only

" only wanted fome inftructive *fact* to convince
" them of the tendency of what they were about,
" and to incline them to fhew themfelves the harm-
" lefs profeffors of a peaceful religion. Such a
" fact has happened, and the nation is waiting to
" fee what effect it will have on them. If it is fuch
" as to fhew that they have erred through want of
" confideration, an act of oblivion is ready to be
" paffed on all their former mifconduct. But if
" the fame reftlefs and turbulent fpirit is ftill feen
" working among them, farewel candour, forbear-
" ance, and concord. There will be an extinction
" of all the charities that chriftianity inculcates be-
" tween the different perfuafions, and hoftilities will
" commence, that will probably never end till the
" one has effected the deftruction of the other."

What could Dominic himfelf have faid more to
his purpofe, at the head of his crufaders? And what
have we done more than the perfecuted Albigenfes
did to provoke this violence? What have we done
more than the primitive chriftians, or than the reformers from popery did, in their time, that is,
write in defence of our principles, and with a view
to this, expofe thofe of our adverfaries, and almoft univerfally when they were the aggreffors, and
we were treated in the moft infulting manner? For
this all candour is profeffedly abandoned, and deftruction threatened.

At length, then, we are come to an iffue. And
fince with us refiftance would be in vain, and in

our

our opinion unchriftian, we muft bear all the malice of our enemies, or abandon the country. For we fhall never abandon the defence of our principles as we have hitherto done, that is, by *writing*.

According to this writer, Diffenters muft neither write about religion nor politics. " As to the improvement of the conftitution," he fays, p. 49, " leave it to other hands." *This*, then, is a thing that we have no intereft in. Confequently, we are already to be confidered as no better than *aliens*, which is another reafon why we fhould go to fome country, where we may be treated as *citizens*.

Inconfiftently enough, however, with the declaration of hoftility quoted above, this writer fays, p. 22, " The unitarian Diffenters are not yet of fuf-" ficient confequence to give any apprehenfions." Why then all this rage, and buftle ? Is the Britifh lion fo tormented with a fly ? Have the high church people burned our meeting-houfes and dwelling-houfes, with every thing belonging to us, without the excufe of having fomething to *fear* from us ? What then would they do if we gave them real caufe of fear ?

In the opinion of this writer, and all of his party, it was I who was the proper caufe of the riot, and of all the mifchief that was occafioned by it. " Tis you," fays he, p. 16, in his farcaftic way, " meek divine, peaceable philofopher, that did, in " faƈt, fet the populace afloat, and bring it down

I 4 " upon

" upon a crouded town, like a deſtructive engine,
" that threatened general devaſtation. In vain,
" therefore, you ſeek to ſhift off the blame of this
" event from yourſelf, by endeavouring to fix it on
" others. The country conſiders *you* as the prin-
" cipal cauſe of the miſchief, and the utmoſt that
" candour itſelf can ſay in your behalf is, that per-
" haps you did not intend the conſequences, and
" are, independent of the loſſes you have ſuſtained,
" ſincerely ſorry that they happened."

From reading this, any ſtranger would naturally conclude, that it was I that raiſed the rioters,
and headed them, but that afterwards they turned
upon myſelf; and not that they were raiſed and inſtigated by my enemies, and that I was their firſt
victim. On the idea, however, that I was the
aggreſſor in this buſineſs, and taking it for granted,
that I muſt ſee it in the ſame light as himſelf, he is
ſurprized, p. 3, 17, to find nothing of *penitence* in
my *Letter to the Inhabitants of Birmingham.* But
what have I to repent of? Is it my writings, in
defence of truth and liberty? I am ſo far from
repenting, that I glory in them, and in the ſame
circumſtances, I would have done the ſame; and
while I am capable of writing at all, I ſhall continue to write in the ſame manner, as opportunity
offers. With reſpect to the riot, if I repent at all,
it muſt be for the crimes of others. But though I
cannot repent of them, I can truly ſay I am deeply
concerned for them, and deſirous that thoſe who are
guilty may repent. As things are, it is enough for
me,

me, as a chriftian, to forgive thofe who have offended me, whenever *they* repent. More than this
is not required of any man. Let thofe then who have
burned my houfe, or have inftigated others to burn
it, do their duty, and I fhall be ready to do mine.

This writer himfelf, this abettor of the burning
of houfes, libraries, and philofophical inftruments,
as an anfwer to *arguments*, only pretends to find my
inftruments of deftruction in my writings. "Cu-
"riofity," he fays, p. 16, "would prompt the
"people to read for themfelves" (I only wifh they
were difpofed to do fo, efpecially at Birmingham)
"where a man that was diftinguifhed by fuch fen-
"timents" (whatever, then, it was that was dangerous about me, they were but *fentiments*) "was
"an inhabitant. They opened one of his books,
"and there found that the man who had quietly
"enjoyed the exercife of his religion threatened the
"deftruction of theirs." But did not I allow to
others the fame liberty that I took myfelf; and how
did I threaten others, except in the fame manner as
others had threatened me, viz, by writing?

In the fame manner, in vindication of the juft-
nefs of his charge againft me as the proper author
of all the mifchief, he fays, p. 17, "I call the whole
"nation to witnefs." Now what can the whole
nation witnefs befides my writings, which are open
to them all, and which I fincerely wifh they would
all read ? *

* He likewife fays, p. 17, that this charge againft me can be
"fubftantiated by producing the papers of the offender." If by *papers*
be

That the whole of the turbulence this writer ascribes to me consists in nothing but my *writings*, is farther evident from his censure of my treatment of civil establishments of christianity in my *Letter to Mr. Burke*, in which, replying to an orator, who had not been sparing of his metaphors on the other side, I had made use of some which appeared to me to be applicable on mine, comparing those establishments, which were unknown in the primitive and founder ages of the church, but were introduced in a late and more corrupt state, to a *fungus*, &c. " How remote," says he, p. 18, " is this from " the language of a peaceable man." But, surely, it is not more remote from peace, than the burning of a house is from the answering of an argument. However, it is evident that, in this writer's idea, I cannot write at all, at least to any purpose, and employ either *reason* or *imagination*, without breaking the peace, and incurring the penalties annexed to that offence. I should have been happy, however, if my conduct had been considered in that light, and my enemies had contented themselves with prosecuting me in any legal method for breaking the peace. It would have been a curious trial, and would not, I presume, have ended as did the riots at Birmingham.

---

be meant *manuscript papers*, found in my library, when the rioters plundered it, of which this writer seems to have had the inspection, let them be produced. I have a perfect consciousness that there exists nothing of my writing, found either there, or in any other place, that can furnish just matter of crimination against me, though, as was the case with the immortal Algernon Sydney, papers so found should be admitted as legal evidence. I will not, however, answer for papers that may have been written by others in order to be found in my library, any more than for the *forged letter* that was read to the mob, to instigate them to do the mischief.

As

As a farther reafon why I fhould not have written any thing againft the church (which, it feems, does not like to be molefted) he alleges my *not being of it.* " This pacific divine, and phi- " lofopher," he fays, p. 6, " meddles with the " concerns of a fociety to which he does not be- " long." But do the clergy govern themfelves by the fame maxim? Have they never volun- tarily attacked the Diffenters? Did Mr. Madan get himfelf admitted into any of our focieties before he wrote againft us? Was not he, then, guilty of med- dling with the concerns of a fociety to which *he* did not belong, even more than myfelf, as he was the aggreffor in the controverfy. But the maxim itfelf is abfurd. It becomes every man to defend truth, and attack error, wherever he finds it. Every man is of the fociety of mankind, and fhould not fee his brethren go aftray, or in any refpect injure themfelves, without endeavouring to ferve them. Did not the primitive chriftians meddle with the affairs of the heathens, and the Proteftants with thofe of the Catholics, though they did not belong to their focieties? And did they not meddle with them in the fame manner in which I have med- dled with the church of England, viz. by fpeaking and writing: and many of them wrote in a much more irritating manner than I have ever done, and were univerfally admired for it.

Diffenters, however, have juft caufe of med- dling with the church of England, fo long as it is a *national church,* and they, as well as the reft of
the

the community, contribute towards the maintenance of it. For every man is concerned to fee
that he has the value of that for which he gives
his money. The Diffenters are much more a fociety with which the members of the church of
England have no bufinefs to meddle, as they do
not contribute to the fupport of our worfhip.
According to this writer, Diffenters have nothing
to do with either the *church* or the *ftate*, but muft
be paffive lookers on in every thing; patiently
bearing every burden that is laid upon them.

From the whole of this performance, which,
whether coming from any authority or not, evidently fpeaks the language of all the high church
party, it is evident that we are to receive blows
for words, and fire and fword for argument. Let
them then go to their purpofe, and proceed as they
have begun to burn, viz. our houfes and meeting-
houfes, and ourfelves too, if they can find us in
them; for that was their intention at Birmingham.
We alfo fhall defend ourfelves as we have hitherto
done, i. e. with more writing, and more arguments.
All men, and all animals, naturally have recourfe
to fuch weapons as they find themfelves furnifhed
with, and are moft expert in the ufe of; and infignificant as ours may appear, in comparifon with
theirs, they will be found more effectual. We
will fay as the noble Florentine faid to the French
king and his officers, " Do you found your trum-
" pets, and we will ring our bells."

This

This writer fays, p. 12, that " as a philofopher " I know fomething of human nature, and how " irritable men are on the fubject of their national " religion;" and p. 51, that my " political ani-" madverfions did not act merely on the under-" ftandings of men, but that they took hold of their " paffions." This, indeed, we have found to our coft. But it is likewife well known that paffion predominates moft where there is the greateft de-ficiency of reafon. The primitive chriftians alfo, and the firft Proteftants, found that their adverfaries had paffions, which they were always ready to oppofe to the dictates of reafon; and that, having as little to fay for themfelves, they were as irritable as the high church party at Birmingham. But this cir-cumftance was no fufficient motive with the pri-mitive chriftians, or the Proteftants, for filence, nor will it be any with us; and if this writer, or his friends, imagine that the riots in Birmingham will filence us, and produce no writing, he will be greatly miftaken indeed. I forefee a deluge of pamphlets on the occafion, and if he had wifhed that there fhould be no writing on our fide, he fhould not have publifhed on his.

If this writer be furprized at finding nothing penitential in my Letter to the Inhabitants of Bir-mingham, others, will be as much furprized on finding nothing of *commiferation* in his pamphlet, except for the wretches whom he expected would be executed for what they did in the bufinefs. Of

this

this he has drawn an affecting picture indeed, as of the sufferings of so many martyrs to the church, and to religion. "This riot," he says, p. 3, " will " be followed with the sacrifice of many lives on " the altar of public justice. Disconsolate women " are soon to take their last embrace of their huf- " bands, children to shriek at the sight of their fa- " thers suspended before their own doors, and heart- " broken parents to follow their sons to the fatal " tree, some of whom, had they not been put in " motion by the ferment his writings have contri- " buted to raise, had never disturbed the peace of " society. Had there been any sympathy in the " heart that dictated the letter, on the events that " must draw such calamities after them, there had " furely been one line expressive of such a sensation. " Let the reader find it, if he can." And let the reader look through this whole pamphlet, and find, if he can, any thing like such a fellow-feeling for the innocent sufferers, that he here expresses for the wicked authors of their sufferings. In a Note, however, on this passage (which I suppose he thought too eloquently written to be lost) the author is happy " to find that his ideas were not fully justi- " fied by the issue of the late assizes held at War- " wick." Indeed, the incomparable behaviour of the magistrates and of the jury, and the proper re- presentations made to the king, have happily saved this writer and his friends much of the pain which they expected from the cruel and unmerited suffer- ings of their *fellow churchmen.* Had our sufferings

been

been ten times greater than they have been, fo much greater would have been their pious exultation over us.

I do not undertake to animadvert upon every thing that deferves animadverfion in this pamphlet, but I cannot conclude thefe ftrictures without obferving that, as a compliment to the church of England, againft which Diffenters muft not write, the author fays, p. 11, " lays it any reftraint on the " fpirit of enquiry, and how then is it hoftile to " the cleareft truth?" Is then fubfcription to the thirty-nine articles at an age in which it is impoffible for perfons to have ftudied them, no reftraint on the fpirit of enquiry; and is not every reftraint on the fpirit of enquiry neceffarily hoftile to truth? But no man can fee the darkeft fpot on his own forehead. Otherwife this writer could not but have been fenfible of this, and many other moft glaring abfurdities in his publication.

APPENDIX.

APPENDIX.

N° I.

Copy of a Hand-bill privately circulated in Birming-
ham, a few Days before the Riots.

MY COUNTRYMEN,

THE fecond year of Gallic liberty is nearly
expired. At the commencement of the third, on the 14th
of this month, it is devoutly to be wifhed, that every enemy to civil and religious defpotifm would give his fanction
to the *majeftic common caufe*, by a public celebration of the
anniverfary. Remember that on the 14th of July the Baftile, that " High Altar and Caftle of Defpotifm" fell. Remember the enthufiafm *peculiar* to the caufe of Liberty,
with which it was attacked. Remember that generous
humanity that taught the oppreffed, groaning under the
weight of infulted rights, to fave the lives of oppreffors!
Extinguifh the mean prejudices of nations; and let your
numbers be collected, and fent as a free-will offering to
the National Affembly.

But is it poffible to forget that your own Parliament is
venal? Your Minifter hypocritical? Your Clergy legal
oppreffors? The reigning Family extravagant? The Crown

K of

of a certain great Perfonage becoming every day too weighty for the head that wears it? Too weighty for the people who *gave* it? Your taxes partial and exceffive? Your reprefentation a cruel *infult* upon the facred rights of property, religion, and freedom?

But on the 14th of this month, prove to the political fycophants of the day, that You reverence the Olive Branch; that You *will* facrifice to public tranquility, till the majority *fhall* exclaim, *The Peace of Slavery is worfe than the War of Freedom.* Of that moment let Tyrants beware.

N° II.

My Letter to the Inhabitants of Birmingham.

My late Townfmen and Neighbours,

AFTER living with you eleven years, in which you had uniform experience of my peaceful behaviour, in my attention to the quiet duties of my profeffion, and thofe of philofophy, I was far from expecting the injuries which I and my friends have lately received from you. But you have been mifled. By hearing the Diffenters, and particularly the Unitarian Diffenters, continually railed at, as enemies to the prefent government, in church and ftate, you have been led to confider any injury done to us as a meritorious thing; and not having been better informed, the means were not attended to. When the *object* was right, you thought the *means* could not be wrong. By the difcourfes of your teachers, and the exclamations of your fuperiors in general, drinking confufion and damnation to us (which is well known to have been their frequent practice) your bigotry has been excited to the higheft pitch, and nothing having been faid to you to moderate your paffions, but every thing to inflame them; hence, without any confideration

fideration on your part, or on theirs, who ought to have known, and taught you better, you were prepared for every fpecies of outrage; thinking that whatever you could do to fpite and injure us, was for the fupport of government, and efpecially the church. In *deftroying* us, you have been led to think, *you did God* and your country the moft fubftantial *fervice*.

Happily, the minds of Englifhmen have an horror of *murder*, and therefore you did not, I hope, think of *that*; though, by your clamorous demanding of *me* at the Hotel, it is probable, that at that time, fome of you intended me fome perfonal injury. But what is the value of life, when every thing is done to make it wretched? In many cafes, there would be greater mercy in difpatching the inhabitants, than in burning their houfes. However, I infinitely prefer what I feel from *the fpoiling of my goods*, to the difpofition of thofe who have mifled you.

You have deftroyed the moft truly valuable and ufeful apparatus of philofophical inftruments, that perhaps any individual, in this or any other country, was ever poffeffed of; in my ufe of which I annually fpent large fums, with no pecuniary view whatever, but only in the advancement of fcience, for the benefit of my country, and of mankind. You have deftroyed a library correfponding to that apparatus, which no money can re-purchafe, except in a long courfe of time. But what I feel far more, you have deftroyed *manuscripts*, which have been the refult of the laborious ftudy of many years, and which I fhall never be able to re-compofe; and this has been done to one who never did, or imagined you any harm.

I know nothing more of the *hand-bill*, which is faid to have enraged you fo much, than any of yourfelves, and I difapprove of it as much; though it has been made the oftenfible handle of doing infinitely more mifchief than any thing of that nature could poffibly have done. In the celebration of the French Revolution, at which I did not attend, the company affembled on the occafion, only expreffed

K 2 their

their joy in the emancipation of a neighbouring nation from tyranny, without intimating a defire of any thing more than fuch an improvement of our own conftitution, as all fober citizens, of every perfuafion have long wifhed for. And though, in anfwer to the grofs and unprovoked calumnies of Mr. Madan, and others, I publicly vindicated my principles as a Diffenter, it was only with plain and fober argument, and with perfect good humour. We are better inftructed in the mild and forbearing fpirit of chriftianity, than ever to think of having recourfe to *violence*; and can you think fuch conduct as yours any recommendation of your religious principles in preference to ours?

You are ftill more miftaken, if you imagine that this conduct of yours has any tendency to ferve your caufe, or to prejudice ours. It is nothing but *reafon* and *argument* that can ever fupport any fyftem of religion. Anfwer our arguments, and your bufinefs is done; but your having recourfe to *violence*, is only a proof that you have nothing better to produce. Should you deftroy myfelf as well as my houfe, library, and apparatus, ten more perfons, of equal or fuperior fpirit and ability, would inftantly rife up. If thofe ten were deftroyed, an hundred would appear; and believe me, that the church of England, which you now think you are fupporting, has received a greater blow by this conduct of yours, than I and all my friends have ever aimed at it.

Befides, to abufe thofe who have no power of making refiftance, is equally cowardly and brutal, peculiarly unworthy of Englifhmen, to fay nothing of chriftianity, which teaches us to do as we would be done by. In this bufinefs we are the fheep, and you the wolves. We will preferve our character, and hope you will change yours. At all events, we return you bleffings for curfes; and pray that you may foon return to that induftry, and thofe fober manners, for which the inhabitants of Birmingham were formerly diftinguifhed.

I am your fincere well-wifher,

London, July 19, 1791.   J. PRIESTLEY.

N° III.

*An Account of the Origin of the Riots in Birmingham,
from a Newfpaper called the* THE TIMES.

Tuefday, July 19, 1791.

BY every account which has arrived from Birmingham, and from authenticated facts in corroboration of what
we have already afferted, it is an indifputable truth, that the
motives which occafioned the havoc already made among
the Diffenters at Birmingham, and which is ftill in continuance, folely fprung from the loyalty of the people, and
the utter abhorrence in which the principles of a republican
fyftem of government are held by the public at large.

The public were determined before they proceeded to
violence, to have fome further proof of the intention of
thofe commemoration men. The hand-bill might be a
forgery,—or might be an infidious fcheme to raife a mob
for the purpofe of plunder ;—they therefore waited until
they heard what was faid at table—how the political
complexion of the company would manifeft itfelf,—and
whether any thing more than a mere fcene of commemoration conviviality was intended.

They had indeed their fufpicions, and thofe fufpicions,
after the firft courfe were realifed, by the following toaft
being drank ;—

' DESTRUCTION TO THE PRESENT GOVERNMENT—AND
THE KING'S HEAD UPON A CHARGER !'

The inhabitants, and they were almoft to a man refpectable houfekeepers and manufacturers, who waited out-
fide the Hotel to watch the motions of the Revolutionifts
within, no fooner had this treafonable toaft made known
to them, than LOYALTY fwift as lightning fhot through
their minds, and a kind of electrical patriotifm animated
them to inftant vengeance. They rufhed into this con-
venticle of treafon, and before the fecond courfe was well

laid

laid upon the table, broke the windows and glaffes, pelted and infulted thefe modern reformers, and obliged them to feek for fafety in immediate flight.

An inflammatory bill in Doctor Prieftley's handwriting was found among his papers, and has been tranfmitted to the Secretary of State....The Doctor is at Kidderminfter, to which place it is faid the populace mean to follow him. His doctrines, they avow, were meant to fubvert the Conftitution.

Mr. Parker, a very eminent attorney, is the perfon who fent up the inflammatory and treafonable paper found in Prieftley's houfe, and in the Doctor's own hand, which it is thought is a full ground for profecution.

N^o V.

Mr. Ruffell's Letter to the Editor of the Morning Chronicle.

SIR,

BEING in London, and feeing in *The Times* of yefterday the moft atrocious calumny that was ever laid before the public, I feel it my duty immediately to contradict it in the moft pointed terms. I do therefore declare, that the narrative of the Birmingham Conftitutional Dinner is materially untrue; and that the account given of the *firft Toaft*, in *The Times*, is a moft flagrant falfehood. It was, *The King and Conftitution.*

The Meeting broke up without the leaft riot or difturbance.—That the public may judge, whether the proceedings of the day, and the Toafts, were or were not reprehenfible, the following true narrative is now produced, the authenticity and truth of which I will vouch for.

The

The proceedings of the day were preceded by an advertifement in the Birmingham Chronicle, publifhed that morning, of which the following is a copy:

Birmingham Commemoration of the French Revolution.

Several Hand-bills having been circulated in the Town, which can only be intended to create diftruft concerning the intention of the Meeting, to difturb its harmony, and inflame the minds of the people; the Gentlemen who propofed it, think it neceffary to declare their entire difapprobation of all fuch Hand-bills, and their ignorance of the authors. — Senfible themfelves of the advantages of a free Government, they rejoice in the extenfion of Liberty to their neighbours, at the fame time avowing, in the moft explicit manner, their firm attachment to the Conftitution of their own Country, as vefted in the Three Eftates of King, Lords, and Commons: Surely no *free-born Englifhman* can refrain from exulting in this addition to the general mafs of human happinefs. It is the caufe of *humanity*, it is the caufe of the people.

Birmingham, July 13, 1791.

In the morning, however, after this was publifhed, many rumours of the probability of a riot were brought to the friends of the Meeting; and as there was too much reafon to think that means had been ufed to promote one, they determined to poftpone the intended Dinner, and accordingly agreed to put it off, and prepared a hand-bill for that purpofe, of which the following is a copy:

Intended Commemoration of the French Revolution.

The Friends of the intended Feftivity, finding that their views and intention, in confequence of being mifconceived by fome, and mifreprefented by others, have created an alarm in the minds of the majority of the town, and it is thought, endangered its tranquility, inform their neighbours that they value the peace of the town far beyond the gratification of a Feftival, and therefore have determined to give up their intentions of dining at the Hotel upon this occafion; and they very gladly improve this renewed opportunity of declaring that they are to this hour entirely ignorant of the Author, Printer, or Publifher, of the inflammatory Hand-bill circulated on Monday.

This was fent to the Printer; but before he had compofed it, Mr. Dadley, the Mafter of the Hotel, attended,

in

in confequence of having the Dinner countermanded; and reprefented, that he was fure there was no danger of any tumult, and recommended that the Dinner might be had as was intended; only propofing, that the gentlemen fhould take care to break up early, and then all danger would be avoided. This meafure was then adopted, and orders given to the Printer to fupprefs the hand-bill. Accordingly there was a meeting of eighty-one gentlemen, inhabitants of the town and neighbourhood, at the Great Room in the Hotel, where they dined and paffed the afternoon with that focial, temperate, and benevolent feftivity, which the confideration of the great event, which has diffufed liberty and happinefs among a large portion of the human race, infpired.

The following Toafts were drunk, and were agreeably intermixed with fongs, compofed and fung by fome of the company.

1. The King and Conftitution.

2. The National Affembly and Patriots of France, whofe virtue and wifdom have raifed twenty-fix millions from the mean condition of fubjects of defpotifm, to the dignity and happinefs of freemen.

3. The Majefty of the People.

4. May the New Conftitution of France be rendered perfect and perpetual.

5. May Great Britain, Ireland, and France, unite in perpetual friendfhip, and may their only rivalfhip be the extenfion of Peace and Liberty, Wifdom and Virtue.

6. The Rights of Man. May all nations have the wifdom to underftand, and the courage to affert and defend them.

7. The true Friends of the Conftitution of this Country, who wifh to preferve its fpirit, by correcting its abufes.

8. May the People of England never ceafe to remonftrate, till their Parliament becomes a true National Reprefentation.

9 The Prince of Wales.

10 The United States of America. May they for ever enjoy the Liberty which they have fo honourably acquired.

11. May the late Revolution in Poland prove the harbinger of a more perfect fyftem of Liberty extending to that great Kingdom.

12. May the Nations of Europe become fo enlightened as never more to be deluged into favage wars, by the mad ambition of their rulers.

13. May

13. May the fword be never unfheathed, but for the defence and liberty of our country, and then, may every man caft away the fcabbard, until the people are fafe and free.

14. To the glorious memory of Hampden and Sydney, and other heroes of all ages and nations, who have fought and bled for liberty.

15. To the memory of Dr. Price, and of all thofe illuftrious fages who have enlightened mankind on the true principles of civil fociety.

16. Peace and good-will to all mankind.

17. Profperity to the town of Birmingham.

18. A happy Meeting to all the Friends of Liberty on the 14th of July, 1792.

It is but juftice to the liberality and public fpirit of an ingenious Artift of this town to mention, that he decorated the room upon this occafion with three elegant emblematic pieces of fculpture, mixed with painting, in a new ftile of compofition. The central piece was a finely executed medallion of his majefty, encircled with a glory, on each fide of which was an alabafter obelifk; the one exhibiting Gallic liberty breaking the bands of defpotifm, and the other reprefenting Britifh liberty in its prefent enjoyment.

A truly refpectable gentleman, a member of the church of England, was Chairman—others of that profeffion were of the company, nor was a fingle fentiment uttered, or, I believe, conceived, that would hurt the feelings of any one friend to liberty and good government, under the happy conftitution we are bleffed with in this kingdom.—I aver this to be a true and juft reprefentation of the proceedings which have been fo fcandaloufly mifreprefented in the Paper above-mentioned; and am,

Sir,

Your obedient fervant,

London, July 20,
1791.

WILLIAM RUSSELL.

N° V.

Mr. Keir's Letter to the Printer of the Birmingham and Stafford Chronicle.

MR. PRINTER,

AS I find that many grofs falfhoods have been circulated through the country, in order to inflame the minds of the people concerning the meeting held laft Thurfday, to commemorate the French Revolution, I will beg leave to ftate what I myfelf have had occafion to know refpecting that fubject.—Some gentlemen in Birmingham had propofed by an advertifement in the newfpapers, to hold a meeting of the friends of liberty and of mankind, at the Hotel, to commemorote the French Revolution, in the fame manner as was done in London, and many other parts in the kingdom. Two days before the time appointed for this meeting, a very refpectable gentleman called on me, and faid he came to tell me, that it was the general wifh of thofe who intended to meet, that I fhould be their chairman on the occafion. I accepted the compliment, and promifed to come to Birmingham to attend, never conceiving that a peaceable' meeting, for the purpofe of rejoicing that twenty-fix millions of our fellow-creatures were refcued from def-potifm, and made as free and happy as we Britons are, could be mifinterpreted as being offenfive to a government, whofe greateft boaft is liberty, or to any who pro-fefs the chriftian religion, which orders us to love our neighbours as ourfelves.—We accordingly met and dined with the greateft peace and harmony, and after drinking fome toafts, expreffive in the firft place of our loyalty to our own *King* and *Conftitution*; and in the fecond place, of our joy at the happinefs which the French have acquired by their new Conftitution, we diffolved the meeting entirely, in the greateft order, between five and fix in the

evening,

evening, and quitted the Hotel, every man retiring fepa-
rately to his home, or to his private affairs. I returned
to my houfe in the country, nor knew of the difturbances
till next day. The meeting in London was conducted
with the fame decorum, nor has there been an inftance, as
far as I know, in the many fimilar meetings throughout
England, of the fmalleft irregularity attempted by them.
Now, Mr. Printer, as actions are the beft interpreters of
men's intentions, it is evident that the malicious infinuations, that thefe meetings were intended to difturb the
peace and government of the country, have been by the
event proved to be falfe and groundlefs.

I have lately heard that it is reported that we drank
difloyal and feditious toafts. Now the very firft toaft that
was given was, *The King and the Conftitution.* I do not
know any words in the Englifh language expreffive of
greater loyalty; and one of the laft was, *Peace and good-
will to all mankind,* which cannot eafily be interpreted to
excite people to tumult. I fhall hereafter publifh a lift
of all the toafts, which were altogether in the fame fpirit of
loyalty, peace, and charity.

A fecond report is, that Juftice Carlefs was infulted
and turned out of the room. The fact is, that Juftice
Carlefs never was in the room, and therefore it is not eafy
to conceive how he could be turned out. I will add, that
I have not the fmalleft doubt, that if that gentleman had
come, he would have been received with due refpect.

A third falfe report was, that a feditious hand-bill had
been diftributed by the members of the meeting, on fome
preceding day. A feditious and truly infamous hand-bill
had been diftributed, it is true, but by whom written or
diftributed is not known. It is heartily to be wifhed that
the perfons concerned may be difcovered, and punifhed
according to law. As foon as the gentlemen of Birmingham, who had concerted the Commemoration Meeting,
faw this hand-bill, they perceived that the effect, and perhaps the intention of it, was to inflame the mob againft
them,

them, and they immediately publifhed in the Thurfday's
newfpaper, an advertifement declaring their difavowal of
this hand-bill, and their own loyal attachment to the
King, *Lords*, and *Commons*.   They alfo fent hand-bills
with copies of this advertifement all over Birmingham.
It was not poffible for them to do any thing more effectual
to prevent any bad effects from this feditious paper, or to
refcue themfelves from the calumny of their being the
authors of it.

The laft falfe report that I have heard relative to that
meeting is concerning Dr. Prieftley's behaviour there. To
this I fuppofe it will be fufficient to anfwer, that *Dr.
Prieftley was not prefent.*

Thefe are all the reports which I have heard, but I
doubt not there may be many others, of the truth of
which every man of common fenfe will judge from what
I have faid of thofe which have come to my knowledge.
Neverthelefs, thefe falfe reports are all the pretences for
the late horrible riots; but the event fhews that they
were only *pretences*, and that the Diffenters were the true
object of the fury of the mob, as many of thofe gentlemen
who have fuffered from the riots were not prefent. For
the bufinefs of the Commemoration meetings had nothing
to do with religious diftinctions, and were in other parts
compofed of churchmen, catholics, and diffenters.   It is
true, that in Birmingham, the majority were Diffenters;
but it is evident that they did not wifh it to be diftinguifhed
as a party meeting, when they did me the honour to chufe
me as their chairman, who, it was evident, muft have con-
formed, in order to qualify myfelf for the commiffions
which I have held in the army, to all the formalities pre-
fcribed by the Teft Act, and who never was prefent in a
diffenting meeting above once or twice in England; although I have the greateft regard for the diffenting individuals whom I know, among whom are feveral of the
late unfortunate victims, men as peaceable, refpectable, and
loyal as any in the kingdom.   But as the fubject of the
                                             commemoration

commemoration meeting was quite unknown to the ignorant part of the people, it gave an opportunity of
raifing any lies that were neceffary to inflame the mob to
execute their horrid purpofes.---But that the proceedings
of the meeting were innocent, peaceable, and honourable, and alfo free from every fubject relative to religious
parties, I folemnly affirm. I am, Mr. Printer,

Yours, &c.

JAMES KEIR.

Weft Bromwich July 20, 1791.

N° VI.

*Copy of a Letter to me, printed in a column oppofite
to my own Letter to the Inhabitants of Birmingham,
and thrown into many houfes in London with the
title of* SELF-MURDER, OR THE DOCTOR TRIED
AND CONVICTED BY HIS OWN EVIDENCE.

SIR,

YOU have appealed to the public in vindication of your conduct, and lamented your loffes with the
feelings of a man; they are great, becaufe in one refpect
irreparable.

But whilft I join with the public in regretting the deftruction of your philofophical property, it pains me to
aver that you have not proved your political innocence.

You and your friends have been charged as enemies
to the prefent fyftem of Government: let us examine
how you attempt to difprove that affertion

You fay, that your friends met to exprefs their joy at
the French Revoluton, and to intimate a defire that an
improvement fhould take place in our couftitution.

Does

Does the inference to be drawn from this, prove you, and thofe of your perfuafion, to be friends to the prefent eftablifhed Government?—Surely not.

By celebrating the French Revolution, you give your fanction to the fyftem adopted in that country. If you did not fanction, you would not celebrate; and by befiring an improvement, at the fame moment, in the Britifh confti-tution, you declare yourfelf inimical to our government in its prefent form. He who is inimical to any matter, can-not be a friend; and the oppofite to that character is, of courfe, an enemy. Your letter has afforded me thefe premifes, and the conclufion is fairly drawn, from that which is fully eftablifhed.

It is not your religious, but your political fentiments which are thought dangerous to the ftate. The Prefbyte-rians certainly approve the conduct of that ufurped autho-rity which decollated the unhappy CHARLES. Our con-ftitution confiders that bloody act of common-wealth ty-ranny, to be a martyrdom. The difference in political fentiments on this great point, can therefore never be re-conciled. It is as oppofite as monarchy and repub-licanifm can make it. Were I to afk you, if the doctrine laid down by Mr. Paine in his *Rights of Man*, coincided with your principles?—you would certainly fay that " it does." You cannot fuccefsfully controvert that affertion.

Now, Sir, this publication of Mr. Paine's is a grofs libel upon the fpirit and letter of the Britifh conftitution, and as it is received into your community as a political truth, and that in approving fuch doctrine, you and your friends cannot difapprove the French Revolution, I wifh to know what fort of amendment you would make to the Britifh government.

You have made a diftinction in your letter, between the conftitutional fubjects of Great Britain and your fect, You divide them by faying, " our caufe," and " your " caufe." The conftitutional fubjects' *caufe*, is the pre-fent government in church and ftate,---your caufe muft

be

be the oppofite to that;---and therefore it is fome other kind of government in church and ftate; and though you have not direatly faid that you ever attacked the ftate, you fairly acknowledge to have given our church a BLOW:—— Your words are, " The church of England, which you " now think you are fupporting, has received a greater " blow by this conduct, than I and all my friends *have* " *ever aimed at it.*" This is a direct avowal that you and your friends have aimed a blow at our religious rights.

Do you call this *peaceably* following your ftudies as a minifter of the gofpel and a philofopher?---No, Mr. Prieftley, it is fuch kind of turbulent conduct that has brought you and your friends into the prefent fituation.

Had you, Sir, and thofe of your perfuafion, quietly at- tended the duties of your refpective ftations, and left the Proteftant church and the Britifh government to the care of thofe who are appointed by the conftitution, as Repre- fentatives of the people, to guard and protect them; you might have enjoyed that eafe, happinefs and peace which every good fubject is entitled to expect from the excel- lence of our laws, and the honour and integrity of thofe men who compofe the three branches of the legiflature.

July 20, 1791.   JOHN CHURCHMAN.

N° VII.

Copy of a Hand-bill diftributed in London the day after I arrived there.

DR. PRIESTLEY is a damned rafcal, an enemy both to the religious and political conftitution of this country, a fellow of a treafonable mind, confequently a bad chriftian: for it is not only the duty, but the glo- rious ambition, of every good chriftian to *fear God and honour the King.*

N°. VIII.

N° VIII.

Copies of two Hand-bills diſtributed among the
. *Rioters.*

Birmingham, July 16, 1791.
Friends and Fellow Countrymen,

IT is earneſtly requeſted that every *true friend*
to the *Church of England*, and to the laws of his country,
will reflect how much a *continuance* of the preſent proceedings muſt injure *that Church* and *that King they are
intended to ſupport*; and how highly unlawful it is to deſtroy
the rights and property of *any* of our neighbours. And
all *true friends* to the town and trade of Birmingham, *in
particular*, are intreated to forbear *immediately* from all
riotous and violent proceedings; diſperſing and returning
peaceably to their trades and callings, as the only way to
do *credit to themſelves* and *their cauſe*, and to promote the
peace, happineſs, and proſperity of this great and flouriſhing town.

....

Birmingham, Sunday, July 17, 1791.
*Important Information to the Friends of Church
and King.*

Friends and Fellow Churchmen,

BEING convinced you are unacquainted, that
the great loſſes which are ſuſtained by *your burning* and
deſtroying of the houſes of ſo many individuals, will eventually fall upon the *county at large*, and not upon the
perſons to whom they belonged, we feel it our duty to
inform you, that the damages already done, upon the beſt
computation that can be made, will amount to upwards
of *One Hundred Thouſand Pounds*; the whole of which
enormous

enormous fum will be charged upon the refpective parifhes, and paid out of the rates. We, therefore, as your *friends*, conjure you immediately to defift from the deftruction of *any more houfes*; otherwife the very proceedings of your *zeal* for fhewing your attachment to the CHURCH and KING, will inevitably be the means of moft ferioufly injuring innumerable families, who are hearty fupporters of Government, and bring on an addition of taxes, which *yourfelves, and the reft of the Friends of the Church*, will for years feel a very grievous burthen.

This we affure you was the cafe in London, when there were fo many houfes, and public buildings burnt and deftroyed in the year 1780, and you may rely upon it, will be the cafe on the prefent occafion. And we muft obferve to you, that *any further* violent proceedings will more offend your King and Country than ferve the caufe of Him and the Church.

Fellow Churchmen, as you love your King, regard his laws, and reftore peace.

GOD SAVE THE KING.

Aylesford	*J. Carlefs*
E. Finch	*B. Spencer*
Robert Lawley	*H. Gref. Lewis*
Robert Lawley, Jun.	*Charles Curtis*
R. Moland	*Spencer Madan*
W. Digby	*Edward Palmer*
Edward Carver	*W. Villers*
John Brooke	*W. W. Mafon*

N° IX.

TO THE KING's MOST EXCELLENT MAJESTY.

The humble Addrefs of the High Bailiff, Clergy, and other principal Inhabitants of the Town and Neighbourhood of Birmingham.

" *May it pleafe your Majefty,*'

" WE, your Majefty's moft dutiful and loyal fubjects, the High Bailiff, Clergy, and other principal inhabitants of the town and neighbourhood of Birmingham, deeply fenfible of your Majefty's paternal care of all your fubjects, beg leave moft humbly to approach your royal throne, with hearts full of gratitude for the recent inftance of that care which your Majefty gracioufly condefcended to afford us during the late riots in this place, by commanding fuch particular attention to be paid to our fecurity, and directing fuch ample relief for our neceffities.

" Rejoicing alfo in every opportunity of teftifying our loyalty to the beft of Sovereigns, and our firm attachment to that noble fabric the conftitution of this country, the envy of all other nations, as it is the glory of our own; We cannot neglect this occafion of pledging ourfelves to fupport your Majefty's illuftrious houfe, and to defend that happy conftitution both in church and ftate, againft every attempt at innovation, at the rifk of every thing dear to us."

N° X.

The Addrefs of the Diffenters to the King.

" Moft Gracious Sovereign,

" WE, your Majefty's loyal and dutiful fubjects, the Proteftant Diffenters in the town of Birmingham, beg leave to approach your Majefty in a moment of ferious affliction and concern, arifing not only from our recent aggravated fufferings, but from our painful apprehenfions left the calumnies of our enemies fhould influence your royal mind, and infinuate fufpicions of our loyalty and affection.

Affured

Assured not of our innocence alone, but of our unalterable attachment to your august person, and to the succession of your Royal House, we respectfully claim your Majesty's continued protection and favour, and beg leave most earnestly to assure your Majesty, we have no thoughts of disturbing the Constitution. We are the descendants of those to whom (as the annals of our country will testify) the Revolution, which secured to your illustrious house the crown of these kingdoms, was greatly indebted. The civil constitution of our country is our pride and our glory; which we have been taught from our infancy to revere, and which we would die to preserve. Indeed, Sire, though deeply afflicted by the late riotous devastations, and by the want of energy in the civil power, yet we speak from hearts that are actuated by the love of law, of peace, of order, and good government. Sensible of your Majesty's goodness, in the vigorous measures which have been adopted for suppressing the outrages, which a lawless banditti were spreading through this place and its environs, we offer you the warmest tribute of our gratitude, for the happy deliverance we have experienced, by the wisdom of the measures planned by your Majesty's ministers, and by the energy and promptitude with which they were so successfully executed.

We feel ourselves deeply thankful to your Majesty, for this very beneficial and decisive instance of your royal attention; and likewise to your great goodness, in the measures which have since been adopted, for discovering and bringing to exemplary punishment, as well the instigators, as the perpetrators of the late atrocious violences; and we firmly and dutifully rely upon your Majesty for the continuance of it, as well as for the exercise of that candour and magnanimity, which will resist the calumnies of our enemies, and continue to us that protection, favour, and confidence, to which we know ourselves justly entitled.

That your Majesty may long reign in peace and glory; that your royal honours may for ages continue to descend

to

to your lateſt poſterity; and that the happineſs of Britain may proſper and improve itſelf under their auſpicious influence, is the honeſt wiſh and fervent prayer of, Sire,

Your Majeſty's moſt loyal and dutiful ſubjects.

N° XI.

From the Committee of Diſſenters.

WHEREAS it now appears, that among other inſidious and unwarrantable practices made uſe of during the late riots, to delude the populace, and inſtigate them to acts of violence and deſtruction, letters were forged, charging the Diſſenters with a treaſonable deſign to overthrow the preſent happy conſtitution of this kingdom, and pretending that the whole body of them were combined together, and had appointed to aſſemble on the 16th of Auguſt, " to burn the churches, blow up the parliament, " cut off the head of the King, and aboliſh all taxes:" And whereas it is now well known, that ſuch forged letters were pretended to be found among the papers of the Rev. Dr. Prieſtley, and William Ruſſell, Eſq. and the words above quoted formed part of one of the forged letters which were brought and read by two perſons on horſe-back at Showell-green, the houſe of Wm. Ruſſell, Eſq. whilſt the ſame was in flames, in order to inſtigate the rioters to further acts of violence: Notice is hereby given, that the Proteſtant Diſſenters of Birmingham, in addition to the reward of One Hundred Pounds, graciouſly offered by his Majeſty for diſcovering the inſtigators of the late horrid violences, will give a further reward of One Hundred Pounds for the diſcovery of the perſon or perſons who wrote the ſaid forged letters, or any one of them, ſo that he, or they, may be convicted thereof, and brought to puniſhment.

THOMAS LEE, Junior,
Secretary to the Committee of Proteſtant Diſſenters
Birmingham, Aug. 22, 1791.   in Birmingham.

N° XII.

Copy of a Letter addreſſed to the Biſhops, and Members of the Houſe of Commons, mentioned in page 20, of this work.

Sir,

AS I am informed that a *printed paper*, containing *Extracts* from the Preface to one of my late publications, viz. *Letters to the Rev. Edward Burn*, has been ſent by ſome enemies of the Diſſenters, probably by ſome of the clergy of this town, to every Member of Parliament, and alſo to all the Biſhops, and that it made a very unfavourable impreſſion with reſpect to the queſtion before the Houſe, on Tueſday the ſecond inſtant, it will not, I hope, be deemed impertinent, to ſhew you how much you have been impoſed upon by it. For had the *Extracts* been given together with what is *connected* with them, they would have appeared in a very different light indeed. The following paragraph, from p. 15, I give as a ſpecimen of the whole, printing what has been ſelected in the *Roman* character, and what immediately follows it, but which has been omitted, in *Italic*.

" Whether I be more pleaſed or diſpleaſed, with their " preſent violence, let them" (the clergy) " now judge. " The greater their violence, the greater is our confidence " of final ſucceſs. *Becauſe it will excite more public diſ-* " *cuſſion, which is all that is neceſſary for our purpoſe.*"

In the ſame Preface there is the following *Note*, p. 12, which is in perfect agreement with the tenor of all my writings on the ſubject.

" It has always been my opinion, that Diſſenters " ſhould not accept of any civil offices for which the " majority of their countrymen have pronounced them " diſqualified, but patiently acquieſce in their excluſion " from

" from them, till it fhall pleafe God, in the courfe of
" his providence, and by means of our peaceable repre-
" fentations and remonftrances, to open the eyes, and en-
" large the minds, of our countrymen, and thereby give
" them more juft ideas of the natural rights of men, and
" the true interefts of their country."

To a perfon of any fenfe of *honour*, whatever be his
political or *religious principles*, no remarks of mine can be
neceffary to fhew the unfairnefs of this proceeding. Whoever it be that could give thofe extracts as a juft reprefentation of my principles, muft have *meant to deceive*, and
therefore would not fcruple to have recourfe to any other
artifice to gain their point. The paper was fent off in a
private manner, and too late to be difcovered and counter-
acted; but when the fame, or any fimilar queftion, fhall
again come before the Houfe, I hope you will remember
whofe conduct has always been open and manly, and
whofe was infidious and deceitful.

I am,

Sir,

Birmingham,   Your very humble Servant,

MARCH 4, 1790,   J. PRIESTLEY.

N° XIII.

*Copy of a Letter from M. Condorcet, Secretary to the
Academy of Sciences at Paris, to Dr. Prieftley.*

Sir, and moft illuftrious Affociate,

      THE Academy of Sciences have charged me
to exprefs the grief with which they are penetrated at the
recital of the perfecution of which you have been lately
the victim.

They all feel how much lofs the Sciences have experienced by the deftruction of thofe labours which you
had prepared for their aggrandifement. It is not you, Sir,

who

who have reafon to complain; your virtue and your genius
ftill remain undiminifhed, and it is not in the power of
human ingratitude to forget what you have done for the
happinefs of mankind:—they only ought to be unhappy,
whofe guilty conduct has led their reafon aftray, and whofe
remorfe has already punifhed their crimes.

You are not the firft friend of liberty, againft whom
tyrants have armed the very people whom they have
deprived of their rights. Thefe are the only means which
they can make ufe of againft him, whofe difintereftednefs
of mind, whofe elevation of foul, and whofe purity of conduct, equally fhelter him from their feductions and their
vengeance.

They calumniate fuch a perfon when they can neither
intimidate nor corrupt him; they arm prejudices againft
him, when they dare not arm the laws; and that which
they have done in regard to you, is the nobleft homage
that tyranny dares to render to probity, to talents, and to
courage.

At this prefent moment a league is formed throughout
Europe againft the general liberty of mankind; but for
fome time paft another has exifted, occupied with propagating and with defending this liberty, without any other
arms than thofe furnifhed by reafon; and thefe will finally
triumph.

It is in the neceffary order of things, that error fhould
be momentary, and truth eternal. Men of genius, fupported by their virtuous difciples, when placed in the
balance againft the vulgar mob of corrupt intriguers—the
inftruments or the accomplices of tyrants—muft at length
prevail againft them.

The glorious day of Univerfal Liberty will fhine upon
our defcendants, but we fhall at leaft enjoy the *aurora*;
and you, Sir, have contributed not a little to accelerate
that happy event by your labours, by the example of your
virtues, by the indignation which all Europe feels againft

L 4   your

your perfecutors, and by the interest and the admiration which a misfortune has excited, that, although it may wound, cannot subdue your soul.

I am, with an inviolable and respectful attachment,
　　　　Sir, and my very illustrious associate,
　　　　　　Your humble and most obedient servant,
Paris, July 30, 1791.　　　　　CONDORCET.

N° XIV.

Dr. Priestley's Answer.

SIR,

I AM more then consoled for my losses, in finding that the Members of the Academy of Sciences have done me the honour to interest themselves in my affairs, and especially in observing that the friends of philosophy are, what they ever ought to be, the friends of general liberty. With us there is an example of the enemies of the one being also the enemies of the other. Having always been an avowed advocate of public liberty, civil and religious, which led me to write in defence of your late glorious Revolution, the great body of the Clergy in this country, and many of those who call themselves the friends of the King, have long been my enemies; and in accomplishing my ruin, they have not spared the instruments of that *science*, my application to which gave some degree of weight to my labours in another field.

But do not, Sir, suppose that *these* friends of the Church and of the King are the English nation. They are no more than a faction, whom a failure in the way of argument has rendered desperate. The sober part of the nation think more justly, and equally disapprove their maxims, and the methods they take to enforce them. The English nation in general respect the French; and, though too many of them are at present under a temporary delusion, will vie with you in every thing truly liberal, in

whatever

whatever can contribute to the honour and happiness of the country at home, and to its living in peace and good-will with all its neighbours, and especially with yourselves, whose exertions in favour of universal liberty, and universal peace, will for ever endear you to us.

Assure my brethren of the Academy, that, honoured by their choice of me for an associate, and by their generous sympathy on the present occasion, I shall not fail, while my life and my faculties are continued to me, to resume my philosophical pursuits, and endeavour to shew our common enemies, that a genuine love of science, and of liberty, is inextinguishable, except with life, and that un-reasonable and wicked opposition tends to animate, rather than depress, the mind that is penetrated with it.

In perfect confidence that whatever is *true and right* will finally prevail, and that every mode of opposition will only contribute to their more complete establishment, I subscribe myself with respect,

Sir,

Their, and your, very humble servant,

J. PRIESTLEY.

N° XV.

An Address from the Members of the New Meeting to Dr. Priestley.

Rev. and dear Sir.

WE the afflicted and sorrowing members of the New Meeting Society, in the midst of the anguish and anxiety which is inseparable from our present calamities, have greatly regretted that we could not before this day assemble together, to confer upon the deplorable situation of our congregational affairs, and the measures necessary to be pursued in consequence of our persecutions. Being now met together for this purpose, we immediately embrace the opportunity of addressing ourselves to our well beloved

beloved paſtor, and beg to aſſure you how tenderly and affectionately we ſympathize with you in the preſent ſeaſon of ſevere trial and affliction, and that, in the ſpirit of chriſtian love and affection, we moſt tenderly condole with you under your perſonal unmerited and painful ſufferings.

Little did we conceive that the exemplary diligence with which we have ſeen you for the ſpace of eleven years inculcate upon us, and our children, every thing that was good and virtuous, could be followed by ſuch a dreadful cataſtrophe as we now feel and contemplate. Whatever miſconceptions our neighbours may have unhappily adopted reſpecting your various publications, we dare appeal to them, and we teſtify to the world, that your paſtoral labours have uniformly tended to every thing that becomes the chriſtian, or can adorn the man, to a ſincere and fervent piety towards God, and to peace and univerſal good-will to all mankind, without any diſtinction of ſect or party.

You have uniformly taught us to reſpect the government under which we live; and in the devotional ſervice of every Lord's day have never failed to offer up our united prayers for the Divine bleſſing upon the King, his Royal Family, and all that are in authority under him; ſo that from whatever cauſe it may be that you have been marked out for perſecution, and for the grievous calamities to which you are ſtill expoſed, we are ſenſible it cannot originate in any part of your paſtoral labours, which all thoſe ſtrangers who have occaſionally joined us (without ſome of whom ſcarce a Lord's day has paſſed) muſt witneſs as well as ourſelves, have been conducted in the true ſpirit of the Goſpel, in a ſpirit of love and peace, and though diſtinguiſhed by an ardent deſire to promote the cauſe of truth, yet ſtill more uniformly directed to inculcate the great and primary duties of ſincere piety towards God, and univerſal benevolence towards all mankind.

Accept, dear Sir, our unfeigned teſtimony to your exemplary diligence, your eminent abilities, your unremitted

zeal,

zeal, your diftinguifhed humility, your unqueftioned fin-
cerity, and your uniform love of peace, chriftian forbearance and moderation; and permit us to affure you how
affectionately and tenderly we fympathize with you under
your prefent fufferings, and how fincerely we wifh their
removal. And although you are not immediately returning to us, yet we look forward with pleafure to thofe
happier times when you may refume your paftoral labours
here with fafety and fatisfaction.

In the mean time we earneftly recommend you to the
Divine protection and favour, imploring him to watch
over, to guide, and blefs you, and in due time, to reftore
you to us, who are, in the bonds of chriftian love and
affection,

Rev. and ever dear Sir,

Your fincere and affectionate friends,

'(Signed in the Name and at the unanimous requeft of the
Congregation)

Birmingham, Auguft 2, 1791·　　　W. RUSSELL.

Nº XVI.

THE ANSWER.

My Chriftian Brethren,

YOUR affectionate Letter has given me not only
confolation, but joy. I rejoice to fee the effects of thofe
principles in which it has been my bufinefs, and that of
my excellent Colleague to inftruct you; and the fituation
in which we now are, is peculiarly adapted to try their
force, and to fhew the world that religion is not a bufinefs
of mere fpeculation, but that it is capable of fupporting
the mind, and directing the conduct, in the moft trying
circumftances.

I rejoice that after being an example to other congregations of purity of chriftian doctrine, and excellence of difcipline,

line, you are now an example of patience and fortitude in suffering; firmly maintaining the principles for which you suffer, and yet preserving your good-will towards the authors of your sufferings; not forgetting that there is the hand of God, as well as that of man, in every thing that befalls us; and praying that God would forgive your enemies and turn their hearts.

Be assured that in the height of my sufferings I would not (even without any respect to futurity) have exchanged my feelings with those of our persecutors, in the moment of their greatest exultation over us; for I never lost the feelings of pity and benevolence towards them, while I was the object of their hatred and execration, I have even found, as I doubt not yourselves have also done, that these christian sentiments are more easily exercised in great trials than in little ones, as they more effectually call forth the principles from which they proceed.

I rejoice that you are about to re-establish the affairs of our society, and I only wait your summons to assist you in that necessary work. Your call will be to me an intimation of my duty; and then committing my life to him who gave it, and who will not suffer it to terminate unseasonably, I will instantly attend you, and resume the functions of the office with which you have honoured me. I know no satisfaction equal to that which has ever accompanied the discharge of such duties as those I owe to you.

Let what we have mutually suffered teach us the uncertainty of every thing in this world, and the value of those principles which enable us to look beyond it, and not only to bear, but to rejoice in, tribulation; to esteem it an honour to be " counted worthy" to bear reproach, to incur loss, and even to lay down our lives, for the pure faith of the Gospel. May your tribulation work patience, and patience experience, and experience hope, even that hope which maketh not ashamed.

Finally,

Finally, may God preferve and keep you. May your fufferings be for the furtherance of the Gofpel here, and add to your crown of glory hereafter.

I am, my chriftian friends,

In the firm faith and hope of the Gofpel,

London, Auguft 4, 1791.

Your affectionate Paftor,

J. PRIESTLEY.

N° XVII.

An Addrefs from the Young People belonging to the Congregation of the New Meeting to Dr. Prieftley.

Honoured Sir,

THE common principles of humanity would, after what has recently occurred, incite us to communicate our feelings to you. But we feel urged to it by far greater motives. We have feen the great apoftle of civil and religious liberty driven from among us. We have feen the precious labours of a great part of his life deftroyed by a lawlefs mob. We have feen his apparatus and library fhare the fame fate. We have feen this valuable member of fociety in the greateft danger of falling a victim to popular fury; and not yet having perfecuted him fufficiently, we are frequently hearing the vileft invectives againft him, who is fo highly deferving of our gratitude for his perfonal and unwearied efforts to enlighten our minds on the great fubject of religion, and whofe philofophical labours have been fo juftly extolled throughout every part of the civilized world. To attempt a defcription of what we feel on reflecting on thefe circumftances would be as difficult as it would be painful.

To

To aſſure you that we feel extremely for you, would be ſuppoſing you unacquainted with us. But, Sir, there is one circumſtance which much heightens our ſorrow, we cannot think of your abilities without reſpect, we cannot feel the effects of your labours without indulging an ardent wiſh that we may ſtill continue to experience the happy effects of your inſtructions. But when we recollect the indignities you have felt, the trials you have had to ſupport, and the irreparable loſs you have ſuſtained; our fears are alarmed leſt ſuch complicated diſtreſs ſhould lead you to ſeek an aſylum, which, Sir, to our inexpreſſible ſorrow, Birmingham hath not afforded you. On the other hand, knowing the chriſtian diſpoſitions you poſſeſs, and the knowledge you have of the human mind, we are convinced that many palliatives will ſuggeſt themſelves, which, to a mind like yours will have conſiderable influence.

Young as we are, we cannot but hope, and expect, that the flame which ignorance and bigotry have kindled, will be ſoon extinguiſhed by an increaſe of knowledge, and that genuine chriſtianity will ſo far take poſſeſſion of the hearts of our fellow townſmen, that they will look upon the perſecution you have ſuffered at their hands, as a ſin againſt the pureſt of the goſpel precepts. Many, very many, we truſt agree with ourſelves in wiſhing your return. Indulge us then, kind Sir, in this fond hope. Should it, however, be delayed, may we ſhew our miſtaken neighbours, that, although Prieſtley is gone, he ſowed good ſeed before his departure, that it fell into good ground, and that it now flouriſhes in the blade and promiſes a plenteous harveſt. May we prove it to them, that argument armed with fire and faggot may produce a temporary ſhock, but that it finally ſtrengthens our cauſe, that it forces us to feel the great juſtneſs of it, and produces actions natural to ſuch a conviction; we truſt we ſhall always follow your great example in candour and moderation, not loſing ſight of that chriſtian fortitude you have ſo uniformly diſplayed ſince we have had the happineſs of your reſidence among us.

us. Accept, dear Sir, our warmeſt expreſſions of gratitude for the great and laſting ſervices you have rendered us as chriſtians, as members of civil ſociety, and as citizens, and be aſſured it is with the greateſt reſpect we ſubſcribe ourſelves,

Honoured Sir,

Your affectionate Pupils.

(Signed, One Hundred and Twenty-one Names.)

Nº XVIII.

THE ANSWER.

My Young Friends,

  I COULD not read your very affectionate Addreſs to me without tears of joy. You were ever the moſt pleaſing part of my charge, and this Addreſs is a proof that the affection I had for you, and the pains that I took in inſtructing you, have not been thrown away. Your example will encourage other chriſtian miniſters, who hear of it to follow mine. The great object of my Lectures, in all your Claſſes, was to give you a juſt knowledge of the principles of religion, as the only ſolid foundation of proper ſentiments and good conduct, and I ſhall want no conſolation under my unmerited ſufferings, while you continue to feel, and to act, as you do.

  The unſettled ſtate of the Congregation, and the conſequent diſcontinuance of our Lectures, you will conſider as a trial of the principles you have already acquired. Give a proof of their ſtrength by a ſteady attention to every means of improvement that is yet in your power. The enemies of our chriſtian liberty have deſtroyed an excellent Library provided for your uſe; but your zeal and liberality will ſupply you with reſources of the ſame kind; and let the more opulent among you aſſiſt thoſe who

are

are lefs fo. Re-perufe the works which I compofed for
your ufe, and fuch others as can be re-purchafed of thofe
which the enemy has deprived you of. Shew them, that
by deftroying books, they cannot deftroy the effects of
reading them; that the love of truth, of virtue, and of
liberty, which you have imbibed, can never be eradicated,
and that lawlefs power can never fubdue fixed principles.

What I more particularly wifh, in your prefent fituation, is, that thofe who are the beft inftructed among you
would fupply my place, in undertaking the inftruction of
others; and many of you, I am well fatisfied, are fufficiently qualified for it; and affure yourfelves of the
Divine bleffing on the weakeft well-meant endeavours.

Young as you are, I truft you are too well eftablifhed
in chriftian principles, to have your faith in a wife fuper-
intending Providence at all fhaken by the calamitous
events which have been permitted to befal us. Chriftianity
did not lofe, but gain ground by perfecution. It is a ftate
excellently adapted to recal to our minds, and to ftrengthen
our regards to, our future and better profpects, while it
loofens a dangerous attachment to the things of time and
fenfe.

The ways of God are unfearchable by us. But be
affured, that nothing can materially harm you, if you be
followers of that which is good. If I be reftored to you,
which is my moft ardent wifh, our mutual fatisfaction
will be doubled by this interruption; and if not, it will
add to the ardour of your wifhes, as it does to mine, to
meet you where the violence of the adverfary can never
feparate us any more..

        I am, my young Friends,

            In the faith and hope of the Gofpel,

                Your affectionate Paftor,

London, Auguft 12, 1791.   J. PRIESTLEY.

A Letter

N° XIX.

From the Members of the New Meeting.

Dear and Rev. Sir,

THE affectionate terms in which you accept our letter of condolance, and the affurance you give us that it afforded you confolation and joy, have caufed us a lively fatisfaction. Your defire to concur with us in our endeavours to re-eftablifh the affairs of the congregation has awakened our anxiety for the feafon when we may urge your return to Birmingham; and although that period has been thus long protracted, yet we think it our duty to remind you, that we exercife a chearful reliance upon your kind declaration, that you only wait our fummons.

The fincere affection we bear you, and the conviction we poffefs of the value and importance of your life to the caufe of truth, and the world at large, will not permit us to confent that you fhould be expofed to any unneceffary hazard on your return hither before the time of tranquility and fafety. Prevented by thefe motives, and thefe alone, from requefting in the moft affectionate terms, that you would refume in perfon your paftoral charge, we affure ourfelves that the interval they occafion, will not be permitted to operate, in any fenfe, to our difadvantage.

Our endeavours to procure a fuitable place to affemble in for public worfhip, until our own is rebuilt, though not altogether fo fuccefsful as we could wifh, will no be difcontinued till the object is fully attained: in the mean time, we have the pleafure of affembling in Carr's Lane each Lord's day, with our brethren and fellow-fufferers of the Old Meeting congregation; and we learn with unfpeakable fatisfaction, that the junior part of our fociety, profiting by your advice and correfpondence, are already affembled in regular claffes, and are conforming to your wifhes, in endeavouring to continue the important

M   bufinefs

busineſs of religious inſtruction among themſelves, agreeable to the plan you eſtabliſhed; ſo that your labours are ſtill flouriſhing among us, even in our preſent ſtate of diſperſion and perſecution; and we hope and truſt it will not now be long, ere your own judgment, and that of your friends, will concur in affording us a renewal of thoſe perſonal exertions by which we have heretofore been ſo much edified, and from the continuance of which, we promiſe ourſelves ſo much future advantage.

We rejoice in the continuance of your health, and in the frequent accounts we receive of your uninterrupted chearfulneſs, and offer our fervent prayers to the Almighty that your eminent abilities may long be ſpared, and your health and chearfulneſs be prolonged with them. With ſentiments of the ſincereſt reſpect, we remain with unalterable attachment,

Rev. and dear Sir,

Your much obliged

And very affectionate friends and ſervants,

Birmingham, September 5, 1791.

N° XX.

From the Young People belonging to the Congregation of the New Meeting.

Dear and reſpected Sir,

PERMIT us to indulge our feelings in again addreſſing you. When aſſurances of gratitude and attachment are not neceſſary, there is a gratification in expreſſing the prevailing ſentiments of the heart; and when you, Sir, are the object, we feel no common ardour. We have too much confidence in your goodneſs, and have had too many proofs of your affectionate regard to our happineſs, to imagine you will think us troubleſome.

We

We have received your affectionate and animating letter. Our tears fpoke our feelings. We cannot exprefs them,—language is feeble and inadequate. But we will bind your inftructions to our hearts. While we remember whofe pupils we have been, we cannot act unworthily. We can never fufficiently exprefs our fenfe of the obligation you have conferred upon us, but we dwell upon the fubject with too much pleafure to omit any opportunity of renewing it. To you, Sir, we are indebted for the defire of improvement. You have given us habits of employing our leifure hours in the cultivation of our underftandings, in purfuits that afford delight and advantage, and which are calculated to raife us higher in the fcale of being. The love of virtue you have implanted in us by precept and example. We will guard and cherifh it; and while we enjoy the fruits of it, our fouls exulting fhall blefs you. You have deprived adverfity of its fting, and have enabled us to extend our views with fatisfaction beyond the world, by imprefling our minds with the ftrongeft evidence of the great truths of chriftianity. Thefe advantages, Sir, we have received from you. We feel their importance, and will diffufe them as far as our influence extends. It fhall be our grand object to endeavour to follow your example in a firm adherence to what we believe to be the caufe of truth; in preferving our minds open to conviction, and in the cultivation of fortitude, patience and charity. We have indeed no flight trial of the latter, when we behold the enlightened and benevolent friend of all mankind, whofe life has invariably exhibited, and whofe inftructions have ever enforced, the practice of every mild and gentle virtue, treated with a cruelty which would difgrace a barbarous age. But we will remember our principles, the principles, Sir, we have imbibed from you, and will fay in the language of philofophy and of chriftianity, Deluded men, we pity you,--- May your hearts be turned, and your errors forgiven.

Your

Your fufferings, Sir, have been great, but we have much confolation in knowing that your mind is ftill greater. The man who can review a life like yours, and fay it has been mine, poffeffes the nobleft fources of joy. You have formed to yourfelf a fanctuary which no ftorm can reach. The venomed dart muft rebound and wound the breaft which aimed it. While the vices of mankind prefent a melancholy picture to your view, and call forth emotions of forrow, in a heart benevolent as your's, you will remember how many have been made virtuous and happy by your means, and that no lawlefs power can deftroy the works you have given to the world, or prevent their operation in promoting the beft interefts of man.

The violence of a mob, or thofe who chofe to act by fuch inftruments, can only give additional luftre to a character known, admired, and revered by the wife and liberal in every part of the civilized world. But eminent talents and diftinguifhed virtue, feldom fail to excite in narrow and interefted minds, the defpicable paffions of envy and fear; and the ignorance of mankind affords, alas! an ample field for them to work upon. The page of hiftory which the recent event is deftined to fill, will exhibit a ftrong contraft in human nature. Pofterity will paufe with aftonifhment when they find that the fame age which witneffed your generous exertions in the caufe of truth and of mankind, produced fuch favage ferocity. Happy would it be for many if the cloud which will hang over their memories were the dark veil of oblivion. But the brichtnefs of your character will render the deformity of theirs confpicuous.

Your propofal that the claffes fhould continue to meet has given us much fatisfaction. We fhall all rejoice in any occafion of giving or receiving inftruction. We hold the advantages we have received too dear to neglect any opportunity of extending and improving them. We have this day met to confider of the beft means of carrying it into execution. The different circumftances under

which

which we now affemble cannot fail to imprefs our minds in a very powerful manner: but we truft they are impreffions which will have a favourable influence on our future lives. We have requefted Mr. Blythe to fupply your place in the fenior clafs till your return, and when he is defirous of it, we fhall willingly relieve him from the fatigue of reading. Mr. Hawkes we have requefted to give us his prefence in the noon clafs, and to take only fo much of the bufinefs of it upon him, as is agreeable to himfelf; fince many of us will gladly give him any affiftance in our power. They have in the moft affectionate manner complied with our wifhes, and next Sunday the three claffes, recommence in their ufual form, every thing previous to their meeting being fettled.

We have had a very full meeting, and many who were obliged to be abfent have requefted to put their names to this addrefs as a teftimony of their gratitude for your kind letter. But we hope, Sir, the time will foon arrive, when you may again appear among us in the fame venerable and endearing character in which we have fo often beheld you. To be feparated from you is an evil we are ill-difpofed to bear. We will hope this trial is not in referve for us. Should infatuation, however, extend fo far, our enemies fhall find that they can never feparate you from our hearts; that our gratitude and attachment has a bafis too ftrong for them ever to fhake, and that the mind is property which no iniquitious power can reach.

With fentiments of the warmeft gratitude and veneration,

We are,

Sir,

Your affectionate pupils,

(Signed with 145 names)

Birmingham, Auguft 22. 1791.

A Letter

Nº XXI.

From the Members of the New Meeting Congregation.

Birmingham, Oct. 22, 1791.

Dear and Reverend Sir,

WE, the Subscribers and Members of the New Meeting Society, being assembled together for the purpose of conferring upon the rumour of an unexpected impediment in the way of your return to us, desire to assure you of the deep and poignant concern these rumours·give us. The·bare apprehension of your leaving us is deeply affecting to us all. Sudden and violent as was the first onset of the persecution and troubles with which you and ourselves were lately assailed, we saw it necessary that you should retire for a season, and we not only acquiesced in your retirement, but rejoiced in your enjoying that safety at a distance which a deluded populace appeared to deny you here; but the thought of these violences operating to the final dissolution of our happy connection, as pastor and people, is really more distressing to us than all our other sufferings and calamities, multiplied and severe as they are, and we cannot but sincerely and earnestly deprecate such an event.

Indeed, Sir, we can truly assure you, that there is no plea to be urged, there is no assurance to be given, there is no inducement to be offered, by a people whose hearts are full of veneration, respect, and gratitude, which we cannot; which we do not now urge and offer to you as the genuine dictate of the most ardent, sincere, and fervent affection. We cannot describe how much our feelings are interested; we cannot tell you how earnest, how sincere, and how fervent our desires are for your return, and how much our best affections are moved upon this truly important and interesting occasion: but we know we may safely rely upon your own feelings to do us justice: we know you will feel for us, and also for those who are

the

the deareſt to us, when we intreat you to recollect your invaluable uſefulneſs among them, and the happy fruits which have been already ſeen to reſult from your exemplary aſſiduities and labours there. But we will forbear; for although we would be ſerious and earneſt, we would not be importunate. We ſhall, therefore, urge you no further—We know your candour, we truſt your goodneſs, and would rely upon your well known ſerious and pious mind for the acceptance of this our ſincere and well meant application.—Perſuaded you will not deem it an intruſion, we offer no apology. On the contrary, knowing and feeling ourſelves that it is the dictate of a pure affection and ardent attachment, we doubt not but you will receive it as ſuch, and that, as it is the genuine reſult of our zeal and ſincerity in the moſt important of all concerns, it will operate with you accordingly.—Hoping that you may ſpeedily return amongſt us, reſume your pen with renewed vigour, and your labours with increaſing ſucceſs, we remain, with the ſincereſt affection, reſpect, and attachment,

> Reverend and ever dear Sir,
> .   Your friends and fellow Chriſtians.

N° XXII.

To the Members of the New Meeting Congregation at Birmingham.

London, Oct. 8, 1791.

My Chriſtian Friends,

I NEVER felt myſelf in a more painful ſituation than the preſent, in conſequence of ſitting down to anſwer your two moſt affectionate Addreſſes, inviting me to return to the exerciſe of my miniſtry among you, after having been driven away by lawleſs violence.

Not only on my leaving Birmingham, but ſome time after my arrival in London, I had no idea but that of a temporary retreat; thinking that the violence of party ſpirit, having had its triumph, would be ſatisfied, and that perhaps, repentance ſucceeding, I might reſume my functions with more advantage than before. But every account that I have received having repreſented the ſpirit of party as more inveterate than I had imagined it to be, ſo that, in all probability, my return would only inflame it, and in conſequence of this, my ſituation, if ſafe, would be uncomfortable, and perhaps hurtful, it is my deliberate opinion, that it will be better for ſome other perſon, leſs obnoxious to popular prejudice, to take my place, and that I may be more uſefully fixed in London, or its neighbourhood.

I hope I need not aſſure you, that it is with the greateſt regret that I at length, after much heſitation, have come to this reſolution, in forming which, conſiderations of a more private nature, but to which no man is, or ought to be, wholly inſenſible, have likewiſe had their influence. Never, I believe, was any chriſtian miniſter more happy in his ſituation than I have been with you. My ſentiments concerning you are not only thoſe of reſpect and affection, but of pride. It has been my boaſt, that no congregation that I have been acquainted with, was ſo candid, ſo well informed, and ſo ready to adopt whatever their miniſters recommended to them for their edification, and that, in conſequence of it, your regulations were the beſt adapted to form intelligent and ſerious chriſtians. Our example was looked up to by other and diſtant congregations, who were excited to form themſelves upon our model. I had, alſo, perfect liberty, which few diſſenting miniſters have, to follow all my favourite purſuits, of every kind, and to preach and write without the leaſt hazard of giving offence, whatever I thought proper. I had, therefore, no other wiſh than to live and die among you.

But as I hope the good that has been done will never be undone, owing eſpecially to the almoſt unprecedented zeal, and excellent ſpirit, of the young people among you, whoſe whofe Addreffes will for ever endear them to me, and whofe example, wherever it is known, muft contribute to inftruct and warm others, I have the lefs regret in now fignifying my intention of refigning my paftoral charge, but not till I have feen your affairs in fome meafure re-eftablifhed, and fome profpect of your being able to do as well without me: and as fome time muft be fixed, I mention Chriftmas next.

As foon then, as you fhall have provided a place in which I can officiate, I fhall with peculiar pleafure refume my functions among you, and continue them, till the time abovementioned; and if it pleafe God that I fhould die in your fervice, I fhall not (feeing no apparent caufe of ap-prehenfion, fuch as would juftify my flight from my pro-per ftation) think it will clofe unfeafonably with refpect to myfelf, or the world.

I am,

My friends and fellow chriftians,

Your affectionate paftor,

J. PRIESTLEY.

N° XXIII.

From the Congregation of the New Meeting, Birmingham.

Birmingham, October 24, 1791.

Rev. and dear Sir,

YOUR truly interefting letter of the 8th inftant has deeply affected us. We are grieved to an excefs at the feparation it announces, and the apparent neceffity of our acquiefcing in it; and in "your own "deliberate opinion, that it will be more for the general "good to have fome other perfon fill your place here, "and that you may be more ufefully employed in London "or its neighbourhood." It is with the moft painful re-luctance that we yield to this truly humiliating conclufion,

without

without importuning you with our intreaties, that you would reconfider it, and refume your firft purpofe of fpeedily returning to us. But feeing it your deliberate judgment, and knowing the circumftances which furround us; we patiently refign our wills; and urging you no farther, moft devoutly pray our heavenly Father, that your profpect of greater ufefulnefs may be realized; that many fouls may yet be added to your faithful miniftry; that your glorious career of ufefulnefs and benevolence may long be continued, and that your final removal from it to the realms of light may be ferene and happy.

You will permit us to add, that the apprehenfions which we have been recently informed fome of our wifeft and beft friends entertain for your fafety, fhould you profecute your intended return to us, neceffarily compel us, to make a farther facrifice of our anxious defires to fee you here. We are, indeed, truly forry to abandon the profpect of your promifed return, though it is but for a few weeks; but we fhould be wanting in affection towards yourfelf, and in refpect to the general good of mankind, were we not to attend to thefe apprehenfions. Indeed, Sir, we fpeak very fincerely, when we declare that we bear you too fincere and fervent an affection, that we have too great a value for your peace and fafety, are far too anxious for your prefervation from infult, to confent, that you fhould upon the prefent occafion expofe your perfon to the hazard of it. Give us leave, then, with hearts full of refpect and affection, to intreat you to forego for the prefent, your purpofe of vifiting us as our paftor, and let us repeat the affurance conveyed by our firft letter, that when the feafon of perfect tranquility and fafety approaches, we fhall moft cordially hail your return to us for any period your other important connexions and engagements may admit. In the mean time, anxious to maintain an intercourfe with you, and defirous of your aid and concurrence in our choice of a fuitable perfon to affift your worthy coadjutor, the Rev. Mr. Blythe, we

request

requeſt that if you know of any gentleman whom you think ſuitable for us, and whom you have reaſon to expect would wiſh for ſuch an eſtabliſhment, you will favour us with your nomination of him. We are, with the livelieſt ſentiments of gratitude, reſpect, and affection,

Dear and Reverend Sir,

Your truly affectionate friends and fellow‑chriſtians.

Nº XXIV.

From the Congregation of Mill-Hill Chapel Leeds.

Leeds, Auguſt 14, 1791.

Rev. and Dear Sir,

WE, the Proteſtant Diſſenters of Mill-Hill Chapel in Leeds, cannot reſt ſatisfied in a ſilent ſympathy with you on the loſſes you have lately incurred from the violence of party rage.

While all the ſincere friends of rational liberty and good order are rouſed to an honeſt indignation, by outrages which have diſgraced our country in the eyes of enlightened Europe, we, having had the happineſs of being under your paſtoral care, feel a perſonal intereſt in your welfare. And as, from this intimate connexion with you, we have had a better opportunity of becoming acquainted with your real character than many others have enjoyed, we the more readily embrace this opportunity of bearing our ſpecial teſtimony to its exemplary excellence. An interval of more than eighteen years has not effaced from our memory the good principles you inculcated upon us, and the affectionate care which you uniformly manifeſted for our advancement in every virtue. It was, in a peculiar degree, the object of your attention, to impreſs upon the minds of the young ſuch ſentiments as are beſt calculated to produce the peaceable and uſeful citizen, in all

the

the departments in life, which many of us, who were then only rifing to maturity, and are now the heads of families, gratefully acknowledge. We alfo recollect with pleafure, that when you inftructed us in the reafons of a Proteftant diffent from the eftablifhed church, you were careful to guard us againft the rancour of an intolerant fpirit, and to form us to the genuine temper of that divine religion, which injoins peace on earth, and good will towards men. And though you always efteemed it your duty to oppofe what appeared to you the erroneous opinions, and fuperftitious practices, of individuals, or bodies of men, you were fo far from entertaining a hoftile difpofition to their perfons or property, that you were folely actuated by a regard to their beft intereft; for which, however, they might think you miftaken, they ought to have felt themfelves obliged. Rejoicing in the fupport which you derive from the ample refources of your own mind, efpecially thofe which are the refult of a good confcience, and earneftly wifhing you every good,

We remain,

Rev. and dear Sir,

Your affectionate friends.

•••••••••••••••

N° XXV.

From the Proteftant Diffenters in Great Yarmouth.

Yarmouth, July 29, 1791.

Reverend Sir,

W E, minifters and members of the three denominations of Proteftant Diffenters in Great Yarmouth, beg leave to exprefs to you the intereft we take in the late calamitous events which have befallen you. Differing in various matters of opinion, we all agree in warm admiration of your high abilities, your zealous refearches after

chriftian

chriftian truth, and your diftinguifhed exertions in the caufe of civil and religious liberty. Thefe qualities, which have made you the peculiar mark of the vengeance of bigotry, render your fafety and welfare proportionably dear to us.

Whilft we lament your loffes, not only as thofe of an individual, but of the public, we receive a confolation in the magnanimity with which you have borne them, and in the teftimony this event has given to the world of the difference between the temper and conduct of thofe who fupport a good caufe, and and of thofe who oppofe it.

What will be the final refult of fo atrocious an act we prefume not to pronounce; but one good effect from it we think we can forefee, that of drawing clofer the bands of union and amity amongft all the different bodies of Diffenters, who muft henceforth feel that they have a common concern in each others welfare and fecurity.

We requeft you to convey our cordial fentiments of condolence to your fellow fufferers, and remain, with fincere efteem, and every good wifh,

Reverend Sir,

Your Friends and fellow Chriftians.

N° XXVI.

To the Members of the New Meeting Congregation, Birmingham.

My Chriftian Friends,

I T adds not a little to my affliction, occafioned by my violent exclufion from a congregation to which I have fo much reafon to be attached, to be deprived of the fatisfaction I promifed myfelf from my propofed vifit to you, and doing what might be in my power towards your future fettlement. But I am more concerned on account of the reafon you affign for it; as it

argues

argues a continuance of that malignant perfecuting fpirit which has been the caufe of all our fufferings. What muft be the government of a country, nominally chrif-tians, in which fuch outrages againft all law and good order cannot be reftrained, and in which a man cannot be encouraged by his beft friends to come to the difcharge of the duties of a peaceable profeffion, without the appre-henfion of being infulted, if not murdered.

Do not, however, think that any thing ftrange, or new, has happened to us. The enemies of the primitive chriftians frequently fet loofe a licentious populace upon them, when they did not think proper to proceed againft them by law; and for this purpofe they raifed fuch ca-lumnies againft them as made them be confidered as the very pefts of fociety. I truft you are fo well grounded in the principles of your religion, as not to be difcouraged at *this*, or any thing elfe that has befallen us. Though the enemy has burned our places of public worfhip, and lighted the fires, as I have been informed, with our bibles, they cannot deftroy the great truths contained in them, or deprive us of the benefit of our Saviour's decla-ration, " Bleffed are ye when men fhall revile you, and " perfecute you, and fhall fay all manner of evil againft " you falfely for my fake."

Be affured that, from the intereft I take in your wel-fare, I fhall not fail to mention to you any perfon that I may hear of, who fhall appear to me proper to fucceed me. Hoping that you will foon be provided with fuch a perfon, and that in confequence of being built up in our holy faith, we fhall have a happy meeting in a better, world, for which all the difcipline and trials of this life are excellently fitted to form us, I am,

My Friends and fellow Chriftians,

Your's affectionately,

J. PRIESTLEY.

ADDENDA

ADDENDA.

IT may be amusing to some of my readers, to see the following account of the riots at Birmingham, written on the spot, and at the time, by a member of the establishment, in letters to a friend of his near Maidstone in Kent, and published in a *Supplement to the Maidstone Journal*, for Tuesday, July the 19th, last, as it shows with how little feeling, or sense of impropriety, some persons can relate the most atrocious actions, in the full view of all their enormity, when they are well wishers to the *cause* in which they are performed. The mistakes and exaggerations in this account are also amusing. I would likewise observe that Mr. Walter, the printer of the paper called THE TIMES, assures me that his account, false and malignant as it is, was written by " a gentleman " of great respectability, at Birmingham, and of " large commercial concerns." But this kind of *respectability* does not always give liberality of sentiment, just notions of right and wrong, or proper feelings.

LETTER

N^o I.

LETTER I.

Thurſday Evening.

"THE deiſts here, after their utmoſt endeavours, ſat down eighty-two. The mob encreaſing in number and ſilence, they broke up in leſs than two hours—their names will appear in white letters and black paper. Some of them were rudely handled. Prieſtley durſt not appear, the encloſed paper * inflamed much. I cannot think we have any thing to fear; we muſt be blind indeed, provided the kingdom is as flouriſhing as Birmingham, for we are richer, and our trade better than ever."

....

LETTER II.

Sunday Noon.

"TO remove your fears on our account, I ſend you the particulars of our commotions: on Thurſday evening the zealous aſſembled in St. Philip's church-yard, and broke a few windows at the Hotel; Dadley appearing, declared himſelf attached to high church and king. It was ſettled for their leader to examine his houſe, and not a diſaffected perſon being there, they went to the New Meeting, which was ſoon in flames; then to the Old Meeting, but they firſt deſired the charity children to be ſent to their homes;— they were informed the houſes on each ſide belonged to loyaliſts, whoſe property they are as cautious of as poſſible: therefore to preſerve whatever belonged to them, they gutted the Old Meeting, laid the wood in a pile in the Meeting-yard, and burnt it there; then took the bricks down with care, which employed
them

* Alluding to the ſeditious hand-bill.

them all night: a party was fent to fecure Dr. Prieftley, who efcaped very narrowly: his houfe with every thing they could find fell a victim to the flames, they then deftroyed Mr. Ryland's houfe, late Bafkerville's; then Bordefley, then Mr. Hutton's. I went by defire of our neighbour Cooper into Hutton's houfe, to requeft they would not fire it, as many loyal people would fuffer. They knew me, fhook me heartily by the hand, and promifed me *no fire*, which was obferved. I am confidently informed that a woman bringing a candle was knocked down; they then went to Mr. G. Humphrys's, Mr. W. Ruffell's, and Mofely Hall, where they waited for the tenant, Lady Carhampton, removing her effects, they then deftroyed the houfe as they had done thofe of the preceding perfons, They are ftill in the country: their objects are the Meeting-houfe at Withwood-heath with the teacher's, Coates's at the Five-ways, late Wefley's, and Lady Wood; and they declare, that unlefs Prieftley is. delivered to them, no Diffenters fhall efcape. On Friday five hundred gentlemen began cudgelling them, and drove them, but this only made them more outrageous, and we have now no hopes of quieting them but from the military; the fame day, they gave notice by their bellman, that every houfe that had not high *church and King*, written upon it, would be deftroyed.

"No money, or any thing elfe has any influence, nor have they been diverted from any one of their attempts; they feem to move quite fyftematically, and fay, they are only doing what their enemies would have done by them. We are, I confider, quite fafe; the only inconvenience we have felt, has been from a few ftragglers, who have taken the advantage of the times, in extorting money, but the *loyal* mob, yefterday, as foon as they were informed of it, fent a party, who beat them feverely, and they are at prefent difperfed.

"P. S. I am informed they are now at Edgbafton, in confequence of their finding a letter of Dr. W. at

N   Ruffell's

Ruffeli's; they now fay they regard no perfuafion, every enemy to high church fhall fall."

·················

Mr. Ryland's houfe, which has been burnt down, was fet fire to on account of his fon's having affifted in the efcape of Dr. Prieftley, whom the mob have purfued in different directions. Should the Doctor not be able to elude their vigilance, it is much to be apprehended that they will murder him, as he is confidered the mif-chievous author of all the treafonable hand-bills that have been circulated about the town, and which firft pro-duced the riot.

The Methodifts and followers of the Countefs of Huntingdon have been all protected. In the beginning of the riots the mob went to fome of their houfes, and queftioned them concerning the doctrines which they profeffed, and on their declaring for *church and King*, they were affured that they fhould remain unmolefted. The church people walk about as ufual, without the fmalleft apprehenfion of danger.

The Hotel belonging to *Dadley*, where the Revolu-tionifts dined, has been only damaged by the windows being broken, the mob refufing to pull it down, becaufe he was a churchman.

Mr. Humphrys, whofe houfe at the turnpike was pulled down, offered the mob 4000 and afterwards 8000 guineas if they would defift; but they declared that money was not their object, and that they pulled down his houfe becaufe they confidered him as a principal perfon con-cerned in the inflammatory hand-bills; perhaps too for his ridiculing the national church by building a cow-lodge in the form of a chapel.

A letter dated Sunday night at eleven o'clock, fays, " Unlefs fome foldiers arrive early to-morrow morning,

we

we are in very great apprehenfion that every Diffenter's houfe in Birmingham will be deftroyed, and with them, no doubt, many other houfes which were never intended. Near one hundred houfes have been fet on fire and pulled down, and about fixty more are marked for the purpofe of being burnt or deftroyed. At nine o'clock laft night it was computed that the damage already done amounted to 250,000l. Thofe which we have mentioned belong to principal people."

N° II.

An Addrefs to Dr. Prieftley, agreed upon at a Meeting of the Philofophical Society at Derby, Sept. 3, 1791.

SIR,

WE condole with yourfelf, and with the fcientific world, on the lofs of your valuable library, your experimental apparatus, and your more valuable manufcripts: at the fame time we beg leave to congratulate you on your perfonal fafety, in having efcaped the facrilegious hands of the favages at Birmingham.

Almoft all great minds in all ages of the world, who have endeavoured to benefit mankind, have been perfecuted by them; GALILEO, for his philofophical difcoveries, was imprifoned by the Inquifition; and SOCRATES found a cup of hemlock his reward for teaching " there is one " God." Your enemies, unable to conquer your arguments by reafon, have had recourfe to violence; they have halloo'd upon you the dogs of unfeeling ignorance, and of frantic fanaticifm; they have kindled fires like thofe of the Inquifition, not to illuminate the truth, but, like the dark lantern of the affaffin, to light the murderer to his prey. Your philofophical friends, therefore, hope that you will not again rifk your perfon among a people, whofe bigotry renders

renders them incapable of inftruction: they hope you will leave the unfruitful fields of polemical theology, and cultivate that philofophy, of which you may be called the father, and which, by inducing the world to think and reafon, will filently marfhal mankind againft delufion, and with greater certainty overturn the empire of fuperftition.

In fpite of the perfecution you have fuftained, we truft that you will perfevere in the exertions of Virtue, and the improvements of fcience. Your fame, already confpicuous to every civilized nation of the world, fhall rife like a phœnix from the flames of your elaboratory with renovated vigour, and fhine with brighter corufcation.

R. ROE, Secretary.

N° III.

THE ANSWER.

London, Sep, 19, 1791.

Gentlemen,

I FEEL myfelf greatly encouraged in my prefent fufferings from the effects of bigotry, by the fympathy expreffed by you, and by other liberal friends of fcience here and abroad.

It will be a new thing in the world if any thing truly valuable lofe credit, or have a lefs rapid fpread, in confequence of perfecution. If any thing will bear to be viewed, and examined, it muft derive advantage from whatever draws attention to it; and fuch, I am confident, is the caufe in which I fuffer.

In confequence of this, far from being difcouraged, I feel myfelf more animated than ever; and I am at this very time fetting about the re-eftablifhment of my philofophical apparatus, and refuming all my former purfuits.

Excufe me, however, if I ftill join theological to philofophical ftudies, and if I confider the former as greatly
fuperior

fuperior in importance to mankind to the latter.   But as
thefe different purfuits have never yet interfered with, but
have promoted, each other, be perfuaded that this will
continue to be the cafe.

I am, Gentlemen,

Your very humble fervant,

J. PRIESTLEY.

———

The perfon high in office, after declaiming againft
me in the manner mentioned p. 58, added, " As
" to Paine, he is no *Diffenter*, and therefore we
" cannot take *him* up." On this I leave my reader
to make his own remarks, and fome of a fufficiently
ferious nature cannot fail to occur to him.

A

CATALOGUE of BOOKS,

WRITTEN BY
Dr. PRIESTLEY,
AND PRINTED FOR

J. Johnson, Bookseller, St. Paul's Church-Yard,
LONDON.

1. THE History and present State of *Electricity*, with original Experiments, illustrated with Copper-plates, 4th Edition. corrected and enlarged, 4to. 1l. 1s.

N. B. *A New Edition of this is in the Press and will soon be published together with a* Continuation of it, and original Experiments by Mr. Nicholson, *in 2 vols.* 4to, *in Boards, 2l. 2s.*—The Continuation will be sold alone, 1l. 1s. in Boards.

2. A Familiar *Introduction* to the *Study* of *Electricity,* 5th Edition, 8vo. 2s. 6d. sewed.

3. The History and Present State of Discoveries relating to *Vision, Light,* and *Colours,* 2 vols. 4to. illustrated with a great Number of Copper-plates, 1l. 11s. 6d. in boards, 1l. 18s. bound.

4. *Experiments* and *Observations* on different Kinds of Air and other Branches of *Natural Philosophy,* connected with the Subject, 3 vols. 1l. 1s. in boards, being the former Six Volumes abridged and methodised, with many Additions.

5. A Familiar Introduction to the Theory and Practice of *Perspective,* with Copper-plates, 2d Edition, 5s. in boards, 6s. bound.

6. A New *Chart* of *History,* containing a View of the principal Revolutions of Empire that have taken Place in the World; with a Book describing it, containing an Epitome of Universal History, 4th Edition, 10s. 6d.

7. A *Chart* of *Biography,* with a Book containing an explanation of it, and a catalogue of all the Names inserted in it, 6th Edition, very much improved, 10s. 6d.

N. B. *These Charts mounted on Canvas and Rollers, to be hung up in a Study, &c. are* 14s *each.*

8. The *Rudiments* of *English Grammar,* adapted to the use of Schools, a new Edition, 1s. 6d. bound.

9. The same *Grammar,* with Notes and Observations, for the Use of those who have made some Proficiency in the language, 4th Edit.

10. *Lectures* on *History* and *General Policy*; to which is prefixed, an Essay on a Course of Liberal Education, for Civil and Active Life, 4to. 1l. 1s. in boards.

11 *Observations*

Books written by Dr. Priestley.

11. *Observations* relating to *Education*: more especially as it respects the Mind; to which is added, an Essay on a Course of Liberal Education for Civil and Active Life, 2d Edition, 3s. 6d. in boards.

12. A *Course* of *Lectures* on *Oratory* and *Criticism*, 4to. 10s. 6d. in boards, 14s. bound.

13. An Essay on the first Principles of Government, and on the Nature of Political, Civil, and Religious *Liberty*, 2d Edition, much enlarged, 4s. in boards, 5s. bound. *In this Edition are introduced the* Remarks on Church Authority, in answer to Dr. Balguy, *formerly published separately.*

14. Letters to the Right Hon. Mr. Burke on his Reflections on the Revolution in France, 8vo. 3d Edition, 2s. 6d. sewed.

15. A *Letter* to the Right Hon. *William Pitt*, First Lord of the Treasury, and Chancellor of the Exchequer: on the Subject of *Toleration* and *Church Establishments*; occasioned by his *Speech* against the Repeal of the *Test and Corporation Acts*, on Wednesday the 21st of March, 1787, 2d Edition, 1s.

16. *Familiar Letters*, addressed to the Inhabitants of the Town of Birmingham, in Refutation of several Charges advanced against the Dissenters, and Unitarians, by the Rev. Mr. Madan.—Also Letters to the Rev. Edward Burn, in Answer to his on the Infallibility of the Apostolic Testimony concerning the Person of Christ. And Considerations on the Differences of Opinion among Christians, in Answer to the Rev. Mr. Venn, 2d Edition, 5s. sewed.

17. An Examination of Dr. *Reid's* Inquiry into the Human Mind, on the Principles of Common Sense, Dr. *Beattie's* Essay on the Nature and Immutability of Truth, and Dr. *Oswald's* Appeal to Common Sense, in Behalf of Religion, 2d Edition, 5s. in boards, 6s. bound.

18. *Hartley's Theory* of the *Human Mind*, on the Principle of the Association of Ideas, with Essays relating to the Subject of it, 8vo. 6s. in boards, 7s. bound.

19. *Disquisitions* relating to *Matter* and *Spirit*. To which is added, the History of the Philosophical Doctrine concerning the Origin of the Soul, and the Nature of Matter; with its Influence on Christianity, especially with respect to the Doctrine of the Pre-existence of Christ. Also the Doctrine of Philosophical Necessity illustrated, 2d Edition enlarged and improved: with Remarks on those who have controverted the Principles of them, 2 vols. 8s. in boards, 10s. bound.

20. A *Free Discussion* of the *Doctrines* of *Materialism* and *Philosophical Necessity*, in a Correspondence between Dr. *Price* and Dr. *Priestley*; to which are added, by Dr. *Priestley*, an *Introduction*, explaining the Nature of the Controversy, and Letters to several Writers who have animadverted on his Disquisitions relating to Matter and Spirit, or his Treatise on Necessity, 8vo. 6s. sewed, 7s. bound.

21. A Defence of the Doctrine of *Necessity*, in two Letters to the Rev. Mr. John Palmer, 2s.

22. A Letter to *Jacob Bryant*, Esq. in Defence of Philosophical Necessity, 1s.

23. A *Philosophical*

23. A *Philosophical Enquiry* concerning *Human Liberty*, by W. Collins, Esq. with a Preface by Dr. Priestley, 2s. 6d.

The three preceding Articles may be properly bound up with the second volume of Disquisitions on Matter and Spirit.

24. *Letters* to a *Philosophical Unbeliever*, containing an Examination of the principal Objections to the Doctrines of *Natural Religion*, and especially those contained in the writings of Mr. Hume. Also a State of the Evidence of *Revealed Religion* with Animadversions on the two last Chapters of the first Volume of *Mr. Gibbon's History of the Decline and Fall of the Roman Empire*; and an Answer to the Letters of Mr. *William Hammon*, 2 vols. 8vo. 7s. sewed, or bound in one volume, 8s.

25. A *Harmony* of the *Evangelists* in Greek. To which are prefixed, *Critical Differtations* in English, 4to. 14s. in boards, 17s. bound.

26. A *Harmony* of the *Evangelists* in *English*, with Notes, and an occasional Paraphrase for the Use of the Unlearned. To which are prefixed, Critical Differtations, and a Letter to the Bishop of Offory, 4to. 12s. in boards, 15s. bound.

N. B. *Those who are possessed of the* Greek Harmony, *may have this in* English *without the* Critical Differtations, 8s. in boards.

The Greek and English Harmony with the Critical Differtations, *complete*, 1l. 1s. in boards, or 1l. 4s. bound.

27. *Institutes* of *Natural* and *Revealed Religion*, in 2 vols. 8vo. 2d edit. 10s. 6d. in boards, 12s. bound.

The third Part of this Work, containing the Doctrines of Revelation, *may be had alone*, 2s. 6d. *sewed*.

28. An *History* of the *Corruptions* of *Christianity*, with a general Conclusion, in two Parts. Part I. containing Considerations addressed to Unbelievers, and especially to Mr. *Gibbon*. Part II. containing Considerations addressed to the Advocates for the present Establishment, and especially to Bishop *Hurd*, 2 vols. 8vo. 12s. in boards, or 14s. bound. Or, *bound uniformly with the three following* Defences *of it, in* 3 *vols.* 1l. 4s.

29. A *Reply* to the *Animadversions* on the *History* of the *Corruptions* of *Christianity*, in the Monthly Review for June, 1783; with Observations relating to the Doctrine of the Primitive Church, concerning the Person of *Christ*, 8vo. 1s.

30. *Remarks* on the *Monthly Review* of the *Letters* to Dr. *Horsley*; in which the Rev. Mr. *Samuel Badcock*, the writer of that Review, is called upon to defend what he has advanced in it, 6d.

31. *Letters* to Dr. *Horsley*, Archdeacon of St. Alban's, in three Parts, containing farther Evidence that the Primitive Christian Church was Unitarian, 7s. 6d. sewed.

N. B. *These last three Articles together in boards*, 9s. *or* 10s. *bound.*

32. An *History* of *Early Opinions* concerning *Jesus Christ*, compiled from Original Writers; proving that the Christian Church was at first Unitarian, 4 vols. 8vo. 1l. 4s. in boards, or 1l. 8s. bound.

33. A *General History* of the *Christian Church*, to the Fall of the Western Empire, in 2 vols. 8vo. 14s. in boards, 16s. bound.

34. *Defences* of *Unitarianism* for the Year 1786; containing Letters to Dr. Horne, Dean of Canterbury; to the Young Men, who are in

a Course

a Courfe of Education for the Chriftian Miniftry, at the Univerfities of Oxford and Cambridge; to Dr. Price; and to Mr. Parkhurft; on the Subject of the Perfon of Chrift, 2d Edit. 3s.

35. *Defences* of *Unitarianifm* for the Year 1787; containing Letters to the Rev. Dr. Geddes, to the Rev. Dr. Price, Part II. and to the Candidates for Orders in the Two Univerfities, Part II. Relating to Mr. Howe's Appendix to his fourth Volume of Obfervations on Books, a Letter by an Under-Graduate of Oxford, Dr. Croft's Bampton Lectures, and feveral other Publications, 2s. 6d.

36. *Defences of Unitarianifm* for the Years 1788 and 1789; containing Letters to the Bifhop of St. David's, to the Rev. Mr. Barnard, the Rev. Dr. Knowles, and the Rev. Mr. Hawkins, 3s. 6d.

N. B. *Thefe laft three* Articles *together, 9s. in boards.*

37. A *View* of the *Principles* and *Conduct* of the *Proteftant Diffenters*, with Refpect to the Civil and Ecclefiaftical Conftitution of England, 2d Edit. 1s. 6d.

38. A *Free Addrefs* to *Proteftant Diffenters*, on the Subject of the Lord's Supper, 3d Edit. with Additions, 2s.

39 An *addrefs* to *Proteftant Diffenters*, on the fubject of giving the Lord's Supper to Children, 1s.

40. A *Free Addrefs* to *Proteftant Diffenters*, on the Subject of *Church Difcipline* ; with a preliminary Difcourfe concerning the Spirit of Chriftianity, and the Corruptions of it by falfe Notions of Religion, 2s. 6d. fewed.

41. *Letters* to the Authors of *Remarks on feveral late Publications relative to the Diffenters, in a Letter to Dr. Prieftley*, 1s.

42. A *Letter* to a *Layman*, on the Subject of Mr. Lindfey's Propofal for a reformed Englifh Church, on the Plan of the late Dr. Samuel Clarke, 6d.

43. *Three Letters* to Dr. Newcome, Bifhop of Waterford, on the Duration of our Saviour's Miniftry, 3s. 6d. fewed.

44. *Letters* to the *Members* of the *New Jerufalem Church*, formed by Baron Swedenborg, 1s. 6d.

45. *An Appeal to the Public*, on the Subject of the late Riots in Birmingham. To which are added, *Strictures on a Pamphlet*, intitled, ' Thoughts on the late Riots at Birmingham, 3s. *fewed.*

N. B. *The preceding* nine Tracts, No. 37 to 45, *inclufive, may be had in 2 vols. boards 16s. 6d. or with No.* 14, 15, 21, 22, *and* 23, *in 3 vols. 1l. 3s. in boards, by giving orders for* Dr. Prieftley's larger Tracts.

46. An *Hiftory* of the *Sufferings* of *Lewis de Marolles*, and Mr. *Ifaac le Fevre*, upon the revocation of the Edict of Nantz, with a Preface by Dr. Prieftley, 8vo. 3s. fewed.

47. *Forms of Prayer*, and other Offices, for the Ufe of Unitarian Societies, 8vo. 3s. fewed.

48. *Difcourfes* on *Various Subject*, viz. On refigning the Paftoral Office at Leeds—On undertaking the Paftoral Office at Birmingham— The proper Conftitution of a Chriftian Church, with a Preface on the prefent State of thofe who are called rational Diffenters—The Importance and Extent of Free Enquiry—The Doctrine of Divine Influence on the Human Mind—Habitual Devotion—The Duty of not living to ourfelves:—The Danger of bad Habits—The Duty of

not

not being aſhamed of the Goſpel—Glorying in the Croſs of Chriſt—
Taking the Croſs and following Chriſt—The Evidence of Chriſtianity
from the Perſecution of Chriſtians, 8vo. 6s. in boards.

49. A *Sermon* on the *Slave Trade*, preached at Birmingham,
1788, 1s.

50. *Reflections on Death.* A Sermon on the Death of the Rev.
Robert Robinſon of Cambridge, 1s.

51. A *View of Revealed Religion.* A Sermon on the Admiſſion
of the Rev. W. Field, of Warwick, with a Charge by the Rev. Tho.
Belſham, 1s. 6d.

52. The proper *Objects* of *Education* in the preſent State of the
World, repreſented in a Diſcourſe delivered April 21, 1791, to the
Supporters of the New College at Hackney, with a Prayer by the
Rev. Mr. Belſham, ſecond Edition, 1s.

53. A *Diſcourſe* on occaſion of the death of Dr. *Price*, delivered
at Hackney, May 1, with a ſhort ſketch of his life and character,
and a liſt of his writings, 1s.

54. A *Diſcourſe* on the Evidence of the Reſurrection of Jeſus, 1s. 6d.

55. A *Catechiſm* for *Children and Young Perſons*, 5th Edit. 4d.

56. A *Scripture Catechiſm*, conſiſting of a Series of Queſtions,
with References to the Scriptures, inſtead of Anſwers, 2d Edit. 4d.

57. Dr. Watts's Hiſtorical Catechiſm, with Alterations, 2d Edit. 9d.

58. *Conſiderations* for the Uſe of Young Men, and the Parents of
Young Men, 2d Edit. 2d.

59. A *Serious Addreſs* to Maſters of Families, with Forms of
Family Prayer, 2d Edit. 9d.

60. An *Appeal* to the ſerious and condid Profeſſors of Chriſtianity,
on the following ſubjects, viz. 1. The Uſe of Reaſon in Matters of
Religion. 2. The Power of Man to do the Will of God. 3. Original
Sin. 4. Election and Reprobation. 5. The Divinity of Chriſt ; and
6. Atonement for Sin by the Death of Chriſt, a new Edition; to
which is added, A Conciſe Hiſtory of thoſe Doctrines ; and An
Account of the Trial of Mr. Elwall, for Hereſy and Blaſphemy, at
Stafford Aſſizes, 3d.

61. A Familiar Illuſtration of certain paſſages of Scripture, relating
to the ſame Subjects, 2d Edit. 6d.

62. A *General View* of the Arguments for the *Unity* of *God*, and
againſt the Divinity and Pre-exiſtence of Chriſt, from Reaſon, from
the Scriptures, and from Hiſtory, 2d Edit. 2d.

63. A *Free Addreſs* to Proteſtant Diſſenters as ſuch. By a Diſſenter.
A new Edition, enlarged and corrected, 1s. 6d.

64. A *Free Addreſs* to thoſe who have petitioned for the Repeal of
the late Act of Parliament in favour of the *Roman Catholics*, 2d. or
12s. per Hundred to give away.

N. B. The laſt Ten Tracts, No. 55 to 64, *may be had together, in
boards*, 5s, *by giving Orders for* Dr. Prieſtley's ſmaller Tracts.

Alſo publiſhed under the Direction of Dr. Prieſtley.

THE THEOLOGICAL REPOSITORY,

Conſiſting of Original Eſſays, Hints, Queries, &c. calculated to promote Religious Knowledge, in Six Volumes, 8vo. 1l. 19s. in boards,
or 2l. 5s. bound.

AN

APPEAL

TO

THE PUBLIC,

ON THE SUBJECT OF

The Riots in Birmingham,

PART II.

TO WHICH IS ADDED,

A LETTER FROM W. RUSSELL, ESQ. TO THE AUTHOR.

By JOSEPH PRIESTLEY, *LL.D. F.R.S, &c.*

———

'SED QUÆ CAUSA GRAVIS, QUÆ TRISTIS ORIGO RUINÆ,
FORSITAN IGNORAS. EGO NUNC VERISSIMA PAUCIS
EXPEDIAM.

PETRARCHÆ AFRICA.

———

LONDON:

PRINTED FOR J. JOHNSON, ST. PAUL'S CHURCH YARD.

———

1792.

THE PREFACE.

THE facts advanced in the former part of my *Appeal to the Public relating to the Riots in Birmingham* having appeared to myfelf, and my friends, incontrovertibly true, I did not, at the time that I wrote it, expect that I fhould have any occafion to trouble the world with another publication on a fubject which to myfelf muft be fufficiently difagreeable. But as not only have thofe facts been denied, but much additional cenfure been reflected upon me, and the Diffenters, by the clergy of Birmingham, who have employed the pen of Mr. Burn, I find myfelf under the neceffity of engaging in a controverfy, the termination of which I do not fee. For I think myfelf bound in honour, and in duty to my fellow-fufferers, not to withhold whatever fhall appear to me to be proper for our common vindication.

Let

Let our enemies, then, difpute our facts, and advance their farther calumnies. I fhall not fail to reply to them, till the Public fhall be in poffeffion of all that is neceffary to form their judgment on a fubject that certainly interefts the whole community. For, if any one fet of men may be infulted and oppreffed with impunity on account of their religious perfuafion, if neither the common courts of law, nor the cool opinion of their countrymen, will do them juftice, another fet may, in their turn, be expofed to the fame, and an all-grafping and domineering hierarchy may crufh us all. It behoves us, then, ferioufly to confider our fituation, and let our enemies confider theirs. And the cafe of perfecution for religious principle is no new thing in the world; we have but too many precedents before us to determine our judgment, and direct our conduct.

It will be obferved, and, I doubt not, to our prejudice, that but few *names* appear in this narrative of facts. But, confidering the great prevalence of a violent party fpirit among the more wealthy and powerful in the town and neighbourhood of Birmingham, and

and how much it will appear that fome perfons have already fuffered in confequence of
giving evidence in favour of Diffenters, and
being otherwife friendly to them, it would
be unjuftifiable in me to expofe them to farther injury without very particular reafon.
Every name, however, that is alluded to in
this work is ready to be produced if neceffary. If, in any very particular cafe, I fhould
decline giving my authority, I can only
pledge my own veracity for *having* a fufficient
authority, which my reader will believe or
not, according to his idea of my moral character. Except a very few, all the facts I have
mentioned, are contained in *affidavits* voluntarily tendered; and many more, I doubt not,
will appear when it fhall feem to be fafe to
the parties. However, thofe affidavits which
tend moft to criminate particular perfons
have already been recited by Mr. Whitbread,
and others, when an inquiry was moved for
in the Houfe of Commons into the caufes of
the riot. Knowing, therefore, what is laid
to their charge, it behoves them to take the
proper method of removing the imputations
under which they lie. A good account of
the debate on this fubject may now be feen

in

in the *Parliamentary Regifter*, publifhed by Mr. Debrett. From perufing *this* our country-men will form their own judgment, whether there was fufficient caufe for public inquiry, and whether the members of the Houfe of Commons acted as the reprefentatives of the Diffenters as well as of the other inhabitants of the country, and whether they were dif-pofed to inquire into, and redrefs, wrongs done to *them*.

The plan, and proper origin, of the riot has not yet been difcovered; and many perfons begin to fufpect, as Dr. Parr, in his truly libe-ral publication, has hinted, that it had a higher origin than Warwickfhire. There were pre-dictions in London of what would be done at Birmingham. But, if any perfon in power fhould wifh to opprefs us, we afcribe it to the inceffant accufations of our enemies, efpecially among the clergy; and time will fhew that thofe accufations are mere calumnies, affer-tions deftitute of all foundation in fact.

No blunder is abfolutely impoffible in fome politicians; but I can hardly think that, at this day, any ftatefman could hope to
avail

avail himfelf of the prejudices of the majority of a nation to intimidate and crufh the
minority, when his ultimate views were really
hoftile to the liberties of all, fuch policy is fo
eafily feen through ; and it would be nothing
lefs than infanity to endeavour to intimidate
by *a mob*, the exceffes of which it may be
impoffible to reftrain, and which, once encouraged and excited, may foon take a different, and even oppofite, direction. In no
country in Europe is a mob fo much to be
dreaded as in this, for in no country in Europe are the populace fo ignorant, fo unprincipled, fo prophane, fo improvident, fo licentious, and fo much difpofed to every fpecies of
violence fhort of murder. If our government
be fo excellent as it is boafted to be, how
came this great and formidable evil to exift ?

In general this extreme ignorance and profligacy are to be found in manufacturing
towns, where the poor are taught nothing,
befides their particular art or trade, and
where they have no leifure, or means, of ac-
quiring general knowledge ; where they
work part of their time, and fpend the reft in
the alehoufe, wholly improvident with re-

fpect

spect to futurity, in this life or another. This necessarily forms the most degraded state of human nature. But for this great evil the government, in church or state, should provide some remedy.

Much pains has particularly been taken to represent the Unitarian Dissenters, among whom I class myself, as disaffected to government, in order to make our sufferings the subject of less regret, as if the chastisement we have met with, though not legally inflicted, was nothing more than we deserved; when in reality our tenets have no relation whatever to any thing of a political nature, nor have we interfered in politics more than other persons.

Among other calumniators, Mr. Burke particularly distinguished himself by his invectives against us in the House of Commons; but he only discovered his utter ignorance of our principles and conduct. As some evidence that the Unitarian Dissenters are the enemies of the constitution, he alleged the toasts that were given at the first annual meeeting of the Unitarian society, none of which,

which, however, were at all difloyal, or breathed a fpirit unbecoming Englifhmen,

Mr. Burke was ignorant that the *Unitarian Society* by no means reprefents the Unitarians of England, being nothing more than the affociation of a very few of them for the purpofe of diftributing books, and certainly are not one in a thoufand of the Unitarians in England. That fociety has no political object whatever, and the toafts were quite an accidental thing, owing to the company of fome ftrangers, who chiefly fuggefted them at the time, none of them being provided beforehand; and it was not the intention of the fociety to continue the cuftom,

Unitarianifm bears no relation to any fyftem of politics, and in fact there are Unitarians among the friends, as well as the enemies, of what is called *government*. There are great numbers of them in the church of England, as well as out of it; and there are many profeffed Unitarians who object to the forming of any fociety, fo far are they from wifhing to make themfelves confpicuous, or from being of a factious and turbulent difpofition,

Unfavourable

Unfavourable as the prefent times are to Unitarians and Diffenters, they may change in our favour, and even in a fhort fpace. Events are powerful and fpeedy inftructors, and produce important changes in the fentiments of whole nations, as we have lately feen both in America and in France. This is an age of revolutions, and fhould teach the High Church party in this country not infolence, but moderation.

At all events men fhould do juftice, whatever their own future fituation may be; and it is only juftice that the Diffenters of Birmingham afk of their countrymen. But they have not yet found it, except with refpect to the demolition of the new meeting houfe; though all damages done by rioters fhould be moft amply repaired by the fociety, which is conftituted for the very purpofe of preventing, or redreffing, the wrongs of individuals. It is notorious that the courts of law have by no means given us complete indemnification. We truft, however, there is ftill fo much juftice in the nation, that our reprefentatives will, on cooler reflection, do for us what was done for the fufferers by the riots in 1780,

and

and punifh thofe who may be proved to have been chargeable with a negle&t of duty.

It will be proper in this Preface to give fome account of *Mr. Ruffell's Letter* to me, which is fubjoined to this part of my Appeal, and of thofe articles in the *Appendix* which are not mentioned in the courfe of it.

Mr. Ruffell thought himfelf at one time particularly called upon to vindicate himfelf and his brethren from the accufation of the High Church party in the reply of Mr. Burn, efpecially as he knew that I wifhed to decline writing any more on the fubje&t. But finding that this was impofible, I defired him to throw fome part of what he had written, (containing fuch particulars as he was beft able to fpeak to) into the form of *a Letter to me*, to be fubjoined to my work. And I think myfelf happy in this, and in every opportunity of appearing in company with a man to whom I owe fo much, in whofe fociety I have had fo much true enjoyment, from the mutual communication of fimilar fentiments; and whofe feparation from me I confider as one of the moft unpleafant con-

fequences

fequences of the riot. But we are all at the
difpofal of one who knows where to place us
better than we do ourfelves.

Having, in my former Appendix, given
feveral *Addreffes* to me, thofe who were
pleafed with *them* will not be difpleafed to
fee added to them that from the *Diffenters
and Delegates of the Diffenters in England to
the fufferers in the Birmingham riots*, with the
Anfwer. In the Gentleman's Magazine there
were feveral fneers at me on account of there
being no Addrefs to me from any Diffenters
in London; and it was infinuated that no
fuch thing having taken place, the Diffenters
in general were far from approving my conduct, or condoling with me on the occafion.
This Addrefs, being a full anfwer to thofe
infinuations, was fent by a friend of mine to
the printer of the Magazine, but it was neither inferted, nor any notice taken of its being fent. I hope Mr. Nichols will not in
future pretend to *impartiality* in his conduct
of that work. I could not have a ftronger
teftimony to the propriety of my general conduct as a Diffenter than this Addrefs, and the
anfwer; and it is a particular fatisfaction to
me,

me, that all the denominations of Diſſenters concurred in it.

I ought alſo to obſerve (and the remem-brance of it will give me pleaſure as long as I live) that the firſt congregation to which I preached after the riot was one of Cal-viniſtic Baptiſts at Amerſham, and at the unanimous requeſt of the miniſter and people. The Sunday following I had invitations to preach to two other Calviniſtic congregations. One good effect of the riot has been to pro-mote this liberal ſpirit, ſo becoming all deno-minations of Chriſtians. Though we differ in many things, and lay ſuitable ſtreſs on thoſe points of difference, we are ſenſible that the articles about which we are all agreed are of infinitely more moment ; and on theſe I can with pleaſure enlarge, without hurting the feelings of any Chriſtian whatever.

No. XIV. will ſhew how far Mr. Burn's aſſertion concerning the cauſe of Mr. Curtis's declining to attend a funeral in company with Mr. Scholefield *only* leſt he ſhould afterwards do the ſame with *me*, is from the truth. Now that I have left them the ſame low bigotry continues,

continues, and is openly avowed by them. And No. XIII. will fhow the extreme malignity of fome of the High Church party fince the riot.

The account from Stourbridge, No. XIX. fhows that the fame illiberal fpirit of the High Church party extended to the neighbourhood of Birmingham, and exifted there long before my coming among them, and alfo its continuance and increafe fince that time. The fpirited and excellent publications of Mr. Field fhew that the fame defpicable fpirit prevails at Warwick; and I doubt not every other town in that neighbourhood could furnifh a fimilar hiftory; fo effectually have the clergy infufed their own fpirit into the members of their church; and nothing furely can be more difgraceful in this enlightened age. The bigotry of the Roman Catholic clergy was never greater, or more intolerant, than that of the clergy of the church of England in that part of this proteftant country, and all bigotry is founded in ignorance. Their narrow education, and other circumftances, eafily account for the whole.

The letter relating to the deftruction of

4   my

my library, was written by a perſon who I had heard was on the ſpot, and I imagined had been preſent at the beginning of it, having, though a member of the church of England, gone thither to ſave what he could of my property, and eſpecially my books and manuſcripts. This letter furniſhes the moſt unexceptionable evidence of the ſavage and brutal fury with which thoſe worſe than Goths and Vandals were inſtigated to deſtroy every thing belonging to me.

Mr. Carpenter's letter will exhibit a ſpecimen of the ſufferings of thoſe whoſe names do not appear in any liſt of ſufferers. I wiſh that more ſuch accounts may be collected before the particulars be forgotten. As yet this country has but an imperfect idea of the magnitude and extent of this miſchief. In due time I hope that all the world will have an opportunity of ſeeing it; and let our enemies indulge themſelves in the contemplation of it if they feel themſelves ſo diſpoſed. I hope it will be the laſt gratification that they will have of the kind. Indeed, their wrath is as great, as if *they knew that their time was ſhort,*

Rev.

Rev. xii. 12. This violence will only precipitate their ruin.

Their beft policy would be moderation, and
a hearty concurrence in the repeal of the impolitic Corporation and Teft Acts, which I
hope no Diffenter will ever trouble the country with petitioning for any more. I never
propofed any application to the legiflature for
that purpofe, and I truft all the Diffenters
will now feel as Paul did when he had been
unjuftly imprifoned. Let the country do
away its own difgrace, and provide for its
own greater fecurity, by doing us juftice.

Pofterity will judge between us and the High
Church clergy of this kingdom, not only who
have been the beft friends of the liberties and
true interefts of the country, but even of the
reigning family. It was the fulfome flattery,
and abject principles of the clergy that chiefly
contributed to precipitate the Stuarts to their
ruin, and they are acting the fame part at
prefent. They taught Charles II. to behave
with the moft indecent ingratitude and trea-
chery to the Prefbyterians, who were the

true

true authors of his reſtoration, and they are
dictating the ſame ingratitude to the preſent
reigning family, to which the Diſſenters have
ever been moſt zealouſly attached, while the
clergy were almoſt univerſally diſaffected.

Theſe are facts that lie on the very ſurface
of the Engliſh Hiſtory, and yet the clergy
have the aſſurance to charge *us* with diſaffection. If there be any diſpoſition towards
it, it is what their violence and injuſtice have
driven us to. There are others, we truſt,
who can better diſtinguiſh the *ſigns of the
times* than they, and who will not again
ſacrifice the intereſts of the nation, and the
conſtitution itſelf, to their bigotry, avarice,
and ambition.

Many of the facts introduced into this part
of my *Appeal* will be found to be the ſame
with thoſe that are mentioned, and ſpiritedly
remarked upon, by Mr. Edwards, in his *Letters to the Britiſh nation,* as well as alleged by
Mr. Whitbread and others in the Houſe of
Commons. In reality we had no other than
the ſame authorities. I ſhould not, however,
have thought it neceſſary to have made ſo

b   many

many of the fame obfervations with Mr. Edwards, if this part of my Appeal had not been
printed before I faw his laft Number. I earneftly recommend this laft Number of his
Letters, as containing feveral more particulars
than had come to my knowledge.

I cannot omit this opportunity of congratulating my late congregation on the acquifition of two fuch valuable minifters as Mr.
Edwards and Mr. Jones, whofe firft and
truly excellent difcourfe to them is now before the public. They have, in a great meafure, verified my prediction, in my *Letter to
the Inhabitants of Birmingham*; and the increafing numbers and fpirit of the Unitarian
Diffenters in that town muft have already convinced the bigoted High Church party there,
that they have been far from gaining any thing
by the riot, or by my expulfion from the
place. Such has ever been, and fuch, from
the nature of things, muft always be, the effect of intolerance and perfecution. But bigotry
will neither read nor reflect, fo that to this
dæmon, equally furious and blind, the inftructive page of hiftory is unfolded in vain.

Mr.

Mr. Burn charges the Unitarians, p. 102, with " inviting the aid of perfecution." If we have given the invitation, the High Church party at Birmingham have been as ready to give as we to afk, and have thereby given us the affiftance that we found we wanted. And though Mr. Burn fays, as a proof that I have not been *perfecuted*, that " I have not fuffered as a Chriftian;" my cafe is fo far common with thofe who are ufually termed *Proteftant Martyrs* in the reign of queen Mary, in this country, and of Philip II. and Louis XIV. abroad: for none of them fuffered as Chriftians. We have this, however, in common with the proper Chriftian martyrs, that we equally fuffer *for confcience fake*. " Much lefs," adds Mr. Burn, " has it been made to appear that the " *clergy* were acceffory to his misfortune." When I wrote the former part of this Appeal, I did not confider them as acceffory to it, but now, in a certain fenfe, I do fo; and they are called upon either to vindicate themfelves, or to bear the imputation; and they will, no doubt, do that which they will find the eafieft to them. If it be true, as they now pretend, that *they* lament the riot in

Birmingham

Birmingham (which the total failure of their object may now perhaps lead them to do) numbers of their brethren in many parts of England do not. I could enlarge greatly in my evidence of this, if it were prudent fo to do. No other event in modern times has fhown fo decifively what fpirit the High Church clergy of this country are really of. It is the fpirit of church eftablifhments univerfally, and truly *Anti-Chriftian.*

I deferred the printing, and after that the publication, of this work, which was compofed in Auguft, with a view to give my readers an account of the complete termination of every thing relating to the riot in Birmingham; hoping that the very inadequate compenfation that was awarded us would have been paid at leaft before this time. But finding this to be ftill delayed, and that there is no near profpect of the bufinefs being difpatched, though the term fixed by the law for this purpofe is expired, (it being now nearly a year and a half fince the difafter, and eight months fince the caufe was heard) and many of my friends and my enemies too call for the work, I have confented to withhold it no longer.

I fhall

I ſhall cloſe this preface with repeating what I have obſerved more than once in the courſe of the work, viz. that depending, as I neceſſarily muſt, on the information of others, with reſpect to the *facts* introduced, or alluded to, in it, it is very poſſible that I may have been miſled. But I wiſh to give our adverſaries an opportunity of exculpating themſelves, if they can, from the charges brought againſt them; and certainly they are under obligation to me on this account; it being always an advantage to know what our adverſaries ſay, and believe, concerning us, as we may then either defend ourſelves, or neglect the accuſation, as we think proper.

Clapton, Jan. 1, 1793.

CONTENTS.

APPENDIX.

A P P E N D I X.

ERRATA.

Pref. p. xii. l. 7, for *Diffenters,* read *Delegates.*

P. 5, l. 8, for *or,* read *as.*

26, l. 10, for *and, as* read *or, as.*

32, l. 7, (b.) for *members,* read *member.*

61, l. 12, (b.) read *the king has fent us word.*

63, l. 12, read *a toaft.*

63, l. 18, dele *perhaps at the fame time.*

81, l. 1, (b) for *affert,* read *infert.*

104, l. 10, (b.) for *Rofe,* read *Hope.*

N. B. (b.) Signifies *from the bottom of the page.*

AN APPEAL

TO

THE PUBLIC,

ON THE SUBJECT OF

THE RIOTS IN BIRMINGHAM.

PART II.

<hr/>

SECTION I.

Introduction, and of the exaggerated Charges in Mr. Burn's Reply.

I DO not remember that I ever entered upon any compofition with fo much reluctance as I do upon this, though not in the leaft from any apprehenfion of not being able to acquit my-felf to my own fatisfaction in it. Indeed, in this refpect, no tafk ever appeared to me more eafy and inviting, as I dare fay my impartial readers (and fome fuch I hope to find) will be fufficiently con-vinced as I proceed. But I wifh to look back as little as poffible to an unpleafant fcene, excepting in fuch a manner as to derive benefit from my reflec-tions upon it. Being, however, loudly called upon

B   by by the clergy of Birmingham, who have employed the pen of Mr. Burn, and who fanction his performance, I find myfelf under a neceffity of vindicating what I advanced in my *Appeal* on the fubject of the riots in that town.

I long entertained hopes that this might be unneceffary, on account of the candour with which my Appeal was written; and, circumftanced as I was, it would naturally be concluded, that I would be as guarded as poffible with refpect to all the facts that I had occafion to introduce; and as I had no vindictive feelings, I imagined that, confidering what I had fuffered (more in fome refpects than moft perfons now living could be made to fuffer) I wrote in fuch a manner as my enemies themfelves would think to be temperate. And, indeed, I have the fatisfaction to find, that not only my particular friends, but many who were not previoufly difpofed to be my friends, thought that the temper with which I wrote was not unbecoming a Chriftian. Notwithftanding this, the clergy of Birmingham exprefs a very different idea of my performance, and it is on nothing but an appeal to *facts* that the propriety of what I advanced before, and of what I fhall now advance in defence of it, muft depend.

What I have had moft occafion to complain of, ever fince my writings have drawn any degree of attention upon me, has been unfounded calumny,
flanders

ilanders of the moſt malignant nature, of which no evidence could be produced, but to which confident aſſertion procured credit. One of theſe, reſpecting my converting Silas Dean to atheiſm, is acknowledged in this *Reply* to my Appeal. That ſtories grow by paſſing from one hand to another, and that by this means mere ſuppoſitions come to be conſidered as undoubted facts, is not uncommon; and it is not eaſy to aſcertain the degree of guilt in any of the relaters. But to be charged with aſſerting the very contrary of what a writer does aſſert, and in the very publication replied to (which is of courſe immediately under the eye of the perſon who profeſſedly replies to it) is much more extraordinary, as it argues ſuch a force of prejudice as the evidence of a man's own ſenſes will not remove; and there are more, and more ſtriking, inſtances of this violent prejudice in Mr. Burn's reply to my Appeal, than I have ſeen in any piece of controverſial writing whatever. If he ever had read my work, he had quite forgotten the contents of it at the time of his writing, and could never have compared the two together. I ſhall, therefore, do it for him, and let the reader judge between us.

Mr. Burn ſays, p. 41, the great object in the narrative part of my work was " to criminate the " clergy," and that I moſt evidently do this, p. 3, " without diſcrimination." Now I do not know how it was poſſible for me to diſcriminate more

expreſsly

expressly than I have done in the account that I gave of the conduct of the clergy; calling some of them *my friends, engaged in the same cause*, Preface, p. xxiii. and even acknowledging, p. 68, that some of them were " among the first to afford me substantial assist-" ance." If, therefore, I had any where censured the clergy in general, it ought to have been under-stood with this limitation, which had been sufficiently expressed before. But I think it will be found that every separate passage, if the scope of it be attended to, is sufficiently guarded, and conveys no censure on the clergy as a body, but only on certain descrip-tions of them. Mr. Burn should, at least, have quoted some passage in which this censure seems to be general, and unqualified; but he does no such thing, contenting himself with asserting it, without producing any evidence of it at all.

The picture that he represents me as having given of the clergy of Birmingham in particular, has no existence but in his own imagination, which, with respect to exaggerated charges, is sufficiently fruitful. " Dr. Priestley's account of the clergy, &c." he says, p. 47, " is of that kind which makes the worst " things he can say of them probable. The idea of " the present clergy of Birmingham," p. x. " will " but exhibit the detested image of a junto degraded " by their vices from the rank not of ministers " merely, but even of men. Either the clergy of " Birmingham," p. 1 , " have forfeited their rank " in

" in fociety, and their claim on its protection, or
" Dr. Prieftley has, in the face of his country, in-
" curred the guilt of accufing the innocent, on the
" ground of invented facts, and of giving plaufibi-
" lity to the compofition, by the affectation of can-
" dour and chriftian meeknefs. It is not permit-
" ted," p. 101, " to the clergy of Birmingham,
" thus publickly arraigned, or the abettors of the
" late riots, to throw in their mite of concern at the
" outrages that have been committed on property,
" on the feelings of individuals, on general fcience,
" and on the plaineft dictates of humanity. Thefe
" are interefts in which, if our accufer may be cre-
" dited, we can feel no concern. It feems, in the
" opinion of Dr. Prieftley, that to be, and to act,
" as a man of principle in the eftablifhed church,
" deprives a man, by a kind of profeffional necef-
" fity, of every claim to the character of humanity,
" and levels him at once to the condition of a
" brute."

Now this frightful idea of the clergy of Birmingham is as far from having any countenance in my
Appeal, as it is from my thoughts. I never had,
or expreffed, any worfe idea of them than that
fome of them were *bigots*; and there are many very
honeft and worthy men, of whom it cannot be denied that they are fo : i. e. perfons who are fo fully
perfuaded, though without reafon, of the truth of
their own principles, that they think much too ill

of thofe of others, and are thereby led to fupport their principles by methods which cannot be juftified.

With refpect to the riot, the worft that I ever thought, or expreffed, concerning the clergy of Birmingham, was that fome of them had reprefented the Diffenters in general, and myfelf in particular, in fuch a light, as, confidering the previous ftate of men's minds in that part of the country, could not but tend to inflame them againft us, and prepare them, though unintended by themfelves, for the outrages that were committed afterwards; and of this I fhall prefently produce ample proof. If I have faid any thing more than this, let my words be quoted, and their fenfe afcertained. But all that the reader has yet feen in the above extracts are the words of Mr. Burn, and not mine.

Mr. Burn, however, fays, p. 124, " the blame " muft, as ufual, fall upon perfons of better condi- " tion, and among thefe the clergy muft of courfe " be regarded as principals in the guilt of the " above horrid tranfactions." But what is ftill more unaccountable than this, he fays, p. xiii. " he has commenced a regular attack upon four " clergymen by name, whom he accufes, by the " moft direct implication, as having been the chief " movers of the popular tumult and outrage, as " incendiaries, and pillagers of houfes, &c. &c. If " the clergy," he fays, p. ix. " whofe names have " been

" been brought forwards on this occasion really are,
" or should even be suspected to be, the wretches
" which Dr. Priestley represents them, their guilt
" must form an anomaly in the history of crimes."

Now I have been far from accusing any clergymen whatever as principals in promoting the riot;
and what Mr. Burn can mean by saying that I have
" commenced an attack upon four clergymen by
" name," I am utterly unable to guess. I do not
know that I have mentioned four of the clergy in
any view, and certainly not as promoters of the
riot; and yet two of them, Mr. Curtis and Mr.
Madan, make a separate defence of their conduct,
as if they had been formally arraigned. It is easy
to answer accusations invented on purpose to be answered; but of what consequence is this, except to
those who are imposed upon by the exaggerated and
false representation, reflecting blame upon the ac-
cuser, instead of answering the proper accusation?
In all that I have quoted from Mr. Burn, he has
only added to that *calumny* with which I have been
already sufficiently loaded, and I publicly call upon
him to vindicate himself from this charge.

I must, however, acknowledge that Mr. Burn's
reply to my Appeal, considered as written with
their concurrence, gives me a much worse opinion
of the clergy of Birmingham than I was disposed to
entertain before. It bears too evident marks of real

malignity.

malignity. It fhews the unrelenting temper of thofe who have done an injury; and on the whole, if I had my choice of the two (harfh as is the cenfure implied in what I am going to fay), I had rather go out of the world with the difpofition of the brutal but ignorant rioters, than with theirs.

It is equally untrue, and unjuft, in Mr. Burn to infinuate, p. iv. that I reprefented Mr. Madan as " an unprincipled favage;" in confequence of which fome perfons, he fays, " having conceived this idea " of him, were aftonifhed when they were affured, " that the urbanity of his manners, and the bene- " volence of his character, rendered him univer- " fally refpected." For certainly, this is the very idea that I myfelf have given of Mr. Madan in my *Familiar Letters*; and my obfervation on it is, that if fuch men as he can be fo inveterate an enemy to the Diffenters, where are we to look for candour, or juftice? For any thing that appears to the contrary, Bonner and Gardiner might be polite, and even good-natured men.

Mr. Burn feems to have imagined that my idea of himfelf and his brethren is fuch as he has conceived of *me*, and this is fhocking enough. But, ill as I have been ufed, I think much better of them, and even of the rioters themfelves. In my next fection I fhall inform my reader what that idea is, and for this I fhall not, like him, produce a picture from

from my own imagination, but quote his own words. It is not a little remarkable that, though Mr. Burn profeffes to write an anfwer to my Appeal, he exprefsly quotes very little of it, but replies to fomething which he gives his reader to underftand is contained in it, but which it will be in vain for him to look for there. Many, however, will read his Reply who will neither read my Appeal, nor this defence of it; and with fuch readers his method of writing will anfwer well enough. This is not the way in which I treat Mr. Burn, or any of my opponents. Whether my replies be fufficient or not, at leaft I let my reader fee what it is that I reply to, and in their own words. Of this fair method this defence of my Appeal will be a fpecimen.

When Mr. Burn fays, p. 34, that in his Reply to my Letters to him he anfwered my *arguments*, but paffed by the *abufe*, he quotes nothing, but leaves his reader to fuppofe that I had written fomething that might be termed *abufe*. I wifh his readers would look into thofe Letters. They will be much at a lofs to conjecture what it is that Mr. Burn meant to reprefent in that light. But I fuppofe that any thing that gives pain, from the difficulty of anfwering it, Mr. Burn will call *abufe*, as a libel is faid to be no lefs a libel, though it be ever fo true.

In that work of his to which my Letters were an anfwer, he thought himfelf at liberty to give the

moft

moſt unfavourable idea of my ſentiments, evidently calculated to excite the reſentment of his readers againſt me, aſcribing to me the worſt deſigns, as well as the groſſeſt miſtakes, and yet in *him* this muſt not be termed abuſe. Though my only ob-ject in every thing that I wrote about the perſon of Chriſt was to aſcertain what the teſtimony of the apoſtles concerning him really was, and I conſtantly appealed to their teſtimony as deciſive, he ſtrangely repreſented me as denying the *infallibility of their teſtimony,* which he undertook to defend againſt me; and with as little pretence, though it ſerved to excite an alarm at my principles, he deſcribed them as leading to all vice and wickedneſs. But there are readers with whom any repreſentations from a cler-gyman, in ſuch a cauſe, will have weight.

Abuſive as Mr. Burn repreſents my polemical writings to be, I have never yet charged any of my opponents with bad intentions, or queſtioned the goodneſs of their underſtandings; but I have always imputed their miſtakes to *prejudice,* the effect of early impreſſions: and if my own opinion, as I muſt ſuppoſe, be right, and conſequently thoſe of my op-ponents be wrong, what leſs offenſive hypotheſis could I frame for it?

One would think that Mr. Burn had never read my Appeal, to which he profeſſes to reply, all his charges are ſo totally void of truth, or ſo ſhamefully exaggerated.]

exaggerated. Speaking of my obfervations on the addrefs to the rioters *as friends and fellow-churchmen,* he calls it, p. 63, " a tranfaction moft fhamefully " reprefented by the author; and that, in confequence " of the impofition contained in Dr. Prieftley's ftate- " ment, this tranfaction was brought forward in par- " liament." " It is remarkable," he fays, p. 65, " that the obvious policy of feeming to coincide in " fentiment with a mob, for the purpofe of influenc- " ing their opinions, and controlling their conduct, " fhould have been actually conftrued into a real " defign of promoting and inflaming their vio- " lence." After calling the rioters *the fynagogue of Satan,* he fays, p. 69, " If there be any thing " doubtful remaining, it muft appear to every im- " partial obferver, to be the integrity of that man's " motives, who can thus, to anfwer a purpofe, make " churchmen of rioters, and in the fame breath too " in which he declares it to be queftionable whe- " ther fuch mifcreants can be faid to be of any " church."

Now all that I have made of this circumftance was to fhew that the rioters were confidered as churchmen, and that their object was the deftruc- tion of Diffenters. I believe, indeed, and I fhall prove, that there was pofitive encouragement given to the rioters by churchmen of better condition, but I do not fay that their defign in this particular

4   part

part of their conduct was to promote and inflame
their violence. Certainly, however, to addrefs them
without giving any intimation that what they had
hitherto done was wrong, was not likely to prevent
their proceeding farther.

SECTION II.

*Of Mr. Burn's Accufation of me, and his challenging
me to defend myfelf.*

LET us now fee what kind of language
Mr. Burn makes ufe of in his Reply to my Appeal, which he will, no doubt, fay contains nothing
that can properly be termed *abufe.*

Speaking of what I fay of the clergy of Birmingham, he calls it, p. 99, " a malignant hypo-
" thefis." In p. 84, he fpeaks of " the unequalled
" malignity and injuftice of my reprefentations."
He calls the language I hold with refpect to my
enemies, p. xv. " the moft complete infolence,
" and abufe, that malignity itfelf could have fuggefted." According to him, p. 100, I am " an
" accufer of the innocent, not merely without fuf-
" ficient evidence, but in open defiance of the
" moft palpable and uniform feries of facts." Of
my

my *Letter to the Inhabitants of Birmingham*, he fays, p. 39, " it was as great an outrage upon charac-" ter, as the conduct of the rioters was upon pro-" perty."

One of the moft curious infinuations of Mr. Burn is his reprefenting me as fo overbearing, that it was an offence, p. 77, in the clergy of Birmingham to think for themfelves without my permiffion. This is the more extraordinary, as he fays, p. 37, " No " man has done more than I have to invite, and " even to provoke difcuffion." Would I have done this, if the controverting of my opinions had been fo very offenfive to me? But while Mr. Burn quotes nothing, and only gives his own idea of me, and of my writings, he has no check upon him befides his own difcretion. I will venture to affert, that all who are really acquainted with me will fay that Mr. Burn's account is the reverfe of my character.

But the moft injurious of all Mr. Burn's infinua-tions are thofe by which he would give his readers to underftand, that my writings are calculated to difturb the peace of the country, and that I am in-tending fomething more than the mere difcuffion of theological or political queftions. Of the Preface to my Letters to him, he fays, p. 27, " it is written " with more freedom, in the opinion of many, than " is practically confiftent with the intire peace of " the country." This was alfo the object of the

Extracts

Extracts that were made from the Preface, which were sent to all the bishops and members of the House of Commons, as every thing in that Preface that shewed that my only object was free and calm discussion, was omitted, and the other passages were so put together, as to be calculated to excite alarm.

With the same unfairness Mr. Burn represents my *Letter to Mr. Pitt,* p. 21, as " menacing, " and insolent, most unconstitutionally infringing " upon freedom of debate; a personal invective, " and not an answer to arguments. It was," he says, p. 19, " a fair developement of what I would " be at, and in the judgment of sober men marked " with some degree of precision the boundary of " my ambition." Now as few men write more intelligibly than I do, it is very easy to see the extent of my views, in that, or in any other of my publications; and this has always been to state my own opinions on any subject, and to invite the fullest discussion of them. What can be my *ambition,* when I plead for abolishing all civil establishments of religion, as hostile to the genius of it, and a burden to the state; and when I claim nothing for myself but what I equally plead for all persons without exception? Besides, in all my proposals for the reformation of the greatest abuses, I expressly say that I would have no man disturbed in his present possession, but that the retrenchment should affect the successor only. Is this ambition? Is it not the greatest moderation?

But

But in me nothing can be moderation. It muſt be ambition, or ſomething equally bad.

Perhaps the moſt perverſe of Mr. Burn's conſtructions of my writing, is his inferring from what I have ſaid of the French " having no court for the " nobility and clergy to look up to, and to depend " upon," that I conſider it, p. 30, " as the duty of " Engliſhmen to renovate this part of their conſti- " tution, which lodges the government in the " hands of an individual;" that is, that it is my wiſh, and I doubt not, he would add, that it will be my endeavour, that there be no king in Eng- land. It is very fortunate for me that I never wrote a Roman Hiſtory: for had I expreſſed any approbation of the conduct of the Romans in baniſhing the Tarquins, Mr. Burn's inference of my antipathy to all kingly power would have been much ſtronger, as they left no hereditary power in the country; whereas there ſtill is a king in France *, though not ſuch a king as the nobility or clergy can look up to for much emolument. Mr. Burn can ſee no medium, at leaſt in me, be- tween retrenching exorbitant power, and taking it away entirely. At all events, I muſt be repreſented as a republican; and with many republicaniſm is ſynonymous to every thing that is dreadful and de-

---

* This was written before the revolution of the 10th of Auguſt, which, in the circumſtances of France, was a happy and neceſſary completion of that of the 14th of July.

teſtable,

teftable, perfect anarchy and confufion, to fay the leaft.

It is generally deemed fair to interpret particular expreffions in one part of any perfon's writings by his declared fentiments in others of them. Now in my political writings, which however are not numerous, I have again and again praifed the Englifh conftitution, as confifting of the three eftates of King, Lords, and Commons. What candour or juftice, then, is there in fuppofing that I wifh the fubverfion of it? I thought it neceffary to premife thefe obfervations, which demonftrate a difpofition in Mr. Burn and the clergy of Birmingham, with whofe concurrence he wrote, to put the worft conftruction on every thing I fay or do, which, if I may adopt their language, is an outrage on character fimilar to that which the rioters committed on my property.

Let us now come to the examination of the *facts* which I have advanced, the evidence for which is fo loudly called for by Mr. Burn. And furely, if there be any thing wrong in producing this evidence, that is, what I take to be fuch, the blame muft lie with thofe who called for it. With refpect to accufation unfupported by facts, Mr. Burn expreffes himfelf very properly, though without reflecting to whom his cenfure applies. " If a character," p. 26, " muft

at

" at any rate be defamed, nothing in the world can
" be fo convenient for the purpofe of invented ca-
" lumny, as an appeal to anonymous report. The
" introduction of anonymous report," p. 25, " whe-
" ther true or falfe, into this ferious argument, is
" more than impertinent; it is infidious."

Mr. Burn's challenge of me to produce authorities for what I have advanced is fuch as becomes a
diligent inquirer after truth, and one who would
not fhrink from it. " If," fays he, p. 26, " the
" doctor would convict by evidence, we invite him
" to the proof of his charge. Let him," p. 59,
" produce inftances from the conduct of the upper
" clafs of people, whom he thus gravely accufes.
" He is, no doubt, in poffeffion of the facts." With
refpect to what I faid of fome of them being concerned in the infults offered to me, he fays, p. 35,
" Let him then come fairly to the proof, or let
" him expunge all illiberal infinuations from the
" lift of his charges." When I faid that the cleareft
facts fhew that there was more than remiffnefs on
the part of many perfons of better condition, and
that nothing they did fhewed a real difapprobation
of the conduct of the mob previous to the deftruction of my houfe, Mr. Burn fays, p. 67, " Then
" produce them. On this fubject," he fays, p. 95,
" be explicit, fir;" and " of this affertion he pro-
" duces no evidence." This is the moft material
article in the queftion that is now before the Public,

an

and therefore I ſhall endeavour to do what Mr.
Burn challenges me to do, viz. to ſupport what I
have advanced, by an appeal to facts.

Mr. Burn inſults me, p. 81, with not having
" proceeded againſt the magiſtrates legally, but
" contented myſelf with venting my ſpleen in to-
" lerated ſlander." But the hiſtory of the aſſizes
at Worceſter and Warwick, and of what paſſed in
the Houſe of Commons itſelf, will, I hope, juſtify us
in not appealing to the laws of our country in ſuch a
caſe as this. Though, however, we have no proſpect
of ſucceſs *there*, we ſhall venture to appeal to a higher
and more reſpectable tribunal, " our countrymen
" in general," as Mr. Burn quotes my own words
in his motto, " the world at large, and eſpecially
" poſterity."

I have not, in my Appeal, ſaid much of the
conduct of the clergy of Birmingham: Mr.
Burn, however, ſuppoſes that I have ; and on
that ſuppoſition he ſays, p. 103, " Dr. Prieſtley
" ſtands forward as the accuſer of the clergy of
" Birmingham, and he is now called upon as pub-
" licly by one of that body, either to ſubſtantiate, or
" retract, his charge. The author of this reply," he
ſays, p. 103, " will not ſhrink from the inquiry.
" He invites it. If there be any one motive that
" influences him more than another in this affair,
" it is the hope that, by promoting this diſcuſſion,
                                                    " in

" in vindication of the character of the innocent, he
" may at the fame time affift Dr. Prieftley and the
" Public, in a clear and full detection of the guilty."
I fhall be much obliged to him for this affiftance.

With refpect to what I have faid of the paffions
of the lower order of the people being inflamed by
the preaching of the clergy, Mr. Burn fays, p. 38,
" We do aver from our own practice, from the
" practice of our brethren in general, prior to the
" late unhappy affair, that this reprefentation of the
" conduct of the clergy is not a true one. For the
" truth of this declaration we can cheerfully appeal
" to the conftant experience of our hearers." This
is fufficiently bold; and I fhall anfwer the challenge,
not by appealing to Mr. Burn's hearers, but to
printed documents, fermons preached at the time,
and now extant. *Litera fcripta manet.*

Thus publicly and boldly called upon, I fhall
proceed to the vindication of what I have advanced
in my Appeal; firft with refpect to what paffed previous to the riot, and the probable caufe of it;
then what took place during the riot, and fubfequent to it. I only requeft an impartial attention to fuch facts as I fhall produce; and it muft be
confidered that, not having been myfelf a witnefs of
what I fhall relate, I muft neceffarily depend upon
the teftimony of others; and as in this I may,

through

through mifinformation, be miftaken, I fincerely
wifh to hear what may be alleged on the other fide.
I cannot wifh to be mifled myfelf, nor would I
knowingly miflead others; and the prefs is as open
to my opponents as it is to myfelf. After this it will
be in the power of our readers to judge whether I
be what Mr. Burn, p. 106, calls me, " a public flan-
" derer," or not.

SECTION III.

*Of Events previous to the Riot, and of the more diftant
Caufes of it.*

THAT there exifted in Birmingham, and
in all that part of the country, a ftrong fpirit of
party, exceedingly unfavourable to Diffenters,
is evident from a variety of circumftances;
and, independently of any that I have mentioned, it muft appear probable from the hiftory of
thofe counties in this refpect, given at length in an
excellent pamphlet lately publifhed, entitled, Hɪɢʜ
Cʜᴜʀᴄʜ Pᴏʟɪᴛɪᴄs, in which it is fhewn that the
neighbourhood of Birmingham was the head quarters of Dr. Sacheverell; and that, in the reign of
George I. feveral meeting houfes were deftroyed by

rioters

rioters in that town, and others in thofe parts. The facts that I mentioned in proof of the exiftence of this party fpirit, and that it was far from originating with me, or being promoted by me, Mr. Burn has attempted to invalidate. But let the reader judge with what effect.

One of the inftances that I mentioned was that the clergy refufed to walk in funeral proceffions with diffenting minifters. I obferved that Mr. Curtis refufed to do fo at the application of Mr. Scholefield. This Mr. Burn infinuates was not on account of his objecting to doing this with diffenting minifters in general, or Mr. Scholefield in particular, but with myfelf only; " left," as he fays, p. 4, " he fhould be led to act officially with one " whofe oppofition to the doctrines and difcipline " of the church of which he is a member, had car- " ried him into exceffes, in his apprehenfion, in the " higheft degree illiberal and indecent. Of this " clafs he juftly confidered Dr. Prieftley. With " him therefore he could not confiftently act upon " fuch an occafion; and for this reafon folely he re- " fufed to comply in the inftance produced by the " Doctor."

But this inftance of bigotry in the clergy of Birmingham appeared before I went thither. More than forty years ago Mr. Wearden, curate of St. Philip's, expreffed his concern that he could not walk with

C 3

Mr.

Mr. Blythe at the funeral of Mr. Ruffel's grand-
mother, hav'ng, as he faid, received orders to the
contrary from Mr. Vyfe, who was then the rector.

In 1770, Mr. Dovey, rector of St. Martin's, refufed to go into a mourning coach along with Mr.
Blythe at the funeral of Mrs. Webfter; and after
the funeral he faid to Mr. Webfter, that " when the
" Diffenters wifhed their own minifters to attend
" their friends to the grave, they had better not in-
" vite the clergy of the eftablifhment."

After this Mr. Webfter, having the direction of
the funeral of Mr. Haddock, omitted to invite Mr.
Dovey, and alfo to 'fend the hatband, fcarf, and
gloves, which it had been ufual to give the attending clergyman. Unwilling to lofe thefe perquifites,
Mr. Dovey fent to inform Mr. Webfter, that,
though he did not choofe to attend the funeral
along with the Diffenting minifters, he did not
mean to refufe what was ufually given on thofe occafions. Mr. Webfter, however, very properly withheld them.

At the funeral of Mr. Stephens of Deretend, Mr.
Aufted refufed to ride before the hearfe along with
the diffenting minifter, and haughtily bade him
ride behind the hearfe.

At the funeral of Mr. Gifborne, when Mr. Dovey
refufed

refufed to walk in proceffion with Mr. Bourn, a man
of activity and fpirit, the following pleafant circumftance happened: Mr. Dovey meeting the corpfe,
and finding Mr. Bourn walking before it, directed
him to walk behind. Mr. Bourn not complying with
this order, Mr. Dovey endeavoured to outwalk him,
but Mr. Bourn, being as nimble as he, kept up with
him, till, the Rector quickening his pace, they both
fairly ran for it, till they got to the church door. Mr.
Dovey was fo much offended, that, after the funeral,
his pride getting the better of every other confideration, he fent back the hatband and fcarf, and even
the pins that had been ufed on the occafion.

Thefe inftances certainly fhow that the refufal of
the clergy of Birmingham to walk in funeral proceffion with diffenting minifters did not arife from any
objection they had to myfelf in particular, as Mr.
Burn intimates; but from an abfurd bigotry of
long ftanding in the place; and I believe hardly
known in any other part of the kingdom.

Befides, if Mr. Curtis had fo violent an objection
to myfelf in particular, why did he come to hear me
preach, or meet me at the committee of the library,
of that for the abolition of the flave trade, and on
other occafions, on which he always behaved to me
with great civility? And at the time that he refufed
to walk with Mr. Scholefield, which, Mr. Burn fays,
was folely on my account, he gave a reafon which

affected

affected all diffenting minifters; and I had not then done any thing to make myfelf more obnoxious than I had when he came to hear me. I am alfo credibly informed that Mr. Curtis himfelf, on reading my Appeal, declared that I had given a juft account of his conduct, that it was the bigotry he found in the place that led him to act as he had done, and that he had not himfelf any objection to walking with diffenting minifters at funerals. How this is to be reconciled with his giving his fanction to Mr. Burn's Reply is no bufinefs of mine.

Another inftance of the High Church bigotry of the town of Birmingham that I mentioned, was the fubfcribers to the Sunday fchools having refcinded a law which permitted the children to go to any place of public worfhip that their parents chofe. On this Mr. Burn fays, p. 66, " It has happened, " unfortunately for his purpofe, that either through " mifinformation, or a fettled plan of perverting and " rendering odious the conduct of others," (and this is the turn that Mr. Burn generally choofes to give to all my accounts of things) " he has totally " mifreprefented this plain bufinefs. The fact," he fays, p. 81, " was that the law was never refcinded " at all;" and after giving a detail of pretended proofs to the contrary, he fays, p. 12, " Let Dr. " Prieftley, by facts, confute this ftatement if he " can." He alfo fays, p. 9, " To refcind the above " law, was an act for which no committee was com-
" petent

" petent, and there, unqueftionably, never was a ge-
" neral meeting held for any fuch purpofe." Mr.
Riland, another clergyman, fays, p. 106, " I have
" no doubt but that your reprefentation" (writing
to Mr. Burn) " is perfectly right, and his" (mine)
" is totally wrong."

Though this reply of Mr. Burn was written with
the concurrence of Mr. Curtis, it is now clearly
proved that my account is ftrictly true. A general
meeting of the fubfcribers to the Sunday fchools
was held (though Mr. Burn fays there unqueftionably
was not) without any previous notice of the bufinefs
that was to come before them. When it was propofed to refcind the law, the votes were equal, and
Mr. Curtis, being in the chair, decided in favour of
refcinding it. The evidence of the refcinding is a
public advertifement in the Birmingham newfpaper, immediately after the tranfaction, as was noticed
by Mr. Scholefield, with proper obfervations with
refpect to the dependance there could be on other
bold affertions in Mr. Burn's reply. This will be
found in my Appendix, No. I.

I do not fay that even this palpable falfehood
was a wilful one, as Mr. Burn, or Mr. Madan,
would not fcruple to fay with refpect to me ; but it
argues fuch a defect of memory as may be hereafter
quoted as one of the moft remarkable things of this
nature in the hiftory of the human mind. It is the

more

more fo, as, when Mr. Burn himfelf applied to Mr. John Lawrence for his fubfcription, and was refufed on account of the refcinding of the rule above mentioned, Mr. Burn immediately faid to a perfon who accompanied him, " I told you how it would be. I " am forry for it;" he himfelf having difapproved of the conduct of the High Church party in this bufinefs. Indeed I never confidered Mr. Burn as a bigot; and, as having been both a Methodift and a Diffenter, rather a friend to both. The fact abovementioned was related to me by Mr. Lawrence prefently after it happened.

The defect in the memory of Mr. Curtis is as remarkable as that of Mr. Burn; and that two men fhould labour under the fame defect, with refpect to the fame thing, is more extraordinary ftill. For he was not only chairman at the meeting in which the rule was refcinded, and decided the queftion himfelf; but when, after this, he called upon Mr. Punfield for his fubfcription, he was refufed, and was informed that it was for the fame reafon.

That this conduct in the fubfcribers to the Sunday fchools arofe from the moft contemptible bigotry, no perfon of the leaft degree of liberality will deny; and that this bigotry was of long ftanding in Birmingham, in the opinion of Mr. Curtis himfelf, was evident from the following circumftance, which I fhall relate from my own recollection. When a

friend

friend of mine was going to that meeting of the fubfcribers, at which it was agreed to permit the fcholars to attend whatever place of worfhip their parents fhould choofe, he was joined by Mr. Curtis;
and talking about the bufinefs of the meeting, Mr.
Curtis, who was then a friend to the propofal, faid
he was afraid they fhould not be able to carry it,
" there was fo much of the *old leaven* yet remaining
" in Birmingham." I have no doubt but Mr. Curtis would have acted with the liberality becoming a
perfon of a diffenting family, if he had not found fo
much of what he properly termed the *old leaven* in
Birmingham. That he had not the fortitude to act
agreeably to the natural dictates of his own mind,
by which it would have been in his power to expel
that old leaven, is much to be lamented. My houfe
and meeting houfe would have been ftanding, and
I fhould now have been at Birmingham, much more
agreeably employed than I am at this moment.

When Mr. Scholefield publifhed a copy of the refolution of the fubfcribers to the Sunday fchools
refcinding the rule above mentioned, and which Mr.
Burn, Mr. Riland, and, in effect, Mr. Curtis alfo
(by joining in the fanction of the other clergymen of
Birmingham to Mr. Burn's Reply) folemnly declared never to have been refcinded at all; Mr.
Burn does not acknowledge the plain inference
from the fact, viz. the exiftence of a fpirit of High
Church bigotry in Birmingham, independently of
any

any thing that I could have done to excite it (and it
was with this view that I mentioned it at all) but
only defires of his readers, what they would certainly
do without his defire, that "that part of his ftate-
" ment, &c. may not be confidered as weighing any
" thing in his general argument againſt me." What
was it but a degree of bigotry of the moſt extravagant kind to refcind a rule by which the fcholars
were permitted to attend public worſhip where their
parents chofe, when in no one inſtance had any of
them, in fact, attended any other worſhip than that
of the Church of England.

The bigotry of the church people at Birmingham
appears, perhaps, more clearly in their conduct of
a charity fchool which has been eſtabliſhed there
upwards of forty years; not only as it is a rule in
the inſtitution of this fchool, that no children ſhall be
admitted that are not of the eſtabliſhed church, but
that they ſhall not be bound apprentices to any Diffenter.   Nay, in two inſtances, the managers of this
charity even refufed to accept of the fubfcriptions of
Diffenters voluntarily offered them.   Both Mr. La-
kin and Mr. Peyton, to their great furprife, had their
money rejected.

I confider it as a proof of High Church principles, unfavourable to civil and religious liberty, that
the centenary celebration of the revolution in 1688,
was not attended by any of the clergy of Birmingham,

ham, and they did every thing in their power to render it unpopular. Their favourite toaſt of *Church and King* was objected to. The meeting was attended by a Catholic clergyman, and the Diſſenting miniſters.

The laſt inſtance I ſhall mention of the exiſtence of a high party ſpirit in the clergy of Birmingham is, that one of that body, of a more liberal turn, when he left the place, declared it was on that account, and that for this reaſon he could not live in comfort in it.

This extreme bigotry is not peculiar to the town of Birmingham, but extends to the neighbouring counties. As a curious inſtance of this, I ſhall obſerve, that Mr. Mould, of Meaſham, near Aſhby de la Zouch, refuſed, the laſt year, to officiate at the funeral of a child of John Bancroft, a Diſſenter; and declared, that no Diſſenter ſhould be buried by him. In conſequence of this, the child was put into the grave without any thing being ſaid at the place; and the mother was ſo much affected, that ſhe was taken home very ill. It is happy that this clergyman has not the keys of the gates of heaven, nor wholly thoſe of the grave.

That I ſaw, lamented, and endeavoured to allay, this party ſpirit in the town of Birmingham, by perſuading the Diſſenters to give up the diſpoſal of the civil

offices

offices, is well known to all my acquaintance, though
Mr. Burn is incredulous on the subject. " This," he
says, p. 16, in his insulting manner, " considering the
" Doctor's natural diffidence of power, and the ex-
" treme readiness which himself and principal friends
" have ever discovered in giving up authority once
" obtained, must appear a very probable, as well as
" interesting story. It is, however, strictly true. To
mention no more, Mr. Ruffel, Mr. G. Humphrys,
the two Mr. Hunts, and the three Mr. Rylands,
who thought as I did on the subject, will bear me
witness, as well as others, who were not Diffenters. I
may add all my particular acquaintance, without exception, know that I constantly blamed the Diffenters for keeping that power in their own hands.

That the Diffenters of Birmingham were not so
attentive as they might have been to retain the
power they once had, appeared in their conduct with
respect to king Edward's charity school in that
town; the governors of which were once Diffenters,
and it was in their power to have admitted no other
among them; but they always chose to take some of
the principal of the church people to act with them.
It happened, however, that at one particular meeting,
at which those church people made a point of attending, while some of the Diffenters were absent, they
took that opportunity of choosing another churchman, by which they became the majority; and from
that time, except in the single case of Mr. Ruffel,

they

they have never chofen any Diffenter into their body, and have repeatedly declared they never would. Let not then the church people at Birmingham upbraid the Diffenters with a love of power.

I had a view to the bigotry of the town of Birmingham, and hoped to fucceed in allaying it, by means of the public library, in the eftablifhment of which I particularly interefted myfelf; as that would neceffarily bring the reading and thinking part of the town better acquainted with each other. The annual advertifement, which was drawn up by me, and which was continued for fome time by the High Church party, after they gained the afcendancy they now have in that library, but which they have fince dropped, I fhall infert in the Appendix, No. II.

With refpect to the bufinefs of the library, in which it was not poffible for any man to act with more liberality than I did, Mr. Burn fays, p. 14, " We never faw great talents fo degraded by party " confiderations as in the conduct of Dr. Prieftley " in fome part of that bufinefs." But, in his ufual manner, he does not fay what thofe parts of my conduct were. As a fmall pamphlet, which I publifhed on occafion of a motion to prevent the purchafe of books of religious controverfy, will give the reader fome idea of the fpirit with which I acted in this bufinefs, I fhall give the whole, or a confiderable part of it, in the Appendix, No. III.; and let

4   Mr.

Mr. Burn, if he pleases, republish the pamphlet which one of the clergy wrote on the occasion, and signed M. S.

What it is that Mr. Burn alludes to, when he says that I degraded my great talents, I believe it will not be very easy for any person, acquainted with the facts, to conjecture. Had I, as Mr. Curtis did, openly canvassed the subscribers for the purpose of getting a committee to my mind, I should indeed have degraded my talents, whether they had been great or small; but it is well known that all my proceedings were fair and candid. The harshest thing that I said of the clergy who withdrew from the library because my *History of the Corruptions of Christianity* was voted into it, was that their conduct was childish. The subscribers seem to have thought as I did; for though Mr. Curtis, in the note he wrote on the occasion, expressed his wish, " that all the mem-" bers of the church of England would follow his ex-" ample;" not one of them, except the clergy, did so.

Another childish and paltry instance of bigotry, in some members of the church of England on that occasion, was striking out the title of *Reverend* prefixed to Mr. Scholefield's name and mine in the list of the committee. A subscriber found the ink with which the rasure had been made, not quite dry; and inquiring who had been in the library, was informed that only Mr. Curtis and Mr. Lloyd, a

Quaker,

Quaker, had been there. Being interrogated on the fubject, they both denied having done it. If notwithftanding this, Mr. Curtis was generally believed to have done it, the fault is not mine. As little regard has been paid to his moft folemn affeveration by Dr. Parr, a brother clergyman.

Without the leaft regard to truth Mr. Burn fpeaks of me, p. 21, as having been " adopted the cham-" pion and leader of the whole body," (viz. of Dif-fenters), " in the bufinefs of the application to par-" liament for the repeal of the corporation and teft " acts;" and he adds, that " after organizing the " whole body of Diffenters, and bringing them to " act as one man, their future conduct in this affair " was to be governed, as unqueftionably it has been, " and efpecially in this, and the neighbouring coun-" ties, by the maxims of his policy."

In all this Mr. Burn fhews his utter ignorance of this whole bufinefs; and, though he pays no regard to what I have before faid on this fubject, viz. that I had very little to do in it, he fhould have procured information from fome other quarter, and have mentioned his authority. Of the many *letters, refolutions,* &c. relating to this affair, that were drawn up at Birmingham, I did not write one. I attended but few of the meetings even there, and though I attended one at Nottingham, it was becaufe I had bufinefs of my own in that place. I affifted, indeed, in drawing up the refolutions that were agreed

upon

upon there, but faid little or nothing at the meeting. Indeed, it is well known that I am very backward to fpeak in public ; being, on feveral accounts, efpe-cially a tendency to ftammering, unfit for public fpeaking.

On the failure of this application to parliament, Mr. Burn fays, p. 18, " Circumftances did arife " which tended extremely to expofe the true tem-" per and views of Dr. Prieftley, and to fink him " prodigioufly in the opinion of his townfmen." I wifh Mr. Burn had faid what thofe circumftances were, and I now call upon him to name them. I had no views that were peculiar to myfelf, or that were not common to all Diffenters; and what I did to promote thofe views was nothing peculiar to my-felf, and lefs than was done by many others; not a hundredth part, I may venture to fay, of what was done, and ably done, by Mr. Walker of Notting-ham, not to fpeak of others. Indeed, it is well known that I was never folicitous about the object. But it is Mr. Burn's manner to make general affer-tions without appealing to any fpecific facts, capable of being fcrutinized.

The difcourfe which I preached and publifhed on this occafion I called " the moft calm and mode-" rate that ever was written on a political fubject." This Mr. Burn does not deny; but as nothing good can come from me, he gives it the following turn, p. 23. " They perceived, indeed, that his gird at the " minifter

" minifter had taught him circumfpection, and that
" his wounds received in the encounter being
" yet frefh, he fought cautioufly; but the true de-
" fign of this piece of management was too pal-
" pable to be miftaken." In this he alludes to my
Letter to Mr. Pitt, by which that minifter might
receive a wound, but it will not be cafy to find the
fcars of any that I received. If I had wounds, they
did not prevent my continuing to fight on (if I
muft purfue Mr. Burn's metaphor) and what I
wrote afterwards in my *Anfwer to Mr. Burke*, and
my *Familiar Letters*, betray no diminution of vigour
or fpirit. But that the temper with which I delivered and publifhed that fermon was not artfully
affumed for the occafion, as Mr. Burn infinuates,
but habitual to me, will appear from what I wrote
refpecting the fame fubject in one of the earlieft of
my publications, viz. my Addrefs to *Proteftant Diffenters as fuch*, a part of which I fhall for this
purpofe infert in my Appendix, No. IV.

Mr. Burn would in vain charge *me* with even
alluding to facts that I am not prepared to authen-
ticate. With refpect to the report of my converting Silas Dean to atheifm, Mr. Burn fays, p. 26,
" Will he oblige the public with the names of fome
" of thofe clergymen in the town and neighbour-
" hood by whom this account was fo induftrioufly
" circulated?" Now I doubt not Mr. Burn knows
much more of this bufinefs than I do. I will men-

tion,

tion, however, that Mr. Swainſon of Rowley, and a clergyman dining at Stratford, both ſtrongly recommended the pamphlet in which that ſtory was publiſhed, as did Mr. Curtis at the library room in Birmingham. The perſon who heard him is ready to atteſt it.

Let the reader judge from theſe particulars whether I have given a falſe account of the temper of the members of the eſtabliſhed church in Birmingham in general, or of that of the clergy in particular. It was the extreme of bigotry, the ſame that had exiſted in the place long before I went thither, what I in vain endeavoured to allay, what exiſts there at preſent in as great violence as ever, and will I fear continue a long time; for it appears to have been greatly inflamed by the late riot.

SECTION IV.

Of the prediſpoſing Cauſes of the Riot.

I CONSIDER the view that was perpetually exhibited of the Diſſenters, and eſpecially of the Unitarians in general, and of myſelf in particular, by the clergy of Birmingham, and others who occaſionally preached in their pulpits, as a principal prediſpoſing cauſe of the riot; as they neceſſary led the people to conſider us as the very peſts of ſociety;

from

from which the wifh, and the endeavour, to extermi-
nate us, as fuch, was but too obvious and natural.
Mr. Burn, in what I have already quoted from
him, ftrongly denies the fact. But there is evidence
of it now exifting in the printed fermons of Dr.
Croft and Mr. Madan, which are well known to
have been in the fame ftrain with many others delivered in the pulpits at Birmingham while I refided
there; and it will not be fuppofed that what they
have printed was lefs guarded than what was not.

Mr. Madan, who fays that his difcourfe was publifhed " at the requeft of many before whom it was
" delivered," which is a proof of *their* party fpirit, as
well as of his own, fpeaks with particular approbation of the fermons of Dr. Croft, and Mr. Clutton; the latter of which he laments was not printed,
and which I remember to have heard fpoken of as
peculiarly violent; as the fermons of Mr. Curtis
were alfo faid to be. The reader may therefore
judge of the inflammatory tendency of thefe fermons
of the clergy in general, by the following extracts
from thofe of Dr. Croft and Mr. Madan.

They both agree in reprefenting the principles of
the Diffenters as " unqueftionably republican."
" Thofe of the Socinians," which Mr. Madan fpeaks
of as evidently gaining ground, he fays, p. 10,
" are certainly no lefs dangerous to the ftate than
" the tenets of popery." Both thefe preachers re-

D 3   prefent

present our principles as not only theoretically, but
practically seditious. Of the sentiments of Dr. Price,
Dr. Croft says, p. xii. " They spread jealousy and
" discontent through the kingdom, and were little
" short of blasphemy. The Dissenters," he says,
p. 33, " wish to destroy the whole fabric of our
" constitution." Mr. Madan also represents us as
no better than *king killers* in general. " Is there no
" reason," he says, p. 13, " to receive with suspi-
" cion their declarations of reverence to the govern-
" ment, and of loyalty to the king, however plau-
" sibly and spontaneously announced, when the
" amount of that reverence has been exactly ascer-
" tained by the woful experience of republican ty-
" ranny, and the extent of their loyalty has been ex-
" actly delineated by the blood of a king." He
also says, p. 8, that he " always regarded our prin-
" ciples as pointedly hostile, and dangerous to our
" happy constitution."

When he was called upon by me to defend these
strange and injurious aspersions, which are in con-
tradiction to all history, and even to recent facts,
and especially to all my principles, as contained in
my writings; he appeared willing, indeed, to except
from his charges the more moderate, or Calvinistic
Dissenters, but by no means myself, and others whom
he terms " the more violent Dissenters;" and in
vindication of what he had advanced concerning the
king killing principles being still retained by the

Dissenters,

Diffenters, he fays, p. 35, that " principles are a
" long lived generation;" and infinuates that therefore, they muft now exift fomewhere among us.
" Thefe principles," he fays, p. 22, " are ftill at
" work." When I appealed to my own peaceable
behaviour, he replied, p. 16, that " Guy Fawkes
" would have done the fame;" plainly fuggefting a
comparifon between him and me.

Both Dr. Croft and Mr. Madan reprefent in a
moft extravagant light the very innocent objeft of
the application of the Diffenters to parliament for
the repeal of the corporation and teft acts, and they
intimate, that fo far from giving us more liberty, it
were to be wifhed that we could be deprived of
fome of the privileges that we now enjoy. Mr.
Madan alarms the public by calling the bufinefs of
this application a " great conftitutional caufe."
The poffeffion of offices, which we plead our right
to a participation in, he fays, p. 12, would be " in-
" compatible with the fafety of our civil govern-
" ment;" and he fpeaks of our third application as
" an extraordinary fubjeft, now a third time ob-
" truded upon the legiflature."

- Dr. Croft fays, p. 36, " It would be fatal to reli-
" gion, if the legiflature fhould by any act of indul-
" gence declare all opinions innocent. It is unfor-
" tunate," he fays, p. xiv. " that the right of vot-
" ing at elections, and of fitting in parliament, can-

" not

" not be taken from the Diffenters.   It would be
" defirable," p. 30, " to exclude from the Britifh
" fenate all thofe who are led away by their plaufible
" arguments, and to caution every Britifh youth
" againft their civil and religious maxims of go-
" vernment."   He particularly fays, p. xi. that
" if the Unitarians were reftricted from fpeaking in-
" decently of the doctrine of the Trinity, and if they
" were enjoined upon certain pains and penalties, it
" might be deemed perfecution by them, but could
" not be thought a hardfhip by others."   Mr. Madan alfo fays, p. 9, " Are we not juftly upbraided
" with a paffive and fupine conduct, in a caufe of
" the moft interefting and facred nature ?"

Of my own character nothing more injurious
could be infinuated than was done by Mr. Madan.
He defcribes me as a man of extraordinary talents,
indeed, but as actuated by *malevolence*; and how elfe
would he have defcribed Satan himfelf?   " When
" I fee," he fays, p. 26, " your blindnefs in any
" point of hiftory, I much fufpect it to be wilful;"
which is to reprefent the worft principle of my
conduct as, in all cafes, more probable than any
other.   What muft the inhabitants of Birmingham, who juftly refpected Mr. Madan more than
any other clergyman in the town, think of the Diffenters in general, and of myfelf in particular, when
we were defcribed in this manner, and when the account was introduced with fuch uncommon folemnity,

p. 2, as given " from the fettled principles of his
" heart, as he hoped for mercy from the God of
" truth ?"

To what can we compare this conduct of the
clergy, but (to adopt that metaphor of mine which
has been fo much carped at, and mifreprefented,)
laying gunpowder, not grain by grain, but by hand-
fuls, in that magazine which exploded on the 14th
of July? For what outrage muft not many of the
common people, who read none of my writings, but
heard them fpoken of by the clergy as highly dangerous, and unfit to be read by them, have been
prepared, when for years together they heard the
Unitarian Diffenters in general, and myfelf in particular, pointed at as the enemies of their country,
ready on the firft opportunity to overturn the government under which we lived, and even to embrue
our hands in the blood of our fovereign? Could
they help concluding that the perfons who defcribed
us in this manner wifhed to have us deftroyed, that
it was even meritorious to deftroy us; and when in
any cafe the *end* is thought to be juft in itfelf, the
propriety of the *means* will be lefs attended to? If
violence be employed to gain any end, there are
thoufands in all parts of this country ready to join in
it, without any regard to the end, but merely for
the fake of mifchief and plunder. It is an army
ready to act on the fide of any whom they think
they can ferve with impunity to themfelves.

3   It

It is, therefore, in this fenfe, though in this only, that I accufe the clergy of Birmingham, and efpecially Mr. Madan, as having been the promoters of the riot; and if it fhould terminate in that deftruction with which I am ftill threatened, I fhall charge them with being the caufe of my death.

The methods that were taken to excite the populace of Birmingham againft the Diffenters, previous to the riot, were various, and but too fuccefsful. Among others, I fhall only mention one, as a fpecimen of ingenuity as well as of the malignant party fpirit, which prevailed in the place, while nothing was done by us but what was calculated to allay it. The following paper was much circulated in Birmingham two years before the riot.

" To thofe factious and republican fpirits, who " are at this time infidioufly endeavouring to un- " dermine the grand bulwark of our moft excellent " conftitution, a plate of their *Coat of Arms* is de- " dicated, by a friend to *church and king*.

" *Blazoning of the Diffenters Coat of Arms*.

" Field fable. A diffenting magiftrate fits with " a table before him, holding in his right hand a " pen, in his left hand a ferpent. On his fhoulder " fits a toad dictating to him. Over his head is a " pair of fcales broken, Or within, and argent. One

" hornet

" hornet and fix wafps, reprefenting the feven united
" congregations. Creft, the head of Janus, party
" per pale, fable, and or, before a thorn and a thiftle,
" iffuing proper. Motto. *To him we owe our power.*

" *Supporters.*"

" Fraud reprefented with the body of a woman,
" with a double face young and old, prefenting the
" moft fafcinating to the unwary objects her prey.
" Her attributes are an angle rod, with a fifh caught,
" and in her left a ferpent. She is always defcribed
" with the legs and claws of a vulture, and the tail
" of a fcorpion. Deceit is reprefented by an elder-
" ly matron gayly dreffed, holds a mafk before her
" face, and on her breaft two hearts, black and red,
" denoting the neceffity of an external appearance
" to cover the defigns of a corrupt mind."

N. B. There is fome incorrectnefs in this copy;
but I have not feen any other.

SECTION V.

*Circumftances previous to the Riot, and more imme-
diately connected with the Caufe of it.*

SEVERAL circumftances, previous to
the riot, fhow that fome fuch thing was expected by the High Church party, while no Diffenter, though expofed to the mifchief, apprehended
any fuch matter. A clergyman dining at the An-
chor, at Worcefter, July 13, faid that, " If there was
" any

" any dinner at Birmingham the next day, fome-
" thing would fhew itfelf at night, and that it was
" then brewing." A perfon of Birmingham faid,]
" there will be the devil to pay at the Hotel to
" day. There are about two hundred Prefbyte-
" rians met there, but we are ready for them, and
" fhall be their mafters yet."

Mr. Burn reprefents the dinner at the Hotel, and
the hand-bill, publifhed a few days before, as the true
caufes of the riot. " The promoters of the dinner,"
he fays, p. 51, " were chiefly Diffenters; and as the
" defign of that meeting was ftrongly fufpected,
" thofe gentlemen became the object of popular re-
" fentment." But that both the dinner and the hand-
bill, were the mere pretences for the violences that
were committed, is evident from the cry of the
time, which had no relation to the dinner. Had the
fufferers been obnoxious as having been concerned
in the dinner, thofe of the church of England, who
joined in it, would have been doubly fo, as men who
had deferted their friends, and joined their enemies;
but no member of the eftablifhment, though prefent
at the dinner, fuffered at all; and the only fufferers
were that very defcription of men againft whom the
popular refentment had been excited feveral years
before, viz. the Unitarian Diffenters in general, and
myfelf in particular, whether we were prefent at the
dinner, or concerned in promoting it, or not.

Of

Of the principal fufferers, who were ten in all, only three were at the dinner, and their houfes were the laft that were deftroyed. On thefe ftriking facts no comment favourable to Mr. Burn's hypothefis can be made.

Mr. Burn fays, p. 52, that " the effect which the " hand-bill might produce on the lower orders, " was very juftly and ferioufly apprehended." Now it is to the laft degree improbable that any ferious effect was ever apprehended from it. All that it invited to was the celebration of the French Revolution; yet he ftrangely fays, p. 47, " The object of it " was, in the apprehenfion of the populace, nothing " lefs than the immediate overthrow both of Church " and State." This famous hand-bill is ftill extant, and has been publifhed a thoufand times more by the enemies of the Diffenters than by their friends; and if it had really been calculated to do much mifchief, it muft have appeared long before this time.

At any time before the riot it was exceedingly difficult for any Diffenter to procure a copy of the hand-bill, while it was circulated with great induftry among church people. If the magiftrates really apprehended a riot from the effects, either of the hand-bill, which few Diffenters had feen, or from the dinner, which, however, few propofed to attend, why did they not prepare to oppofe it by fwearing more

conftables,

conftables, and ufing other precautions directed in the Riot Act ?

If the governors of this country had really thought this hand-bill capable of doing any harm, would they not have fent foldiers to Birmingham, to be in readinefs for the occafion ? A copy of the hand-bill was in the fecretary of ftate's office three days before the dinner, and that was time enough for the purpofe. Would it have been publifhed at full length in the Gazette? Or would Mr. Dundas have recited it in the Houfe of Commons? This publication, and many other publications of it, clearly fhews that no body ever apprehended any danger from it, and that the ftir that was made about it was only to throw an odium upon Diffenters, who were repreprefented as the authors of it.

A letter of Dr. Tatham's, in which the anniverfary of the French Revolution was called an *illegal. and unconftitutional act*, and which was eagerly circulated in Birmingham before the dinner, contributed much more to the riot than this hand-bill.

The fufpicion of the fabrication of this hand-bill has now generally fallen upon the perfon alluded to by Mr. Burn and Mr. Dundas. It is well known to all our friends that I had no connexion with that perfon, and that he was leaft of all likely to be governed

'verned by my advice. This, however, I will fay for
him, that though he thought freely on the fubjects
of government and religion, he was as far from any
thing properly feditious as Mr. Burn himfelf. I believe him to be an honeft and well meaning man,
though I never thought him the moft prudent. It
is to the difgrace of this country that fuch a perfon
was under the neceffity of leaving it.

At the time of my writing the Appeal, I had not
the leaft fufpicion of this perfon being the author
of the hand-bill, and, therefore, thought it as probable that it might be written by fome of the High
Church party, for the ufe that they actually made of
it, as by the Diffenters who fuffered in confequence
of it. And certainly, they who forged letters for the
purpofe of exciting the rioters to do us mifchief,
were *capable* of doing *this* with the fame view. The
one was not more wicked than the other. Admitting, however, that a Diffenter wrote this celebrated hand-bill, and that it was as heinous a thing
as our enemies reprefent it; it was only the work of
one man, for whofe conduct no other perfon is re-
fponfible. No perfon concerned in the dinner had
the leaft knowledge or fufpicion of it at the time, as
appears by their public advertifement.

Depending upon fuch accounts as were given me,
with refpect to tranfactions at which I could not be
prefent myfelf, I had faid that, befides the dinner at
the

the Hotel, there were other dinners on that day, of perſons of better condition, who did not riſe ſo ſoon, or ſo ſober, as thoſe who celebrated the French Revolution, and that the riot commenced at the breaking up of theſe companies. " This," ſays Mr. Burn, p. 58, " is, to ſay the leaſt, an idle fiction." " The " magiſtrates," he ſays, 59, " dined at one of our " inns on that day, and for the expreſs purpoſe of be- " ing on the ſpot, in caſe their interference ſhould " be found neceſſary, in order to keep the peace."

Now I do not find, on farther inquiry, that there was more than one ſuch dinner as I have deſcribed, viz. of *perſons of better condition*, the reſt being of the lower orders, though not all of the loweſt, whoſe aſſembling, whoſe horrid execrations, and whoſe intoxication, Mr. Burn cannot deny. But that the other dinner, though attended by the magiſtrates, anſwers ſufficiently to my deſcription, there is evidence enough.

The High Church party who dined at the Swan tavern in Bull-ſtreet, if I be not miſinformed, uſed the moſt horrid execrations, drank damnation to the Preſbyterians, and propheſied what dreadful havoc would be made. A perſon who heard this perſuaded thoſe who dined at the Hotel to diſperſe; and then returning to the company at the Swan, ſaid, " Gentle- " men, your ſport is ſpoiled, the company is breaking " up;" and this ſeemed to mortify them exceedingly.

That

That the magistrates themselves, and no doubt other persons of their party, were either intoxicated, or worse, at the breaking up of this meeting, the facts I shall presently relate abundantly prove. If they seriously meant to *keep the peace*, their measures, were very ill laid, and certainly had no success. To pretend that they feared a riot from the friends of the revolution dinner is too absurd to be alleged. They were not of that class of people; and there was no dinner, or preparations for any dinner, except at the hotel.

Among other circumstances that indicated a design in the High Church party to promote a riot, I mentioned a report of some shops being shut up, that the workmen might be at liberty for that purpose. Of this Mr. Burn says, p. 51, " If " any instance of the kind does really exist, it has " eluded our research." He adds, that " many " churchmen took pains to keep their men in the " shops." Of this I have no doubt. The generality of the Church people in Birmingham were far from favouring the rioters, nor have I ever given that idea of them. The promoters of the riot were a few, but certainly all of them churchmen.

The state of the town of Birmingham is still such that it is not easy to procure positive evidence against any rioter, or favourer of the riot; nor can it be deemed extraordinary that I should in some

E inftances

inftances have been mifled by the exaggerated reports of the time, when I wrote my Appeal. Whether, however, I wrote without *some* authority, let
the reader judge from the following circumftances.
Mr. Ruffel remonftrating with one of the rioters at
his own houfe, he faid, " What would you have us
" do ? We cannot work, for our mafters turned us
" out of the fhop on Thurfday morning, and de-
" clared we fhould not enter it again all the week."
The name of the man was Patric, and he faid his
mafter was a buckle-maker.

It is poffible alfo, that the Diffenters might get
the idea of the perfons excluded from the fhops being
more numerous than they were, from the following
circumftance, viz. that a little after nine o'clock, on
the 14th of July, Mr. Carles, after faying to the rioters, " Come, my boys, huzza," added, " if they turn
" you out of work, I will employ you." What he
meant by that language he beft knows himfelf. It
is, I own, more probable that his meaning was, that
if the Diffenters fhould turn any perfons out of their
fhops for having been concerned in the riot, he
would endeavour to find employment for them.

That too many, though far from the majority of
the church people in Birmingham, favoured the
riot, and did as much to promote it as the fhutting
up their fhops, though they might not do that fpecific thing, is fufficiently evident; and therefore *this*
could

could not of itself appear improbable; and that great numbers of the common manufacturers were well enough predifpofed for the riot is evident from the following circumftance. On the 13th of July a churchman talking about the intended dinner, faid, " I have got fifty hands in my fhop, and if I was to " go to them to-morrow, and fay, My lads, your " church and king are in danger, they would turn " out every man of them, and break every window " in the hotel."

Another circumftance that I fhall mention is one that I own I do not perfectly underftand; but as it has been mentioned as fome evidence that even Mr. Curtis himfelf expected a riot, that in it re-courfe would be had to fire, and that he did not wifh fuch fire to be foon extinguifhed, I fhall relate it, that Mr. Curtis may have an opportunity of ex-culpating himfelf.

The keys of the fire engine were taken by him out of the cuftody of the perfon who ufually kept them, and delivered to a Mr. Brooke, a clerk in his own church, who, when he was applied to for them, as the rioters were demolifhing the old meeting, faid, that he had orders to let nobody have them. At length, however, an order was procured from the churchwarden, who expreffed much furprife that this fhould be neceffary; when Mr. Brooke (find-ing that he could not refufe them) faid, " If you

E 2   " muft

" muſt have them, you ſhall, but they will do you
" no good;" which was actually the caſe, the engine not being ſuffered to play on any but the
neighbouring houſes.

What makes this ſtory the more extraordinary
is, that it appears from Mr. Curtis's own account
that, in the courſe of that night, the clerk went
to the veſtry, and there wrote a letter, which
he ſent by a ſpecial meſſenger to Mr. Curtis,
to inform him that, at the order of the churchwarden, he had delivered the keys of the engine.
Does not this look like anxiety to make an apology
for having done what he knew would not be pleaſing to his ſuperior? It behoves Mr. Curtis to explain this extraordinary conduct with reſpect to the
fire engine, with which it does not appear that he
had any thing to do.

That ſomething was concerted by the High
Church with reſpect to the Diſſenters previous to
the dinner is evident from this circumſtance, that
a Diſſenter, but not known to be one by Mr. J.
Green, a buſy and not very diſcreet man, going to
him about buſineſs the day before the riot, received
for anſwer, " I have not time to ſettle your account
" now, the damned Preſbyterians give me ſo much
" trouble. There are gentlemen now at my houſe
" conſulting what is to be done with them."

SECTION

SECTION VI.

Circumstances attending the Commencement of the Riot.

I SHALL now proceed to relate some circumstances which immediately preceded, and accompanied the riot, at its first breaking out; and I think they will sufficiently prove not only that there was no exertion on the part of the magistrates, or any of the principal church people in the town, to prevent the riot; but that, not then knowing how far it would proceed, many of them were well-wishers to it. I may, no doubt, be deceived; but all the particulars that I shall mention have been voluntarily declared upon oath, and the reporters are now ready to attest them in any court of judicature, whenever they are called upon to do it. However, let our enemies have an opportunity of vindicating themselves: they have the same access to the Public that I have, and will have a much more favourable hearing.

When the company were going to the hotel, and the mob were throwing at them, the justices, who were present, took no notice of it, and did not endeavour to disperse them. Between seven and eight o'clock Mr. Carles and Dr. Spencer were in the midst of the mob, in passing from the hotel to-

E 3

wards Bull-ftreet, and feemed to encourage them by bowing and nodding to them. When fome of the mob came out of the hotel, where they had been to look for thofe who had dined there, one of the magiftrates, ftanding upon the fteps, took off his hat, waved it round his head, and huzza'd with them, but made no attempt to check them for a quarter of an hour, while the witnefs was with them. When one of them was haranguing the mob on the fteps of the hotel, the other ftood behind him, laughing heartily, and hiding his face with his hat.

When the windows of the hotel were nearly demolifhed, one of the juftices cried, " Well done, my " lads, well done, my lads. We will do what we " can for you; and if I had it in my power I would " make you all drunk." A little after nine he faid to the mob, " Do no mifchief, or murder; and if " you are taken up in a right caufe, and brought " before us, we will acquit you:" and he fhook hands with feveral of them. One of the rioters afked the juftices, if they would give them leave to fhake a little powder out of Dr. Prieftley's wig: and to this they made no anfwer, but laughed, took off their hats, waved them three times, and huzza'd. One of them faid, again " You are all hearty fel- " lows; if I had it in my power I would make you " all drunk." A boy faying, " Damn them, feize " all the Prefbyterians," one of them put his hand

on

on the boy's head, and faid, " Well done, my hearty " chicken: thou art a damned good cock;" and laughed. The mob laughed with him, and huzza'd, crying, *Spencer for ever.*

The moſt ſerious charge againſt one of the ma-giſtrates is the following: while the rioters were throwing at the windows of the hotel, he faid, " My " friends, do not revenge yourſelves upon this man, " who gets his living by making dinners for gen-" tlemen. If you wiſh to be revenged upon *them*, " go to their meetings." On this the mob cried, " To the new meeting; the juſtice will protect us." They were ſo near him, that he muſt have heard them. A young man of my congregation told me before I left my houſe, that he was ſtanding cloſe by one of the magiſtrates when the rioters mentioned going to the new meeting, and that he ſaid nothing to reſtrain them,

While the ſame magiſtrate was walking up Bull-ſtreet ſome of the rioters followed him, and among them was a woman, who cried, " Damn all the " Preſbyterians in the town;" but at this the ma-giſtrate only laughed. Being incommoded by the crowd, one of the juſtices bid them not follow him. On this they cried, " Where muſt we go?" He an-ſwered, " Go down to the meeting to the others." They then went to the new meeting, and joined thoſe who were deſtroying it. He alſo ſaid to them

at the fame time, " Do no other mifchief than pul-
" ling down the meetings, and I will ftand your
" friend as far as lies in my power." Afterwards,
when one of the rioters, who was demolifhing the
new meeting, was told that he would be hanged for
it, he faid, " No; for juftice Carles fent us down
" hither."

    " It is but juftice," fays Mr. Burn, p. 121, " to
" Mr. Brooke, at that time under fheriff, acting
" with the magiftrates, and fince deputed by the
" hundred as their fole folicitor on the trials, to ob-
" ferve, that no individual appears to have rifked
" more by his perfonal exertions during the riots
" than himfelf." I have no objection to admitting
this with refpect to Mr. Brooke, or any other perfon, after the riot had proceeded farther than they
wifhed, in confequence of which they might think
they had particular reafon to be apprehenfive for
themfelves; but the queftion is, how they behaved
at the commencement of the riot; and at that time
there is clear evidence of feveral perfons having
given them too much encouragement.

    The mob being affembled before Mr. Brooke's
houfe, which is very near the hotel, a perfon in a
green coat addreffed them in a low voice, defiring
them to go from thence, and faying, that if they
would go to the new meeting, he would order a
aogfhead of ale for them when they came back. They
afking

aſking him for ſomething in hand, he appeared to give them money, having put his hand into his pocket. Of this circumſtance there are two witneſſes. But previous to this he aſked a young man who was in the crowd, whether he thought they knew him. He then held up his arm, and pointed towards the new meeting, and they immediately cried, " To the new meeting;" whither they went, and in five minutes few were left behind. Before this, when the mob were breaking the windows of the hotel, Mr. Brooke came out of his houſe, and Mrs. Brooke being apprehenſive of ſome miſchief to him, the rioters ſaid, " We will not hurt Mr. Brooke; " we will pull down any houſe Mr. Brooke has a " mind." This, however, they might have ſaid with reſpect to a perſon with whom they had had no previous communication.

SECTION VII.

Of the Conduct of the Magiſtrates, and others, after the Commencement of the Riot.

THE facts related in the preceding ſection ſufficiently prove that there was no diſpoſition in the magiſtrates, or the high church party in general, to check, but rather to promote, the riot at its commencement. Other facts as clearly prove that this diſpoſition continued till the deſtruction of both

the

the meeting houfes, and of every thing belonging to me. When the rioters proceeded to attack the houfes of Mr. Ryland and Mr. Taylor, there is no doubt that the greateft enemies of the Diffenters were alarmed, and wifhed to fupprefs the rioters; but having encouraged them before, they were at a lofs how to proceed, and at all events were determined not to have recourfe to *fire-arms*, though there was no doubt but that *this* would have been effectual in any period of the bufinefs. After the pofitive encouragement given to the rioters, the reafon of this conduct was evident.

Several of the circumftances that I fhall now mention alfo clearly fhew that the proper object of the riot was *the Diffenters*, and nothing relating to the dinner, or the French revolution. The handbill, alfo, which had no relation but to the French revolution, would have been as much forgotten as the dinner, had it not been for the idea of its being written by myfelf or fome other Diffenter. Thofe things had fufficiently anfwered their purpofe, and the mob proceeded on its natural and original principle, the bigotry of the church people againft the Diffenters. In what follows I fhall firft relate the circumftances that refpect the conduct of the magiftrates, then that of the clergy, and afterwards that of other perfons.

About five o'clock in the morning of the 15th, when the rioters were deftroying my houfe, one of
the

the magiſtrates rode up to it, raiſed his arm, and beckoning to them, ſaid, " Come hither, my good " hearty boys." When they were gathered round him, he bade them take off their hats, and huzza, which they did, and he did the ſame ſeveral times. He then ſaid, " I commend you for what you have " done, and will protect you for it. No fire ; re- " turn to your work." They huzza'd, and when he was gone, they returned to the houſe, and continued to demoliſh it, crying, as my ſon, who heard them, ſaid, " Spencer for ever." The reaſon he gave why he would not have them hurt the houſe was, that it belonged to Mr. Lloyd, a quaker. It had lately belonged to him, but had been ſold to Mr. William Humphrys.

Between nine and ten the ſame day the other magiſtrate coming along *Dale End* in a chaiſe, and the people gathering round him, he took off his hat, waved it out of the window, and cried, " *Church* " *and King for ever, my lads.* Be true to your " cauſe; ſtick to your cauſe. Be of my determi- " nation, to loſe the laſt drop of blood in your bo- " dies: it is my determination to loſe the laſt drop " of mine. Do not leave theſe Preſbyterian dogs " a place ſtanding." He then huzza'd again, cry- ing, *Church and King*, and the mob did the ſame. At two o'clock, however, on the ſame day, when Mr. Ryland's houſe was burning, he ſaid to the rioters, " You have gone paſt what you were or- " dered."

" dered." Both the magiſtrates ſaw a man ſeized for carrying off three bottles from Mr. Ryland's houſe without taking any notice of it; and the man was ſet at liberty.

That the rioters took it for granted that the magiſtrates favoured them there can be no doubt; though it is natural to ſuppoſe that, liking the buſineſs, they would make the moſt of every circumſtance of that kind. Some of the rioters being taken into cuſtody at Hay-hall, the reſidence of Mr. Smith, others came, as they ſaid, by order of Mr. Carles, to demand their releaſe, ſaying they did not come to do any damage to the houſe.

At my houſe the rioters ſaid, " The juſtices " will protect us; we ſhall not be hurt; we may do " what we pleaſe, but not burn the houſe." They repeatedly ſaid in the courſe of that night, " We " wiſh we had the doctor locked up in one of the " rooms, we would burn him alive; or if he had " come to the hotel, we would have killed him."

Mr. Carpenter, of Woodrow, at ſome diſtance from Birmingham, meeting a party of the rioters who did not know him, ſaid they were going to burn his houſe by orders from juſtice Carles. On his remonſtrating to them, they perſiſted in ſaying they had juſtice Carles's orders for it, and down it ſhould come. On Mr. Carpenter applying to Mr.
Carles

Carles afterwards for the affiftance of the foldiers, he infulted him, by afking him if he ever knew an honeft Prefbyterian on the Lickey ? his houfe being on a hill fo called. He was not only refufed the foldiers for whom he applied, but could not obtain leave to feize any of the rioters without them.

That the rioters had been led, by fome means or other, to imagine that what they did was agreeable to government, is as evident as that they thought they were pleafing the magiftrates. Soon after the riot, one man was heard to fay to another, " Well, " if any body is hanged for it, the king may fight " for himfelf another time : for I am fure nobody " elfe will fight for him." ,At the time that the rioters were demolifhing the old meeting, one of them faid to another, " This is not right;" but the other replied, " Nay, but the king has fent us, and " if we do not do it, he will foon lofe his crown." On the Saturday, when the rioters were hunting fome ducks, and were talking of the foldiers coming, one of them faid, " What if they do, they will " not hurt us, as we have been fighting on their " fide. The juftices are for us. Did you not fee " how they laughed ?"

That the magiftrates were determined not to have recourfe to fire arms, though this appeared to be the only effectual method of quelling the mob, was evident from the beginning to the end of the bufi-

nefs ;

nefs; and that they fhould not have done this, if they had been confcious to themfelves that they had given no encouragement to the rioters, I cannot well conceive.

In the afternoon of the fifteenth, Capt. Maxwell propofed to Mr. Carles to collect all the foldiers in the town, and head them himfelf, faying he had no doubt but that he fhould be able to put a fpeedy ftop to the riot; but Mr. Carles turned from him with ftrong marks of difapprobation in his countenance. Mr. Ruffel, as early in the bufinefs as poffible, applied to Mr. Carles to fend for a military force to quell the mob, and likewife propofed to head any number of men furnifhed with fire arms. He wrote to him to defire that twenty men might be fent to affift in the defence of Mr. Humphrys's houfe. But no requeft of this kind was ever liftened to, and at twelve o'clock on Saturday he received a note from Mr. Carles, informing him that both himfelf and Dr. Spencer were determined upon pacific meafures. Mr. Hutton's fervant having pricked one of the rioters with a bayonet, and the party afterwards coming before the juftices, Mr. Carles remarked, and Dr. Spencer acquiefced in it, that he had no right to ufe arms, except the other perfon had been armed in the fame manner.

That any of the *clergy* of Birmingham had the leaft concern in the riot, or were at all well-wifhers

to

to it, I was far from having any idea at the time of writing my Appeal, though Mr. Burn has more than infinuated this. I only thought they had contributed to raife the fpirit which produced the riot. Circumftances have fince occurred which, I own, do lead me to think that Mr. Curtis was not wholly innocent. At leaft, whatever might be his meaning, his behaviour contributed not a little to encourage the rioters. One circumftance I mentioned in a preceding fection, and two others I fhall recite here.

Being with a party of the rioters oppofite to St. Martin's church, he thanked them for what they had done in protecting the church and the king. He then took off his hat, joined in three huzzas, and wifhed them to follow him, which they did.

On Friday, as the mob were returning from the deftruction of Mr. Ryland's houfe, Mr. Curtis harangued them at the top of Temple Street, faying, " We thank you, my brave fellows, for the " zeal you have fhown for the church and the king. " You have now fufficiently punifhed your enemies, " and we beg you will difperfe, and go peaceably " about your bufinefs." Being thanked for what they had done, they might think that they could not be blamed for doing a little more.

Mr. Curtis, willing to appear friendly to the Dif-

fenters,

fenters, during the riot, now fays in Mr. Burn's
pamphlet, p. 90, " During the riots my houfe
" at Solyhull was open to a Diffenter and his
" family, and the children of another family were
" literally clothed by Mrs. Curtis." That Mr.
Curtis had a real good will to many individuals
among the Diffenters, I have no doubt, and that he
wifhed the deftruction of any of us I do not believe.

But there was little to boaft of in his conduct in
the cafe to which he refers. The Diffenter that he
received into his houfe was old Mr. Smith of Hay
Hall, a man univerfally refpected, and who, I believe, has no enemy; fo that he ran no rifk in receiving him. Confcious, however, that he himfelf
was not very popular in his parifh, and that many
perfons might wifh for a pretence to do him mifchief, at Mr. Curtis's own requeft, Mr. Smith removed to the houfe of Mr. Eyre, another clergyman
of the place, who was ready to run all rifques in
protecting him. There, and not at Mr. Curtis's,
Mr. Smith flept; and the next day, to the great
concern of Mr. Eyre, Mr. Smith was induced, from
the alarm of the neighbours, to remove.

As to Mrs. Curtis literally clothing the children of
a family of Diffenters, I have no doubt of her readinefs to do it in a cafe of real charity. But it will
not be fuppofed that, in *this* cafe, fhe could look
for

for no recompenfe except *at the refurrection of the juft*, when it is known that thefe children were thofe of Mr. Taylor. They had gone out during the riot with the maid fervant who attended them, and were brought to the houfe of two ladies, who lived not far from Solyhull. Thefe ladies, being un-married, had no change of clothes for children, and therefore they fent to Mrs. Curtis to borrow fome while their own were wafhing, and fhe fupplied them. It would have been very extraordinary, in-deed, if fhe, or any other perfon, who had chil-dren's clothes in the houfe, had refufed fuch a re-queft as this.

When the rioters were demolifhing the new meet-ing, another of the clergy is faid to have encouraged them by faying, " Well done, my lads. When you " have done here, go and pull down their houfes " too."

Mr. Burn fays, p. 94, " Mr. Lawrence (a cler-" gyman in Birmingham) and another gentleman " exerted their utmoft endeavours to fave the Doc-" tor's laboratory." That Mr. Lawrence was no rioter, and did not himfelf affift in the deftruction of my property, I readily acknowledge. But it does not appear that he took any pains to reftrain the rioters when they were demolifhing the houfe. On the contrary, they confidered him as their friend. Mr. Lawrence was alfo obferved to be read-ing feveral of my MS. papers, and to put them

F   into

into his pocket. What he did with them afterwards does not appear. He muſt have known that, being my property, he ought to have returned them to me, or to my friends. If they were letters, he ought not, as a man of honour, to have read them at all.

In what light the rioters conſidered Mr. Lawrence, may appear from the following circumſtance. When he went to the houſe the ſecond time, in the morning of the fifteenth, the rioters at my houſe repeatedly ſaid that Mr. Lawrence had been there, that they were ſure he thought they were doing right, for he laughed at them, and they would be damned if they would not go on. Some of them ſhook him by the hand, crying out, " The curate " of the new church. By God. By God." They continued to ſurround him, and to ſhake him by the hand near half an hour, while he only deſired them to looſe him, but expreſſed no diſapprobation of their conduct.

At the ſame time that, in my own vindication, I mention theſe particulars of the conduct of ſome of the clergy of Birmingham, with the greateſt ſatisfaction I do juſtice to Mr. Darwell, who was indefatigable in his exertions in favour of Mr. Jukes, and I believe of other Diſſenters.

That the rioters conſidered the clergy as being favourable to them, may eaſily be inferred from every circumſtance,

circumſtance, which ſhewed that the Diſſenters, as ſuch, were the objeсt of their malice. When Mr. Ryland's houſe was burning one of the magiſtrates, pointing to the church, ſaid, " You ſee your " church, you have done your beſt for it. Do not " do any more. We are much obliged to you; " you ſee your ſtrength," &c. &c. Mr. Carles ſaid to Mr. W. Ryland, and two other Diſſenters who were following him in the ſtreet, on the fifteenth, that they muſt not come after him, for as they were known to be Diſſenters, it would only irritate the mob, and make them more violent; but when he came to the inn where Mr. Carles had promiſed to meet him, he found the door ſhut againſt him.

That other perſons beſides the magiſtrates and the clergy were favourable to the rioters, and approved of much of what they did, appeared from ſeveral circumſtances. On the fifteenth, about noon, Mr. J. Green ſaid, " We are ſatisfied with what is " done, and now I wiſh they would give over, for " they have done enough." On the ſame day the gentleman in he green coat, one inſtance of whoſe conduсt has been mentioned before, being at the houſe of Mr. Ryland, pulled off his hat, and huzzaed to the rioters, ſaying, " Gentlemen, I applaud you for what " you have done, but ſtop here. This is private " property. Though theſe are the men who wiſh to " overturn the conſtitution, we have other means of

" redreſs."

" redrefs." The mob, however, continued to de-ftroy the houfe.

At Sparkbrook turnpike three gentlemen being on horfeback, were converfing very familiarly with the rioters, while my houfe was burning; when one of them faid aloud, " My lads, you fee your power; " you fee that if any attempt is made againft the " government of this country, you have it in your " power to quafh it."

That fome perfons above the condition of the common rioters were deeply concerned in the bufi-nefs, appeared from many circumftances, befides thofe that are mentioned in my Appeal. The forged letter, which was read at my houfe, in order to in-ftigate the mob to do me mifchief, is alone a proof of this, and a copy of it will appear in my Appendix, No. V. When I was at Warwick, at the time of the affizes, I received a fummons from our opponents, the hand writing of which could not be diftin-guifhed from that of this forged letter. I have no doubt myfelf who the writer of this forged letter was, though no legal proof can be given of it.

Another forged letter was read at Mr. Ruffell's houfe, a copy of which could not be procured, but the following account of it is given upon oath. Two men were on horfeback while the houfe was burn-

ing,

ing, and one of them read a paper, which he declared he had found in the houſe, purporting that
" the Preſbyterians intended to riſe, to burn down
" the church, blow up the parliament, cut off the
" king's head, and aboliſh all taxes." The paper
was ſigned *E. Jefferies*, No. 24, *St. Thomas's Street*,
London. The 16th of Auguſt, they ſaid was the
time fixed for the inſurrection. The perſon who
read the paper ſaid, " Damn it, you ſee they
" would deſtroy us. It is right that we ſhould
" cruſh them in time."

They had alſo another letter, which one of the
perſons preſent ſaid was to know how many forces
Mr. Ruſſel could collect by the tenth, and that they
ſhould be ready to join in concert with their friends
in Scotland. This letter was ſaid to be ſigned by
the ſteward of the Revolution ſociety. He that
had this letter ſaid, " Damn them, we will deſtroy
" every Preſbyterian's houſe in England." A
ſtranger, who was preſent, ſaying that ſome of the
rioters would be hanged for what they were doing,
one of them anſwered, " How can they hang us,
" when the juſtices ſet us agait ?" Being aſked
what juſtices, he ſaid, " Maſter Carles and Maſter
" Spencer, and I muſt do the juſtices' work, and by
" God I will go to the pay table to night, for I
" have worked damned hard. Wont you, Tom ?"
Tom anſwered, " And by God will I." The per-

fon who read one of thefe forged letters was fo defcribed as to be well known in Birmingham.

The following circumftances alfo fhew that there
were promoters of the riot among perfons of better
condition, and that they difguifed themfelves for the
purpofe. While the New Meeting was deftroying,
a perfon was there who had the appearance of a
gentleman, his linen being fine, and with ruffles
tucked up. He was very anxious to have the meeting-houfe confumed, and ftood two hours viewing it.
The fame perfon was feen at Mr. Ruffell's, but differently dreffed, and on horfeback.

After the rioters had entered the Old Meeting, a
perfon was feen in the gallery, who had the appearance of a gentleman, but who endeavoured to
difguife himfelf with a great coat, the cape of
which he buttoned up as high as he could, and his
hat was brought down very low. Three or four
perfons came up to him, and converfed with him in
whifpers. One of the rioters, knowing the witnefs,
aimed a blow at him, fo that he left them.

At Mofely Hall alfo a perfon was feen above the
lower clafs with a riding coat buttoned up to his chin,
and which covered a great part of his head and face.
He went about in a deliberate manner, giving orders, which were obeyed. There were feveral perfons

fons drefſed like gentlemen at Mr. Humphrys's, but eſpecially at Mr. Ruffel's, encouraging the rioters, laughing at them, and ſaying they ſerved the Preſbyterians right, for they deſerved it. The laſt circumſtance that I ſhall mention with this view is, that a lady, in a mixed company, unwarily ſaid, " I very often laugh to think what a figure our " three dons would cut, one in a waggoner's frock, " another with his face blacked, and the other with " his hair cropped." But a hint being given that a Diſſenter was in the company, ſhe proceeded no farther.

SECTION VIII.

Circumſtances ſubſequent to the Riot.

HAVING conſidered what paſſed previous to the riot, and during the continuance of it, as a proof that it originated in the bigotry of the High Church people againſt the Diſſenters, I proceed to what paſſed ſubſequent to it; and it will ſufficiently appear that the ſame malignant ſpirit continued to actuate many perſons in Birmingham, in its vicinity, and indeed through the whole kingdom; ſo that the news of it was far from being ſo diſpleaſing as it ought to have been.

The conduct of the magiſtrates, which has been ſhewn to have been ſo criminally remiſs, to ſpeak in

the

the moſt favourable manner, could not but have been known to the generality of the people of Birmingham, and yet at a public town's meeting, " certainly," ſays Mr. Burn, p. 80, " one of the " moſt numerous, unanimous, and" as he adds, " reſpectable, ever convened at Birmingham, called " for the expreſs purpoſe of thanking our magiſ- " trates, there did not appear any one fact that " would juſtify them in withholding their warmeſt " acknowledgments from thoſe gentlemen."

That any public meeting ſhould be called to thank perſons whoſe conduct was ſo culpable, as that of Mr. Carles and Dr. Spencer, involved all concerned in that meeting (though I believe a ſmall part of the inhabitants of Birmingham) provided they were acquainted with the circumſtances above mentioned, in the guilt of the riot. Mr. Burn himſelf, by joining in this approbation, voluntarily takes his ſhare in this guilt; and I ſhould not otherwiſe have thought of charging him with it.

A proof of bigotry, and of an approbation of the riot, ſimilar to that which is implied in the thanks to the magiſtrates, is the reward that was given to Mr. Brooke, in making him ſole ſolicitor to the hundred. To this lucrative office he was recommended by lord Alesford, " for the zeal that he had " ſhewn in the cauſe of the Church and King." A club has ſince been formed in Birmingham, intitled,

The

The Church and King Club, of which Mr. Brooke is fecretary.

Mr. Burn would infinuate, p. 67, that my con-duct, in criminating the High Church party in Bir-mingham, is condemned by thofe Diffenters who in a public advertifement thanked thofe members of the eftablifhment who had exerted themfelves in their favour. As many of them certainly did fo, thofe thanks were well deferved, and proper. " But " from this," Mr. Burn fays, p. 68, " it fufficiently " appears, that Dr. Prieftley, in his infidious ma- " nagement of this bufinefs, acts as much in oppo- " fition to the avowed opinion of the refpectable body " of Diffenters in Birmingham, as he has done to " the cleareft dictates of candour and truth." This, indeed, is true: becaufe it does not yet appear that I have in any inftance acted contrary to the dictates of candour and truth. I fhould myfelf have cheer-fully concurred in that addrefs of thanks, and I now acknowledge myfelf under much obligation to feve-ral members of the church of England for affifting in faving part of my property, and to Mr. Vale in particular, for materially affifting me in my efcape. But how is this inconfiftent with other members of the church of England being concerned in pro-moting the riot? Becaufe fome, or the majority of any clafs of men, are worthy perfons, does it fol-low that others of them may not be even deferving of the gallows? Such, however, is the reafoning of

Mr.

Mr. Burn, and a specimen of the best of his reasoning in this pamphlet.

That there was a great willingness in some of the principal members of the church of England to criminate *me*, and thereby in some measure to justify the riot, appeared from many circumstances. The following look at least that way. Mr. Carles and Mr. Bond (a justice of peace sent down by government) went on Saturday, July 23, to Mr. Hawkes of the Grove, who had some of my books and papers, and demanded a sight of them. When they had examined many of them, they ordered him to send them to them the next day; but afterwards sent him word, that he did not need to do it.

But the same disposition appeared much more strongly by Mr. Curtis reading some of my MS. papers, and sending them, as he acknowledges himself, to the secretary of state; when seeing what I had already suffered, infinitely more than the sentence of the law, if I had even been convicted of sedition, he ought not to have looked into them. Or if he had, and had thought that they might tend to criminate me, he should have sent them to myself. Such conduct, though, as he was incapable of it, he may have no conception of the thing, would have been magnanimous, and have done him great honour.

The

The fecretary of 'ftate has been guilty of equal meannefs and injuftice in keeping thofe papers from me, whofe property he knows them to be. He alfo knows, though Mr. Curtis was probably ignorant of it, that I am not anfwerable for what other perfons may write to me; and furely I cannot be expected to be the wretch that would divulge any thing fent to me in confidence, to the writer's prejudice.

Though copies of thefe papers, which I underftand are *letters,* written to me by an acquaintance, are circulated among the clergy, I do not find (and what I know of them is from the teftimony of a friend, who was permitted to read them, but not to take a copy) that they contain any thing more than fuch free reflections on adminiftration as perpetually occur in the public newfpapers, and indeed fuch as it is allowable in Englifhmen to write and to publifh, whenever they think the conduct of minifters of ftate to be weak or criminal. I hereby call upon the perfon who detains thefe letters from me to make them as public as he pleafes.

The grofs calumnies againft the Diffenters in general, and myfelf in particular, invented and circulated in juftification of the riot, are another proof of the malignant fpirit that prevailed in the town of Birmingham, and that was the proper caufe of it. Of this kind muft have been the report of my

dining

dining at the Hotel, haranguing the mob out of the window, and drinking *the king's head in a charger*. It is remarkable that this account, which muſt have been a malicious fabrication, was the firſt that was tranſmitted to London, in order to be inſerted in the papers there; and the printer of *The Times* aſſured me, that it was ſent to him by " a re- " ſpectable perſon in the mercantile line in Bir- " mingham."

It was currently reported of young Mr. Hum- phrys, that he had declared his wiſh " to wade up " to the chin in churchmen's blood." This was confidently aſſerted by Mr. William Gem of New Street, Birmingham; and when he was charged with it, he acknowledged the fact, but ſaid he was drunk when he ſaid it. Mr. Humphrys's ſpirited advertiſement in the public papers on the ſubject may be ſeen in my Appendix, No. VI.

Two calumnies of this complexion are retailed by Mr. Burn, p. 113; one that a Diſſenter ſaid, that " kings were expenſive things in this country;" which, however, is certainly very true; but it was interpreted in the worſt ſenſe, or tending to ſedition. The other was, that another Diſſenter, being applied to to pay a church levy, ſaid, " he ſhould not pay " many more." But both theſe ſtories were pro- bably no better founded than that reſpecting Mr. Humphrys, or that of my dining at the Hotel and

, 3   drinking

drinking the king's head in a charger. Mr. Witten was probably the perſon alluded to as having made the laſt of theſe declarations to Mr. Collins the collector. But when he applied to Mr. Burn, he refuſed to name his accuſer, and Mr. Collins denied that Mr. Witten made uſe of the language aſcribed to him, and that what he did ſay was only jocoſely.

Mr. David Blair is underſtood to be the perſon alluded to as having ſaid that kings were expenſive; but though he alſo waited on Mr. Burn, he declined ſaying the converſation referred to him: ſo that in both theſe caſes Mr. Burn himſelf muſt be conſidered as the inventor of the reports. The perſon who was probably Mr. Burn's informer, if he had any, was one who, paſſing by Mr. Blair on the 14th of July, called after him and ſaid, " So you are " going to the Hotel, I find;" and added, " I wiſh " you were all blown up together;" to which nothing at all was replied by Mr. Blair.

What ſtronger proof can be given of this bigotry and malevolence, which appears to have been the proper cauſe of the riot, than its thus driving men to invent and propagate known falſehoods, in order to make the Diſſenters odious? They who thus ſhow that they wiſh to make the Diſſenters appear the proper objects of the riot, may well be ſuſpected of having fomented it.

The

The profane practice of drinking damnation and confusion to the Dissenters is another proof of a violent party spirit, and though instances of it may be unknown, as he says they are, to Mr. Burn, the charge is unquestionably true; and I have no doubt that the practice is still continued and increased. I myself perfectly remember a Dissenter relating to me a conversation he had with Mr. Carles, who said to him, and not long before the riot, " Though in " my cups I do sometimes drink damnation to you, " I would not hurt a hair of your heads." Whatever he might think at the moment, it appears that his good will, or rather his no ill will, to the Dissenters, did not continue long.

When I was at Warwick, at the late assizes, several persons in the Public Hall cried aloud, " Damn " him, there is the cause of all the mischief;" and one man, an attorney in the place, followed me a great way in the public street, then pretty much crowded, and when I was accompanied by the Rev. Mr. Berington, Mr. Galton, and Mr. Keir, three as respectable men as the county can furnish, damning me in the most vociferous manner, and expressing his earnest wish that I had been burned in my house. A toast publicly given and drank with great festivity at the same time was, " May every " revolution dinner be followed by a hot supper." What can be a clearer proof than this, that the

fame

fame fpirit which prompted the riot ftill continues without any abatement, and, if not reftrained, would foon produce another? There were ferious apprehenfions of one while I was at Warwick, and one of the judges, I was informed, was not a little alarmed on that account.

At Birmingham a member of the eftablifhment lately complained to one of my congregation there, of being obliged, when in company, to drink *Church and King*, and damnation to the Prefbyterians.

Mr. Burn calls what I have faid of the clergy having been the firft to calumniate the Diffenters, and to place the conduct of the mob in the moft favourable light, p. 72, " a gratuitous affertion, with-" out even the pretence of evidence." " What evi-" dence," he fays, p. 74, " has Dr. Prieftley to " produce, that they have not done fo," viz. been the firft to preach moderation.

That Mr. Madan preached a very proper fermon after the riot, I have been informed. It was becoming him as a chriftian minifter. But this was not the cafe with Mr. Curtis. One of his conftant hearers was fo much offended at a difcourfe of his, delivered about the fame time, that he declared that " if he had been influenced by it, he " muft have been a ruffian."

Among

Among other inftances of bigotry, and probably that of fome of the clergy at Birmingham, I have been informed that a brick, taken as hot as it could be well handled from the ruins of the new meeting-houfe, was carefully packed up, and fent to the author of feveral works, which fufficiently difcover his high-church principles, and that on a paper which accompanied it, was the word ΑΔΗΛΟΣ, which, being in Greek, muft have been written by a fcholar, and therefore probably a clergyman of the place. I was further informed, that he was advifed to fend this brick to the archbifhop of Canterbury. Whether he did fo or not, I have not heard. Thus have the bigots exulted in the fuccefs of their enterprife. But the ruins of that building will plead againft them with much more energy than all the fermons that could ever have been delivered in it, had it been left ftanding.

I had obferved that the clergy fhould have offered us the ufe of their churches till our meeting-houfes could have been rebuilt. On this Mr. Burn fays, p. 75, 76, " The offer of the churches to the Dif-
" fenters muft have come after my letter to the in-
" habitants of Birmingham, and muft have been
" offered as a compenfation for injuries done to the
" Diffenters, whom they were confcious they never
" injured." It cannot be denied, however, that
we

we were injured, and no doubt by churchmen; for they were not Diffenters who demolifhed the meeting-houfes. And where would have been the impropriety of fome members of the eftablifhment repairing the injuries done to us by others? Would this have been any confeffion of their guilt? This is curious reafoning, indeed. However, the meeting-houfes had been in ruins a week before my letter reached Birmingham. Had the idea then occurred to any member of the eftablifhment? At that time I was far enough from having the leaft idea of any of the clergy promoting the riot, and therefore could not mean that they fhould do any thing as a compenfation for injuries which they had done to us, and their compliance with my propofal would have tended more to exculpate them from any approbation of the riot than any thing elfe that could have been devifed. That I had no very bad opinion of the clergy of Birmingham at the time of the riot, will be evident from a letter which I wrote, to be addreffed to them the day after that to the inhabitants in general. I was, however, diffuaded by my friends from fending it to the printer, they being of opinion that it would not anfwer any good purpofe : but I fhall affert it in my Appendix, No. VII.

SECTION IX.

Observations on the Proceedings in the Courts of Judicature on Occasion of the Riot.

NOTHING, perhaps, shews a more general approbation of the riot, though the approvers were by no means the majority of the church people, than what passed relating to the *trials* which followed. Every possible difficulty was thrown in the way of procuring evidence against the rioters, and every thing was done to screen them from punishment. Also, all that men could do was done to prevent the sufferers from receiving the poor compensation which the law provided for them. It argued some consciousness of guilt, that it was considered as a great point gained by the High Church party when the House of Commons refused to make any inquiry into the cause of the riot, and when the ministry gave no encouragement to the prosecution of the magistrates, and other promoters of the riot. What have innocent persons to dread from the consequences of inquiry into their conduct? Let the reader attend to the following facts, and draw his own inferences from them.

A subscription was made to defray the expence of defending the rioters at the assizes. A letter was drawn up by some of the clergy of Birmingham, addressed to the judges on the circuit, begging them to make a diftinction between thofe of the rioters whofe object was mere plunder, and thofe who acted from a pure but blind motive to ferve their Church and King. One of the clergy, who mentioned this, faid he admired the letter, and had figned it himfelf. Whether it was owing to this meafure, or others of a fimilar tendency, it is a fact, that no perfons have yet been punifhed merely for being concerned in the riot, but becaufe they were the pefts of fociety on other accounts. Confequently, nothing has been done to deter others from committing a riot on the fame account.

Much pains were taken to make Mr. Job Harvey, the evidence againft Hands, or Hammond, (who was condemned for firing the houfe of Mr. Ryland) fay fomething favourable concerning him when he was re-examined before Mr. Bond; and though all that he could fay was, that he had heard fome of the perfons prefent fay, that he was pulling up the boards to let the rioters out from below, and his own proper evidence did not go fo far, Hands was pardoned. Such were not the proceedings with refpect to the riot in London.

Shuker, who had been condemned for firing Mr. Ryland's houfe, abufed J. Elwall, who had been one of the witneffes againft him, in a fhocking manner, ftriking him on the head with his cryer's bell, demo-

lifhing

lifhing his fruit-ftall, &c. &c. by which he loft more than fifty fhillings. When he applied for redrefs to Dr. Spencer and Mr. Carles, it was a long time before they would take his evidence, on the pretence of his not being able to produce a good character. When this was done, in the moft fatisfactory manner, the juftices ftill would not fign any warrant againft Shuker, but contented themfelves with admonifhing him not to infult Elwall any more, on which Shuker behaved in the moft infolent manner, and continued to threaten him.

The fame Elwall was alfo grofsly infulted by one Davis, and others, on account of his evidence; being burned in effigy before his own door, and his family kept in a ftate of alarm feveral nights together; and he was not able to get any warrant from Mr. Carles, to whom he applied for protection. He alfo applied, but in vain, to Dr. Spencer, after Davis had threatened to murder him in a fortnight's time.

Though there is an act of parliament to indemnify thofe who fuffer by riots, and though on other occafions it has been fo conftrued as to afford real relief, fuch was the fpirit that actuated our enemies, and fo fuccefsfully did they exert themfelves, that it has been ineffectual in our cafe. The law was the very fame with refpect to us and the Catholics in 1780; but the iffue of the trials was very different. All

the

the fufferers in London obtained ample redrefs, and
the rioters were rigoroufly punifhed. Money was
even iffued from the treafury for the relief of the fufferers immediately, and long before they could have
received any in the ufual courfe of juftice.

In the very fame year in which the riot was at
Birmingham, there was another at Sheffield, and
Mr. Wilkinfon, a clergyman, was a confiderable
fufferer. But at the fame affizes in which we met
with every difficulty that could be thrown in the way
of our claims, and confequently received a very inadequate compenfation, Mr. Wilkinfon recovered
the whole of his lofs, and had even more offered
him than he chofe to accept; being, as he thought,
more than the real amount of his lofs. In his cafe,
the hundred made no oppofition to his claim, while
in our cafe nothing was fpared to defeat our application for redrefs.

Juftice and equity evidently require that loffes by
riots fhould be moft amply made good, becaufe
double and treble recompence in a pecuniary way
cannot indemnify the fufferers; and becaufe the
great object of all civil government is protection
from lawlefs violence. It was, no doubt, the intention of the law-makers to give ample compenfation; but the act of parliament admitted of much
latitude of interpretation, and in its literal conftruction was not calculated to give us relief. When

this

this was perceived, nothing was more reasonable than that the country at large should be taxed to supply the deficiency, and the inhabitants of the place, which had been disgraced by the riot, should have promoted an application to the legislature for our farther relief. But so far was this from being the case, that a committee was appointed by the hundred in which the riots took place, for the purpose of defending themselves against our claims; and they executed their trust so effectually, that they even put the hundred to considerable expence to do it. It is even supposed that, notwithstanding their success in this measure, by which they reduced our claims between one fourth and one third, the hundred will have little, if at all, less to pay than if our claims had been allowed in their full extent, and no opposition had been made to them.

I shall take this opportunity to state my own case, which was similar to that of all my fellow-sufferers.

My own wish, which I expressed to my friends, was to employ no lawyer in my cause, but simply to carry into the court a statement of what, to the best of my recollection, I had lost in the riot, and leave the country to make me whatever compensation they should think proper. In this method, however, I was told that it would be impossible for me to receive any compensation at all.

I therefore

I therefore confented to do what the other fufferers did upon the occafion, getting eftimates of what I had loft by fworn appraifers, and other competent judges of the different articles; and the difficulty and irkfomenefs of doing *this*, efpecially in the multiplicity of articles in my particular cafe, my own recollection being uncommonly imperfect, is not to be defcribed; without confidering the *time* which it took up, which no ftranger to the bufinefs will readily believe.

To fave fome time, trouble, and expence, I propofed to the Committee who acted for the hundred, by a clergyman, and a particular friend of mine, who was well acquainted with feveral of them, to requeft that appraifers on their fide might meet appraifers on mine in London, and agree on the amount of the lofs. But this reafonable requeft was refufed. I, however, repeated it in as refpectful a letter as I could write to the Committee a little before the trial, but with no better fuccefs; though in that letter I mentioned my former application, and affured them that all the appraifers had been inftructed by me, as they would all bear witnefs, to charge too little, rather than too much, for every article; but that I would willingly abide by the opinion of their own appraifers. I alfo mentioned my original wifh, to have employed no lawyer to plead for me, and my having declined to avail myfelf of the fervice of Mr. Erfkine, or any

other

other able counsel that I should choose, which my friends proposed to be at the expence of; and that I should content myself with such counsel as the other sufferers would employ, and which usually attended that circuit. The judge, apprehensive of some disturbance on account of my cause, expressed his wish that it might be settled by arbitration. To this proposal I immediately signified my hearty consent, and my willingness to abide by the decision of the foreman of the jury, though a high churchman, and a person with whom I had no acquaintance. The judge, I was informed, was pleased with this, but it was not accepted by the opposite party. Consequently the cause took its regular course.

My books were estimated at 432l. 15s. 6d. my philosophical apparatus at 605l. 17s. my manuscripts at 370l. 15s. and my houshold goods, including whatever could be appraised by a common appraiser in my library and laboratory, as shelves, &c. &c. &c. 1277l. 6s. The whole was 2686l. 13s. 6d. But this was far from being the whole of my loss, or of the indemnification that I was entitled to receive, on the idea of being replaced as I had been before on the same spot, which, in equity, ought to have been the rule of proceeding in the case.

Nothing was charged for the carriage and package of such things as could only have been pro-

cured

cured from London, or other diftant places; which in my cafe could not have been lefs than 40l; nothing for damage to books not materially mutilated, or injured, but which will make the books that were preferved (about 2000) of lefs value, if ever they be fold, by, I fhould fuppofe, 50l. Nothing was charged for the recovery of goods difperfed by the rioters, which, to myfelf or my friends, could not, I think, have been lefs than 40l. Nothing was charged for *pamphlets*, which I think muft have been worth 10l. While I was at Warwick I recollected articles in my laboratory, not mentioned in the inventory, worth about 20l. Now that I am refuming my experiments, I recollect many others as I find the want of them, and I expect to do fo for fome time to come. The amount of thefe I fhould conjecture to be about 20l. more. The leafe of my houfe, which had rifen much in value after I took it, was worth at the leaft 100l. If to this be added the expence attending my flight from Birmingham, my removal to London with my family, and the carriage of the goods I recovered, which would neceffarily attend my fettlement in a place fo diftant as London, which can hardly be eftimated at lefs than 100l. the amount of the articles not charged in my eftimate, will be 380l. and will make my whole lofs to be 3066l. 13s. 6d.

In this eftimate nothing was charged for my MSS. more than the money that would have been

given

given for them by a bookseller in case of my death. My sermons, for instance, were only charged half a guinea apiece, though the sermons of a living preacher ought, in equity, to be charged much higher. For I would observe on this occasion, that because the law can give no recompence for any injuries besides *money*, money is often given when the damage is by no means of a pecuniary nature; and there can be no reason why this should not have been done in my case.

When we were at Warwick, and found we had to encounter the most determined opposition of our enemies, who came prepared to litigate every article, and that the law itself, rigorously interpreted, as it would be, was not calculated to redress our wrongs, we all reduced our claims much below our first estimates *. Mine, including that for my house, which I had on lease, (estimated together with the loss of rent, appraisements, &c. &c. at 1426l. 3s. 3d. and which, though not properly mine, was by the rules of law claimed in my name) was reduced from 4492l. 16s. 9d. to 4112l. 16s. 9d.; and the verdict I obtained was 2502l. 18s.; of which I could not do better than allow my landlord 1000l. besides giving up my lease. Consequently, I was,

---

* Previous to this I had employed a person in Birmingham to estimate the household goods; and his estimate, which was considerably lower than that of the London appraisers, was brought into Court.

exclusively

exclufively of cofts, really a lofer, notwithftanding the verdict in my favour, 1563l. 15s. 6d.

The amount of my law expences at Birmingham, Warwick, and London, though the eftimate of my books and inftruments was made by perfons who charged nothing for their trouble, was very near 850l. while the cofts allowed was only 493l. fo that in this article my lofs was 357l. which makes the whole amount of my pecuniary lofs to be 1920l. 15s. 6d. befides being driven into a lefs pleafing and much more expenfive fituation than I was in before. In this country then, the government of which is fo much boafted of, it has not been my fate to receive either protection, or redrefs, and all my fellow-fufferers may fay the fame.

We do not complain of the intention of the law, or of the difpofition of the judges, but of the un-abated malice of our enemies, and the influence they had on the country in general. They fpared no means to prevent our having any redrefs, and our fufferings were fo far from foftening them, and ex-citing any degree of compaffion, that the greateft fufferers were expofed to the greateft infults. I hardly know an inftance of any men deferving bet-ter of any town than Mr. Ruffell and Mr. Hutton, men of the moft difinterefted public fpirit, and in-defatigable in public bufinefs; and yet they were

5   the

the perfons on whom the extreme of malice and grofs abufe chiefly fell.   But fuch, in all ages, and in all countries, has been the fate of great and active worth.

There was fomething particularly, and moſt unreafonably hard in the cafe of Mr. Hutton.   Mr. Ruffell and myſelf were become obnoxious on account of our religious principles, and therefore, in the eye of bigotry, received only *the due reward of our deeds*; but, in this refpect, Mr. Hutton *had done nothing amifs.*   He fuffered the extreme of injuſtice himſelf, for nothing but his unwearied endeavour to procure juſtice for others.

For the beſt ufe of great talents for public bufinefs, and of a higher kind than Mr. Hutton attended to, I have not yet known any man fuperior to Mr. Ruffell, hardly any that, in all refpects, I think to be his equal; and the malice of his enemies is in full proportion to his talents and his virtues.   With refpect to damages in the court, he came off better than Mr. Hutton.

To return to this fubject, our adverfaries not content with the counfel that ufually attended the circuit, at a great expence employed Mr. Hardinge, the Queen's folicitor, who to ferve them neglected his duty as a judge on the Welch circuit, and who fpared

nothing

nothing to inflame the court and the jury againſt us; quoting not only in my cauſe, but in thoſe of the other ſufferers, paſſages from my writings calculated to repreſent me as the peſt of ſociety, and unworthy of protection or of recompence. The firſt judge, Baron Thompſon, endeavoured in vain to check his violence, and therefore Baron Eyre, it is thought, came down on purpoſe; but though he did it in the cauſes of the other ſufferers, when my own cauſe came before the court he was permitted to declaim againſt me and my writings (of which he appeared to know nothing more than the ex- tracts with which he had been furniſhed for the pur-poſe of his abuſe) without any reſtraint, though there was nothing properly before the court but the eſtimate of damages occaſioned by the riot; and if I had been guilty of ſedition, I ought to have been accuſed as ſuch, and ſuffered the penalty of the law.

The legal proof of the articles of my loſs was peculiarly difficult, from the nature and multiplicity of them; nothing of the kind having ever, as I believe, come before a court of judicature before. It was deemed neceſſary that I ſhould prove my having been in poſſeſſion of more than a thouſand different articles, and at the time of the riot. One friend or other could have atteſted my having had moſt of the inſtruments, though not the chymical ſubſtances;

subftances; but it was neceffary they fhould all be prefent in court. Their certificates in writing (and for this purpofe I came provided with them, in the hand-writing of Dr. Heberden and others, who at different times had made me prefents of them) were rejected as no legal evidence; and when a number of articles in my laboratory were claffed together, the oppofite counfel diverted themfelves and the court, expofing their own ignorance, juft as fo many Goths and Vandals would have done. My own leading counfel was as little qualified to defend me, being equally ignorant of philofophy, and declaring in court that he had not read any of my theological or political writings.

The judge, though no chymift, was willing to make allowance for the fingular difficulty in my caufe, as both the catalogue of my books, and the index of fubftances in the laboratory, were deftroyed, together with the books and inftruments; and had any regard been paid to his opinion, confiderably more would have been awarded me. On what principle the jury proceeded is beft known to themfelves, but I believe that very little was allowed for my books, becaufe many of them were deftroyed in another hundred, whither they had been conveyed by my friends, though the deftruction began at my own houfe, and they did not fay what claim I had on the other hundred.

In

In general I thought the judge impartial in summing up the evidence; but in some respects, considering the manifest disposition of the jury, it tended to give too much colour to their injustice. The catalogue of my library being destroyed, together with the library itself, I could only make out a list of the books that were wanting from my own recollection of them, my friends not being able to attest their knowledge of more than a few of them, such as they had occasionally seen or borrowed, though the number of the books lost was sufficiently ascertained. " This enumeration," said the judge, " coming " from the plaintiff himself, and not proved by any " witness, I was bound to reject evidence of that " kind, and could not suffer it to be received." Mr. Payne, my witness, had set a value upon 440 other volumes, which were proved to be missing (though I could not myself pretend to recollect what they were) by supposing them to be of the same value, one with another, with books of the same size in what remained of the library. This, the judge said, was " no measure of value at all, as " it was impossible so to estimate books; and there- " fore he found himself bound to reject that evi- " dence;" adding, however, that " as the plaintiff " could not have been supposed to have collected " trash, the jury might, *if they thought proper*, make " some addition to the sum, upon the ground of da- " mage to the library." But, disposed as they evidently were, they were sure to allow nothing on this account.

I have

I have heard of a judge deciding very differently in a cafe not much unlike this of mine.——A boy had been robbed of a feal which had contained fome precious ftone, of the nature and value of which the boy himfelf was wholly ignorant, being only able to produce the focket in which it had been fet. The judge, however, obferved, that the cafe fhould be interpreted *in damnum fraudatoris*; and he directed that the boy fhould receive the value of the fineft diamond that would fill that focket, becaufe the ftone *might* have been of that value.

Mr. Hardinge alfo (whofe virulent declamation the judge himfelf obferved might, for any thing that appeared in court, be mere calumny) fhould not have been fuffered to proceed as he did, fince it could only tend to prejudice the minds of the jury againft me, and indifpofe them to do juftice. His abufe of me was exactly fimilar to that of Mr. Wedderburn's (now Lord Loughborough) on Dr. Franklin at the privy council, when the caufe before the court related to the conduct of the governor of the province. It was a day of great triumph for the court party. But had they any reafon to exult in it ten years from that time? As little reafon may the *Church and King* party in this country have to exult in the riot at Birmingham, and the affizes at Warwick, ten years from that event.

I was

. I was prefent at that memorable abufe of Dr. Franklin, being accompanied to the privy council by Mr. Burke: he fmiled, and fhook me by the hand, as he went out of the room; and the next morning he obferved to me, that the things for which he had been fo grofsiy infulted were, he believed, among the beft actions of his life, and fuch as he fhould do again in the fame circumftances. I can truly fay the fame with refpect to every thing that has been moft virulently urged againft me.

On the whole, it is evident that, by whatever rule the jury at Warwick went, they allowed me little or nothing for my books, philofophical inftruments, or manufcripts, as the fum that was awarded me would do little more than re-furnifh the houfe as it was before. They refufed to fay what they allowed for the feparate articles of my lofs, except on account of *the houfe*, which I was under obligation to rebuild. For this, which was not mine, it was thought by fome that the allowance was ample enough, being 957l. 18s.

This detail I thought neceffary to go into, in order to explain the confequences of the riot, and the ftate of our laws, and of the actual adminiftration of them in my cafe, that thofe who think it a proper object may provide a more effectual remedy for a fimilar evil in future time.

H   I muft

I muſt add, that though the miſchief was done more than a year ago, I have not yet (Nov. 1, 1792) received any part of the compenſation awarded me, and yet I have been obliged to advance the whole expence of the law-ſuit; ſo that, if any allowance be made for the intereſt of money, my pecuniary loſs will be conſiderably greater than I have ſtated it to be. If I had not been aſſiſted by my friends, I could not have proſecuted my right at all, and therefore muſt have gone without any redreſs. And ſo much trouble and expence have attended this buſineſs, that in caſe of any other misfortune of the ſame kind (from which I am far from conſidering myſelf as exempt) my preſent determination is to ſit down with the loſs, and not to trouble the country on the ſubject. The law, as now adminiſtered, may do all very well for churchmen, but I have found by experience that it is not calculated to protect Diſſenters, as ſuch, or to procure a redreſs of the wrongs done to them.

SECTION

SECTION X.

Of the Approbation of the Riot, and the Extent of High Church Principles, which were the Cause of it, in other Parts of the Kingdom.

THE spirit of party, intimately connected with the approbation of the riot in Birmingham, is even now far from being confined to that town or neighbourhood, especially among the clergy. One of the most speaking and curious instances of this is the following. A clergyman, distinguished by his writings, requested another clergyman, who was going to Birmingham, to procure him a quantity of ashes from the ruins of the meeting in which I had preached; and the request was complied with. What an excellent *Protestant Dominic* would this clergyman make!

So far were the clergy from being moved to any thing like compassion by what I had suffered in the riot, that immediately after this their calumnies were doubled, and their cries for farther vengeance upon me became louder than ever. An instance of this is an extract from the Shrewsbury Chronicle, signed ΟΥΔΕΙΣ ΔΕΥΤΕΡΟΣ, which may be seen in the Appendix, No. VIII.

    This

This virulent paper was, however, very ably anfwered by a perfon whofe fignature was *An enemy to intolerance and perfecution*, though he avowed religious fentiments very different from mine.

Mr. Burn feems to doubt the truth of what I faid of a clergyman calling our fufferings in an Affize fermon *wholefome feverity*. "Had he," he fays, p. 73, " been a Birmingham clergyman, we have no " doubt his name would have appeared." I do not fee why I fhould be more backward, or more ready, to mention his name on this account. But the fermon is now publifhed, though without the name of the author, which was Allen, who refides at or near Illford. The expreffion in the fermon as now printed is not the very fame that was reported, but to the fame purport. He was, however, properly reprimanded for what he delivered by the judge and the counfel afterwards.

That the fame fpirit which prompted the riot in Birmingham pervaded very diftant parts of the country, the following is a curious inftance. During the riot at Birmingham fome officers were in converfation at Dulot's library at Brighthelmftone, when one of them was overheard to fay (on its being fuggefted that it was probable his regiment would be fent to Birmingham to quell the rioters) that he hoped if his men were fent thither

that

that they would not hurt a hair of any of the rioters heads.

Another officer (fuppofed to be of the guards) was heard to declare at Crawford's library at Bright-helmftone, that it was to be lamented that Dr. Prieftley had efcaped; and that, if he had been at Birmingham, he would have gone through the fire, at the hazard of *lofing a limb*, but that the Doctor fhould have loft his life. I am perfuaded, however, that the difpofition of thofe particular perfons is far from being that of the generality of Britifh officers: they have, I truft, better notions of the Britifh con-ftitution, and of that Britifh liberty which they are appointed to defend.

The idea that was generally, and moft affiduoufly, propagated concerning me, and the tendency of my writings, by thofe of whom the beft that can be faid is, that they knew nothing of either, may be conceived from an *epitaph* that was written for me, as was fuppofed, by fome perfon at Exeter, and which, for the amufement of my readers, I fhall in-fert in the Appendix, No. IX.

The perfon who tranfmitted this curious piece to a friend of mine adds, " The virulence of the above " is nearly equalled, if not furpaffed, by what I " have been informed are the fentiments very fre-" quently uttered by the diffipated and the profane

H 3   " bigots

" bigots of Briſtol, and in all parts of the king-
" dom, viz. for the firſt ſentiment at table, *Damna-*
" *tion to Dr. Prieſtley, and ſucceſs to the Birmingham*
" *mob,* or *Damnation to Dr. Prieſtley, and deſtruction*
" *to his writings.*"

Hereafter it will perhaps not be believed that
ſuch barefaced miſrepreſentation and calumny, ſo
entirely void of all foundation, could be publiſhed
in a country in which the means of better information almoſt obtrudes itſelf. Such pains, however,
has been taken to repreſent me as an infidel with reſpect to religion, and a moſt peſtilent member of
ſociety, that I doubt not a great majority of the
people of this country actually conſider me in that
light, the avowed enemy of God and man. But this
will not be thought extraordinary when it is conſidered how great a proportion of the information of
Engliſhmen is derived from the public newſpapers,
and how many of them have abounded with paragraphs exhibiting me in this light from ſome time before the riot, and to this day. I am tempted to give a
ſpecimen of this which fell into my hands by accident, and I preſume it is only of a piece with hundreds of others; but I reſerve it for the Appendix,
No. X.

That ſome perſons muſt make it the intereſt of
the proprietors of the newſpapers to procure, and
inſert, ſuch articles might be concluded à priori.
But

But an acquaintance of mine, being defired to fettle a difference between two of thefe proprietors, faw a lift of names of perfons to be abufed, and among them was mine. Of what clafs of newfpapers this was I need not fay.

Such an unfair advantage, taken to prejudice the minds of the people againft particular perfons or parties, is a circumftance that calls loudly for public inquiry, and punifhment, by the reprefentatives of the nation, who ought, as far as poffible, to provide for the protection of the character, as well as the property, of every individual of the fociety.

The latter part of this paper relates to an impudent falfhood that has been much circulated, though it reflects difgrace upon the late Dr. Johnfon, and not upon me, viz. that when I was at Oxford, he left a company on my being introduced to it. In fact, we never were at Oxford at the fame time, and the only interview I ever had with him was at Mr. Paradife's, where we dined together at his own requeft. He was particularly civil to me, and promifed to call upon me the next time he fhould go through Birmingham. He behaved with the fame civility to Dr. Price, when they fupped together at Dr. Adams's, at Oxford. Several circumftances fhew that Dr. Johnfon had not fo much of bigotry at the decline of life, as had diftinguifhed him before, on which account it is well known to all our

H 4 common

common acquaintance, that I declined all their preffing folicitations to be introduced to him. It were to be wifhed that the church of England would refemble Dr. Johnfon in growing milder and more tolerant in its old age; but, on the contrary, like moft other aged perfons, fhe feems to grow more peevifh and obftinate.

I do not know, however, whether, on the whole, the general prevalence of the High Church party in this country is more clearly manifefted than by its having pervaded focieties of *philofophers*, with whom, in that capacity, I certainly did not ftand ill.

I obferved in my *Appeal*, that the only fociety, not profeffedly formed on the principle of civil or religious liberty, that had addreffed me on occafion of the riot, was the philofophical fociety at Derby, whofe Addrefs I inferted in my Appendix. It ftill ftands a fingle inftance of the kind. Mr. Rofe, a clergyman, and member of that fociety, was, however, fo much offended at it, that, without the knowledge of the fociety, he publifhed an account of the manner in which it had been done, calculated to defeat the effect of it. The other members of that fociety had the fpirit to refent it properly, and to exclude him from the fociety. I fhall infert his *Advertifement*, and the *Anfwer of the fociety*, in my Appendix, No. XI. and XII.

The

The philofophical fociety at Manchefter had not the fame liberality. Though they had not only done me the honour to make me one of their members, but had prefented me with fifty pounds to afiift me in defraying the expence of my experiments; yet when it was propofed to addrefs me on the deftruction of my laboratory, and it was propofed that nothing fhould be contained in the Addrefs that fhould imply any approbation of my civil or religious principles, the motion was negatived by a confiderable majority.

One of the reafons alledged at Manchefter againft the propofed Addrefs was, that none had been fent to me from the *Royal Society.* Many perfons have expreffed their furprife that I had no letter of condolence, or even pecuniary afliftance, from that body, to which I hope I have been no difgrace. I have even been infulted by the High Church party on this account. Had it been a clergyman of the church of England who had been a member of that body, and whofe laboratory had been deftroyed by rioters, whether his labours had contributed any thing or nothing to the ftock of philofophical knowledge, his cafe, I doubt not, would have been confidered by the opulent members of the fociety, or the patron of it. But I was too well acquainted with the political principles of that fociety to expect any thing of the kind in *my* favour. Had I been a fecond Newton, and what I am, and cannot help being,

ing in other refpects, viz. an Unitarian Diffenter, my expectations from that quarter would not have been higher.

I had fufficient evidence of this in the rejection of Mr. Cooper, though originally recommended by Mr. Kirwan, Dr. Crawford, Mr. Watfon, and Mr. Watt, as well as myfelf. As Mr. Cooper's general abilities appear by his publications to be of the higheft order *, and his acquaintance with philofophy and chemiftry was well known, it was evident that his rejection could not have been owing to any thing but his religious or political principles, with which a philofophical fociety had no concern. So confident was I of the merit of Mr. Cooper, and of the fufficiency of his recommendation, not by *gentlemen members*, but by fcientifical perfons, that I had not entertained the leaft doubt of his election, and was never more furprifed than when I heard that it did not take place.

Thinking that a philofophical fociety might, on reconfideration, repent of having rejected a man fo recommended to them, Mr. Cooper's friends thought it right to propofe him a fecond time; and to the former fignatures of his certificate the following were added, viz. Mr. Boulton, Mr. Wedgewood, and Sir G. Staunton; and as it had been

* See his *volume of Tracts*; his *Effays* in the Memoirs of the Manchefter Philofophical and Literary Society; and his *Reply to Mr. Burke's Invective*.

objected

objected before, that the members of the fociety in Manchefter, where he refided, had not figned his certificate, they now all joined in it, viz. Mr. Bayley, Dr. Percival, Dr. White, and Mr. Henry. Notwithftanding thefe additional fignatures, when the day of balloting came, he was rejected by a much greater majority than before.

The ten who figned Mr. Cooper's certificate (without arrogating any thing to myfelf, who firft propofed it to him) are unqueftionably among the firft in the lift of members for reputation as philofophers; and if about as many more were added to them, the reft are, I do not fay improper members, but fuch as the philofophical part of the world has not yet heard much of. When this is confidered, and that Mr. Keir, and other truly effective and diftinguifhed members of the fociety, would have figned Mr. Cooper's certificate if they could have faid, that they had *perfonal knowledge* of him (which the rules of the fociety require) I do not feel myfelf difgraced for having recommended him, nor does he for being rejected.

It has fince been objected to Mr. Cooper, that he is concerned in a manufactory; but when he was firft propofed, his profeffion was that of a barrifter at law, though his purfuits were then chiefly literary and philofophical. Having fufficient leifure, his knowledge of chemiftry induced him to join in a bleaching manufactory

manufactory on the new principles. On the whole, I cannot help confidering the rejection of Mr. Cooper, recommended as he was, by the Royal Society as a moft decifive proof of the influence of High Church principles in this country on a body of men who might be expected to be the moft liberal. Mr. Cooper, though originally educated at Oxford, now clafles with Unitarian Diffenters : he has given noble proofs of his public principles, and his public fpirit, and he has been ftigmatized by Mr. Burke.

It were to be wifhed that the Royal Society would make fome more explicit declaration of the proper qualifications of their members. Some time ago an excellent naturalift, Mr. Rafpe, was expelled for breaking the eighth commandment, of which it was not known before that the members of the Royal Society were the guardians. This would not, however, have been perhaps fo much amifs, if the fact had been proved: but the expulfion had too much the appearance of a royal mandate. Who can tell but that other members may be propofed to be expelled for breaking the feventh, or even the tenth commandment? Mr. Cooper's moral character, however, is irreproachable; fo that his difqualification muft be of another kind. At leaft he cannot be charged with a breach of the firft commandment.

In thefe remarks on the Royal Society I mean no reflection on any particular member, and leaft of all

all on the prefident, who in feveral important refpects fills his ftation in a manner highly honourable
to the fociety and to himfelf. This is an opinion
that I always maintained, when feveral of my particular friends thought differently. If the fociety
muft be both philofophical and royal, I do not know
where we could find a more proper prefident.

I am happy to be able, by the affiftance of my
friends, to have in fome meafure replaced my apparatus, and I am now refuming my experiments.
I have, indeed, loft more than a whole year, befides, in fome refpects, the refult of the labour of
feveral years; but while I live, I fhall continue my
experiments as I have formerly done; and if any
thing worth the notice of the public fhould occur to
me, I fhall communicate it through the channel of
the Royal Society, provided they will receive my
papers. I fhall not quarrel with the inftitution on
account of the prefent adminiftration of its affairs.
The times may change, and that circumftance may
change with them.

In this almoft univerfal prevalence of a fpirit fo
extremely hoftile to me and my friends, and which
would be gratified by my deftruction, it cannot be
any matter of furprife, that a fon of mine fhould wifh
to abandon a country in which his father has been
ufed as I have been, efpecially when it is confidered
that

that this fon was prefent at the riot in Birmingham, exerting himfelf all the dreadful night of the
14th of July, to fave what he could of my moft
valuable property; that in confequence of this his
life was in imminent danger, and another young
man was nearly killed becaufe he was miftaken for
him.   This would probably have been his fate, if
a friend had not almoft perforce kept him concealed
fome days, fo that neither myfelf nor his mother
knew what was become of him.   I had not, however, the ambition to court the honour that has
been fhewn him by the national affembly of France,
and even declined the propofal of his naturaliza-
tion.   At the moft, I fuppofed it would have been
done without any *eclat*; and I knew nothing of its
being done in fo very honourable a way till I faw
the account in the public newfpapers.   To whatever country this fon of mine fhall choofe to attach
himfelf, I truft that, from the good principles, and
the fpirit, that he has hitherto fhewn, he will difcharge the duties of a good citizen.

As to myfelf, I cannot be fuppofed to feel much
attachment to a country in which I have neither
found protection, nor redrefs.   But I am too old,
and my habits too fixed, to remove, as I own I fhould
otherwife have been difpofed to do, to France, or
America.   The little that I am capable of doing muft
be in England, where I fhall therefore continue, as

long

long as it fhould pleafe the fupreme Difpofer of all things to permit me *.

It might have been thought that, having written fo much in defence of revelation, and of Chriftianity in general, more perhaps than all the clergy of the church of England now living; this defence of a *common coufe* would have been received as fome atonement for my demerits in writing againft civil eftablifhments of Chriftianity, and particular doctrines. But had I been an open enemy of all religion, the animofity againft me could not have been greater than it is. Neither Mr. Hume nor Mr. Gibbon was a thoufandth part fo obnoxious to the clergy as I am; fo little refpect have my enemies for Chriftianity itfelf, compared with what they have for their emoluments from it.

As to my fuppofed hoftility to the principles of the civil conftitution of this country, there has been no pretence whatever for charging me with any thing of the kind. Befides that the very catalogue of my publications will prove that my life has been devoted to literature, and chiefly to natural philofophy and theology, which have not left me any leifure for factious politics; in the few things that I

---

* Since this was written, I have myfelf, without any folicitation on my part, been made a citizen of France, and moreover elected a member of the prefent Conventional Affembly. Thefe, I fcruple not to avow, 1 confider as the greateft of honours; though, for the reafons which are now made public, I have declined accepting the latter.

have

have written of a political nature, I have been an avowed advocate for our mixed government by *King, Lords, and Commons*; but becaufe I have objected to the ecclefiaftical part of it, and to particular religious tenets, I have been induftrioufly reprefented as openly feditious, and endeavouring the overthrow of every thing that is *fixed,* the enemy of all order, and of all government.

Every publication which bears my name is in favour of our prefent form of government. But if I had not thought fo highly of it, and had feen reafon for preferring a more republican form, and had openly advanced that opinion; I do not know that the propofing to free difcuffion a fyftem of government different from that of England, even to Englifhmen, is any crime, according to the exifting laws of this country. It has always been thought, at leaft, that our conftitution authorifes the free propofal, and difcuffion, of all theoretical principles whatever, political ones not excepted. And though I might now recommend a very different form of government to a people who had no previous prejudices or habits, the cafe is very different with refpect to one that *has*; and it is the duty of every good citizen to maintain that government of any country which the majority of its inhabitants approve, whether he himfelf fhould otherwife prefer it, or not.

This

This, however, is all that can in reason be required of any man. To demand more would be as absurd as to oblige every man, by the law of marriage, to maintain that his particular wife was absolutely the handsomest, and best tempered woman in the world; whereas it is surely sufficient if a man behave well to his wife, and discharge the duties of a good husband.

A very great majority of Englishmen, I am well persuaded, are friends to what are called *high maxims of government*. They would choose to have the power of the crown rather enlarged than reduced, and would rather see all the Dissenters banished than any reformation made in the church. A dread of every thing tending to *republicanism* is manifestly increased of late years, and is likely to increase still more. The very term is become one of the most opprobrious in the English language. The clergy (whose near alliance with the court, and the present royal family, after having been almost a century hostile to them, is a remarkable event in the present reign) have contributed not a little to that leaning to arbitrary power in the crown which has lately been growing upon us. They preach up the doctrines of passive obedience and non-resistance with as little disguise as their ancestors did in the reigns of the Stuarts, and their adulation of the king and of the minister is abject in the extreme. Both Mr. Madan's sermon and Mr. Burn's reply to my

I   Appeal

Appeal difcover the fame fpirit; and any fentiment in favour of liberty that is at all bold and manly, fuch as, till of late, was deemed becoming Eng- lifhmen, and the difciples of Mr. Locke, is now re- probated as feditious.

In thefe circumftances, it would be nothing lefs than madnefs ferioufly to attempt a change in the conftitution, and I hope I am not abfolutely infane. I fincerely wifh my countrymen, as part of the hu- man race (though, I own, I now feel no particular attachment to them on any other ground) the un- difturbed enjoyment of that form of government which they fo evidently approve; and as I have no favour to afk of them, or of their governors, befides mere protection, as to a ftranger, while I violate no known law, and have not this to afk for any long term, I hope it will be granted me. If not, I muft, like many others, in all ages and all nations, fubmit to whatever the fupreme Being, whofe eye is upon us all, and who I believe intends, and will in his own time bring about, the good of all, fhall ap- point, and by their means execute.

Mr.

DEAR SIR,

I HAVE somewhere read that to argue with a person while he is in a passion, is just as wise as to hold a lanthorn to a blind man. The opponents of myself and of my patriotic companions, on the 14th of July 1791, have evidently been under the most unreasonable phrensy that ever disgraced this nation; and had we been willing to feed it by returning the abuse and calumny that was so outrageously poured upon us, we might have retorted long ago. But as our appeal is to the calmer passions, it appeared necessary to wait till the season of fury was over, and we could hope that the still small voice of truth would be listened to. However the time for a full reply to Mr. Burn's most extraordinary performance is, in my opinion, now come, and I fear any farther delay will be an injury to the cause for which we are suffering. I rejoice therefore to hear that you are preparing a second part of your Appeal, not doubting but that this insidious publication will have a full share of your notice, and be exposed as it deserves.

I 2

This

This leads me, as a friend to fociety, to lament, and I do it very fincerely, that any of the clergy fhould think abufe of the Diffenters is now the road to preferment, and that fo many concurrent circumftances fhould almoft compel others to think fo too. However, while we pity thofe whofe minds are thus debafed, and who can difgrace the talents that they poffefs by fuch an unworthy proftitution, the duty we owe to ourfelves and to the community, calls upon us to guard againft the confequences, by detecting their mifreprefentations and expofing their falfehoods.

I prefume you will recollect the fatisfaction both of us received fome years ago when Mr. Burn firft met us on the library committee, and I well remember the pleafure you expreffed in the hope that he would prove an agreeable acquaintance. Little did I then imagine he could prove the virulent enemy to us both, which his Reply to your Appeal fhows him to be. As to myfelf, though I have very frequently been in company with him fince that period, I never received, or apprehended, the leaft incivility from him before the publication of this laft pamphlet, in which I fee with concern and furprife that I am made the fubject of fome of thofe malevolent farcafms by which the book is diftinguifhed. I cannot therefore but be anxious to engage your notice of them, and to have you informed of what I have to fay in reply; and as I am in poffeffion of a variety

3

of

of information relating to the subject of the riots, and connected with his book, I will detail some of it to you, that you may give the public such part as you think worth notice.

I have often been at a loss to account for the wide extension of the extravagant spirit of declamation and outrage upon the occasion under which we are suffering, and am surprised that Mr. Burn should so readily come forward to join in it, because I was informed that he thought well of the French revolution in the early stages of it. Surely then he should have shewn some consideration for those who still hold his former opinions, as it is possible they may not have the same reasons for abandoning them which have operated upon him. Much do I wish that he had attended to this, and to his character as a minister of peace, which ought to have prevented him from becoming an advocate in a scene of party discord, and a partizan in a business which has not only interrupted the safety and harmony of society, but disgraced the community in which it was transacted. However, as he has thought fit to become the champion of bigotry and the Don Quixote of the High Church party, and I think his motives cannot be mistaken, I sincerely hope he will not be suffered to triumph in his knight errant expedition.

The first part of his Reply, which I feel myself

particularly

particularly called upon to notice, relates to the advertifement refpecting the hand-bill, which he and his friends have endeavoured to reprefent as one caufe of the riots that followed, but which I verily believe would have no more contributed to them than the letter I am now writing to you, had it not been induftrioufly circulated by them, and thereby rendered fubfervient to their own purpofe of creating a difturbance. That hand-bill Mr. Burn tells us was fent to the minifter by the magiftrates. What more then was neceffary for them, or for any one elfe of the party at Birmingham, to do with refpect to it? and if nothing uncommon was meditated, why call out the clergy upon the occafion? Surely the advertifement which followed, offering the 100l. reward, would have been deemed fufficient without their interfering, or without any other fignature than thofe of the magiftrates. But I knew on Wednefday the 13th of July, that feveral others were added: for as I was riding into town on that evening, I accidentally met Mr. Carles on horfeback, who immediately ftopped, and ad-dreffed me as ufual, in a very friendly manner, ac-quainting me with the advertifement which had been agreed upon, telling me that 100l. reward was offered to any one that would difcover the author of the hand-bill, and adding that he had heard we denied any knowledge of, or connection with, the author, and that as he confidered me as the often-

fible

fible perfon for the party I belonged to, he had been much inclined to fend the advertifement to me, that I might add my fignature, but that upon fecond thoughts he had declined doing it, from motives of delicacy, not knowing how I might feel fuch an application.

For this friendly attention I made my acknowledgments, and added, that I thought myfelf obliged by his delicacy, but could affure him that I knew no more of the author than he did, nor had I the fmalleft fufpicion who it was, and therefore fincerely wifhed he had fent me the paper, as I fhould have figned it without hefitation. To this he replied, that he was glad to hear me fay fo, and wifhed he had fent the advertifement, for he was fure I was his friend, and, let what would come, he would not hurt the hair of the head of myfelf or any of the fect I belonged to. This led me to fay that poffibly it might not be too late for me to add my name even then, and that if he approved it, and would give me leave, I would fend Mr. Swinney orders to affix my name to the advertifement, and I would cheerfully pay my proportion towards the expence, fhould the offer be fuccefsful, and the 100l. paid in confequence of it. To this he freely affented, and added, that he wifhed I would, for I was his friend, I had been his friend, and, let what would happen, he would not hurt a hair of my head, no, he would not hurt a hair of my head, or of any of the fect that I belonged to.

The

The tone in which thefe words were repeated, and the attitude in which he rode, whilft repeating them, fhewed me that he had been drinking, and (as ufual) gone fomething beyond the bounds of temperance.   But as he appeared very capable of riding home, I left him, not being at that time impreffed with the fame idea of the fignificance of thefe remarkable words that I have been fince.

After reflecting on what had paffed, and the condition of the perfon with whom I had the converfation, I was in doubt whether fending my name to the printer would not be deemed an intrufion by the other Gentlemen who had figned the advertifement.   In confequence of this, as you will no doubt recollect, I called at Fair Hill, and confulted you as a friend, when you admitted the reafons I had to hefitate, but, upon the whole, thought with me, that it would be beft for me to fend my name, which I accordingly did by a note to Mr. Swinney, telling him that, in confequence of a converfation with Mr. Carles that evening, fince the advertifement relating to the hand-bill was fent, I had been invited by him to add my name to it, that I had given my affent, and accordingly requefted and authorifed him to add it to the others already given in.   Mr. Swinney's return to this note was a printed newfpaper, which I received foon after nine o'clock, and which proved to me that he was much forwarder with the impreffion of his paper than I

had

had any apprehenfion of; and alfo that the opportunity I thought myfelf in poffeffion of was paffed.

. This circumftance, however, leads me to remark, that I gave an incontrovertible and renewed proof of my difpofition as to the author of the hand-bill; and it alfo makes it very evident that fome fcheme had that day been talked of, and that the repeated declarations, that not a hair of our heads fhould be hurt, was the confequence of it*. Thefe words have very frequently and forcibly occurred to me fince the riots happened, and I have had an opportunity of obferving the direction in which the proceedings were conducted. It is now well known to me that a meeting had then been previoufly held at the houfe of a " *Church and King*" partizan for the purpofe of confidering how to punifh thefe " *damn'd* " *prefbyterians.*" Thefe were his own words. It is well known to me that the rioters very frequently and publicly declared, that they had the juftices' protection. It is alfo well known to me, to yourfelf, and to many others, that they had a regular lift of the devoted houfes. Nay, much more than this is known to me and others, though not yet made known to the public; but I truft it will in due time, and that it will appear to every one, that the Diffenters, fo far from being fuch factious, turbulent, and

l

---

* An affociation for burning our houfes and places of worfhip might admit of a condition that our perfons fhould be fafe.

reftlefs

r

reſtleſs characters as they have of late ſo frequently been repreſented, have acted with a degree of forbearance and patience unparalleled in any ſimilar inſtance.   You well know it has not been for want of evidence that proſecutions have not been commenced, but becauſe the Diſſenters committed their cauſe to government, and expected redreſs from thence.

The next inſinuation of Mr. Burn which I am concerned to notice is, that reſpecting the offer the Diſſenters publiſhed of a reward of 100l. to any perſon who ſhould diſcover the author of the handbill.   This, he ſneeringly obſerves, was not advertiſed, but was *" confined to a few corners of the ſtreets " in the town."*   Here again I muſt lament his want of candour or veracity, for his aſſertion is untrue. This offer was not confined to a few corners of the ſtreets; it was printed with a type of the largeſt ſize, and upon paper in proportion; and particular directions were given that it ſhould be paſted up in every part of the town where the proclamation, which offered the ſame reward, was put up.   Nay more than this, it was alſo paſted up in the public ſtreets at Worceſter and Warwick, with the concurrence of the ſolicitor to the treaſury, as ſoon as the aſſizes commenced.   It is true that ſome inſidious wretches very frequently pulled down theſe papers in Birmingham, as they did the king's proclamation, which offered 100l. to any one that would diſ

cover

cover the authors and abettors of the riots. But that does not prove that either the one or the other had not been put up publicly, and very generally too.

I proceed now to the invidious charge in p. 54 and 55, aimed at myself through the means of Mr. Dadley, the master of the hotel. And here again it is necessary to expose Mr. Burn's want of attention, or else his wilful exaggeration of facts. In giving his pretended extract from my letter, he says, p. 54, " Mr. Dadley, it seems, recommended that " the dinner might be had as was intended—he was " sure there was no danger of tumult, provided the " gentlemen broke up early ; *and, on this representa-* " *tion*, orders were given to the printer to suppress " the hand-bill, and *Mr. Dadley's measure* was " adopted."—Now, if you turn to my letter in the appendix of his own book, you may see that the words " and on this representation" are not in my let- ter, as he has quoted them ; nor do I call it Mr. Dad- ley's measure. Surely after such wanton, unprovoked attacks upon private characters as his illiberal pages exhibit, he should have had a little more regard to circumspection. Mr. Dadley's " *solemn deposition*," for such Mr. Burn calls it, and such he would have the world suppose it to be (though it does not appear to me to have been made before any person au- thorised to take it), is contradicted by the testimony of every individual who was present at the conver- sation it alludes to ; and I am fully persuaded that

Mr.

Mr. Dadley would not have interfered on the occasion at all, had he not been folicited by fome of the leaders of the High Church party. To fuch miferable fubterfuges and meannefs does party fpirit carry men whom, in every other character, I can refpect and efteem. Mr. Dadley has fuffered fo much that I pity him; and I have cheerfully joined with my patriotic compeers in giving him folid proof of it. But I fhall not, in return, put him upon maligning others, or expofing himfelf by becoming the tool of a party, which it muft be allowed is extremely ungenerous to require of a man in his fituation of life. Againft his fingle teftimony I now place that of the three gentlemen prefent, who on the 1ft of May laft wrote to me the following note:

"DEAR SIR,

" Mr. Burn having introduced into his Reply to
" Dr. Prieftley's Appeal Mr. Dadley's account of a
" converfation which he fays took place on the
" morning of the 14th of July, with a view to in-
" validate your account of the tranfactions of that
" day, we think it right to declare that the repre-
" fentation there given is not a juft one of what
" paffed between us.—Mr. Dadley was exprefsly
" defired to tell us if he had the fame reafon to ap-
" prehend a difturbance as when we faw him on
" the Monday evening, to which he replied, that
" he had not, and that he then had no fear refpecting

" it,

" it, as he had heard nothing further about it. We
" are fully perfuaded that you could not have, in
" giving your account, the moſt diſtant idea of
" fixing any odium upon Mr. Dadley, or intending
" to make him a party in the dinner. Mr. Dad-
" ley was never conſidered as any way more con-
" cerned in the tranſactions of that day, than when
" he was preparing any other public dinner for the
" various meetings held at his houſe.

    " We are, very reſpectfully,
        " Dear Sir,
  " Your much obliged and obedient ſervants,

Birmingham,	WILLIAM HUNT,
May 1ſt, 1792.	HARRY HUNT,
	JOHN LAWRENCE."

    To this let me add, that I wiſh to aſk **Mr. Burn**,
How long it has been the buſineſs of the clergy of
Birmingham to watch over the concerns of the pub-
licans there? If I have traduced, injured, or offended
Mr. Dadley, pray what have Mr. Burn and his
aſſociated brethren of the cloth to do with it? If
any explanation was neceſſary between Mr. Dadley
and myſelf, it ſurely might have been eaſily ſettled
without this public, and I muſt ſay impertinent attempt to calumniate me, which, though more malevolent than his inſinuations of modeſty and diffidence, is not leſs ſo than his inſidious attempt to
repreſent the dinner as the cauſe of the riots. To his
ſneer about modeſty and diffidence I reply, that an
                             honeſt

honeft man who has no other object than the public good, ought not to feel the diffidence of thofe who have venal purpofes, felfifh ends, or party views, in their public attendances. It is, however, entirely owing to an infirmity in my hearing, that I am not only obliged to place myfelf near the chair at public meetings, but to keep there, if I would contribute my mite towards promoting the general good. And that I have uniformly been governed by that object, and by that alone, in all my numerous and almoft unceafing attendances upon public bufinefs, I now dare to aver, even in the face of the phrenfy and intemperance with which myfelf and my friends are purfued.

Thus much for the impertinent attempt to reprefent me as affuming more than is becoming me. I will frankly confefs, the character contained in another of his farcaftic fneers, gratifies me very highly, that of your " *zealous friend.*" To be called the friend of Dr. Prieftley, and to enjoy an intimacy with him, is an honour that I prize beyond eftimation. And I rejoice in that zeal and activity to which this intimacy has led me, becaufe it has ever been founded in benevolence, and had public ufefulnefs for its object.

The friends of Church and King, as they call themfelves, have burned my houfe, and driven me from the place which it had been my ftudy to improve

prove for twenty-eight years fucceffively, where I had fixed my earthly refidence, and fondly imagined I had fecured a retreat for the decline of life. But though I am thus deprived of my habitation, and driven from the fpot in which I delighted, my principles are in every refpect the fame as before the riots. I am, and will be a truly independent man, a *" zealous " friend"* of truth and liberty. I will ftill ftrive to attain the equal rights of a citizen, to which I know myfelf entitled; and I will always avail myfelf of every opportunity of ferving the caufe of truth and liberty.

The note at the bottom of p. 56 of Mr. Burn's Reply is, I prefume, to be read as a declaration of Mr. Dadley's. But this (as well as my declaration in p. 55, of dining by myfelf, which is printed in italics) is fo ambiguoufly expreffed, that much attention is neceffary to preferve the connexion. To the latter I do not deem it neceffary to make any reply. But, to expofe the former, and fhew the incorrectnefs of the additional note above mentioned, I wifh you to give the public the following declaration, which was figned foon after Mr. Burn's Reply appeared, and will fhew that it was Mr. Dadley's windows only that were mentioned, and about which any apprehenfions were entertained. The declaration Mr. Burn gives by Mr. Dadley, and that of all who were prefent at the time he refers to, is as follows, and I have contrafted it with that of all the gentlemen who were prefent at the time he refers to:

Mr.

Mr. Burn's note, p. 56, containing Mr. Dadley's declaration.

Declaration of Mr. Russell, &c.

" *On the Monday pre-*
" *ceding I had informed*
" *Mr. William Hunt,*
" *Mr. Harry Hunt, Mr.*
" *William Russell, Mr.*
" *George Humphrys, and*
" *Mr. John Lawrence,*
" *who were met at my*
" *house that afternoon,*
" *that it was then gene-*
" *rally thought, if the*
" *dinner should be had, it*
" *would create a general*
" *disturbance in the town.*
" *In answer to which they*
" *all promised to indem-*
" *nify me, provided any*
" *damages or loss should*
" *ensue in consequence of*
" *the dinner being had.*"

" On the Monday even-
" ing previous to the
" 14th of July, when we
" were at the hotel, Mr.
" Dadley informed us
" that he had been told
" by a gentleman, that
" if the dinner was held
" at his house his win-
" dows would certainly
" be broken. We press-
" ed Mr. Dadley to give
" the name of this gen-
" tleman, as there seem-
" ed no doubt that if
" it so happened, this
" prophetic gentleman
" would either be the
" accomplisher of his
" own prophecy, or the
" employer of others for
" that purpose. Mr.
" Dadley, for reasons
" best known to him-
" self, absolutely refused
" naming him. Mr.
Dadley

" Dadley alfo mention-
" ed that he had heard
" a very exceptionable
" hand - bill had been
" circulated in the town,
" but which not one
" of us had at that time
" feen.

" WILLIAM RUSSELL,
" GEORGE HUMPHRYS,
" HARRY HUNT,
" JOHN LAWRENCE,
" WILLIAM HUNT."

I cannot but think that two pofitions advanced by this declaration are worthy of attention, viz. that the parties in queftion had no idea of any indemnification but what related to Mr. Dadley's windows, as he never fo much as mentioned any other objeĉt of apprehenfion; and that we had not on Monday evening any of us feen a copy of the famous hand-bill, of which we have fince heard fo much. Mr. Dadley, as I have already obferved, has received a fubftantial proof of our fympathy, and found us fuperior to the little fubterfuge of fheltering ourfelves under a plea that our promife extended to his windows only, although we never gave him any other. I pity Mr. Dadley, and wifh he had fuffered lefs. I never intended to hold him up

K   · as

as the cause of having the dinner; and therefore wish my letter written in London had been more guarded in that particular. But the extreme hurry in which it was penned, and the assurance which, immediately upon my return home, I gave Mr. Dadley of my intentions respecting it, would, I am persuaded, have satisfied him entirely, had he not been goaded on by the High Church partisans to let them use his name as they have done. All my acquaintance well know that I never concealed my singular exertions in promoting the dinner; and had I conceived that there had been any thing illegal or unjustifiable, either in the dinner or the toasts, I should scarcely have personally avowed myself an advocate both for the one and the other, to his majesty's ministers, and delivered them the original list of toasts, as it was transcribed for the press. But the fact really was so; and this list was in their hands when the infamous libel in the paper called *The Times* was published *.

It was this circumstance, and this alone, which

---

* This libel, as published in the Times on the 19th July, was as follows, viz. " By every account which has arrived from Bir-" mingham, and from authenticated facts in corroboration of what " we have already inserted, it is an indisputable truth, that the mo-" tives which occasioned the havoc already made amongst the Dif-" senters at Birmingham, and which is still making, solely sprung " from the loyalty of the people. The public were determined, before " they proceeded to violence, to have some further proof of the in-" tention of those commemoration men; they therefore waited until " they heard what was said at table. They had, indeed, their suf-" picions; and those suspicions, after the first course, were realised " by the following toast being drunk, " Destruction to the present " government—and the king's head in a charger."

occasioned

occasioned that extreme hurry which I see Mr. Burn had been acquainted with previous to the publication of his book; and has treated with a want of candour on the occasion which I hope it will never be in the power of any man to lay to my charge. Be this as it may, the libellous paper in *The Times* above mentioned, was published on Tuesday the 19th of July, when under an expectation of another audience of the ministers, and receiving from them my list of the toasts on the afternoon of that day, my answer to it was promised for Wednesday's paper. I was, however, disappointed in the expected audience with the ministers on Tuesday; but although I had an appointment, and attended on Wednesday, yet I could not return from the Treasury till near two o'clock, and I knew the answer must necessarily be written, and be delivered at the printer's by three, if it was to appear in the paper of that day, which I had engaged it should. Nay, so much was I pressed for time upon my return from the ministers, that though I hastily wrote, I could not transcribe, the letter, but was obliged to hasten with it myself to the printer's in its rough state, that I might enable the compositor to set it for that day's paper. Now, whatever Mr. Burn may do, I think every candid person who recollects the time and circumstances in which I wrote, will feel little difficulty in making due allowance for any inaccuracy which appears in a letter written in such a short and truly *agitating* period.

K 2

I will

I will therefore rely upon this candour, and go on to observe, that in p. 118 Mr. Burn criticises, with his usual acrimony, upon the toasts, and gives an addition to the 9th toast, " The Prince of Wales." I have no objection at all to this addition. It was, however, added by the chairman, and is not in the original list. But the explanation that respectable gentleman has already given the public upon this subject renders it needless for me to say any more.

As to the meeting breaking up without the least riot or disturbance, which, by way of emphasis, Mr. Burn again prints in italics (see his book, p. 120), I repeat the assertion I made before, " that it did " so." I again aver it to be true, and being called upon for proof, I refer to the company that dined, with a very small exception. I am obliged, however, to make that, because I was repeatedly told, and informed you of the same long ago, that one man was sent by the party to the dinner purposely to insult yourself, and by that means begin a riot within doors, which was happily prevented by your not being at the dinner as they expected.—It is true two of the gentlemen who came from a distance, and on horseback, went out at the back door, as the readiest way to their horses, and I believe were afterwards followed by some of the mob; but neither myself, nor the company in general, who went out together at the front door, met with any rioters, or the least annoyance in

leaving

leaving the hotel; and in repeatedly walking the ftreets fome hours afterwards I did not perceive any difturbance, nor the appearance of any; neither did I ever hear of thofe two gentlemen, who went out at the back door, being molefted till fome time after Mr. Burn's book was publifhed, and occafioned converfation upon the fubject. My own opinion is, that no difturbance would have happened, had not uncommon meafures been ufed to promote it.

In reply to what Mr. Burn advances refpecting the fhort addrefs I took the liberty of adding to our chairman's, upon the breaking up of the company, I fay, that if any part of it was loft through the " perturbed ftate" of the company, as he reports, it is more than I know of. I certainly did lament to them that the people out of doors were fo much mifled as to be brought to infult us as we came to dinner; but I uttered every word I wifhed to fay upon the fubject; and nothing which I fhould be unwilling to repeat again at any time. I fhall only add further upon this topic, that the parties who dined together at the hotel on the 14th of July, may with the utmoft propriety appeal to the whole tenor of their conduct, both before and fince riots, for the refutation of the various c which have been induftrioufly circula their views in holding that meeti

K 3

As to the criminality of that convivial meeting, it is prefumed that this will not be advanced by any one, even in the paroxyfm of paffion. But as Mr. Burn choofes to defcribe this dinner as the caufe of the fubfequent riots, it may be obferved, that as the chairman was a member of the eftablifhment, and many others of this clafs attended, if this dinner was the irritating caufe, how came it to pafs that the firft objet of the rioters fhould be a meeting-houfe where Dr. Prieftley preached, who had nothing to do with the dinner? With more propriety ftill it may be demanded, what was the reafon that thofe gentlemen who were publicly known to have been the firft and moft active in promoting the dinner, were the laft to fuffer in the depredations committed? Mr. John Ryland, Mr. Hutton, and Mr. Taylor, were none of them at the dinner, and yet fo violent was the fury againft the laft, that it was currently reported, and believed among the mob, as well as others, that every mill and farm-houfe which were known to belong to him were threatened; and of a lift which contained feventy-two or feventy-three houfes that were marked to be deftroyed, it is known that the number belonging to this gentleman formed a very large proportion of the whole; whilft myfelf, though amongft the firft at the dinner, was one of the laft that fuffered. And how is it to be accounted for, that, of twelve houfes that have been deftroyed, only

only three of the whole number belonged to gentlemen who dined, and not one to any member of the
establishment?

Here I think it may be proper to observe, that
I have supported a public character in the town
of Birmingham for more than twenty years, and
have ever been disposed to distinguish myself as a
friend to the public interest of the community. In
this character it was that I felt myself impelled to
promote the dinner on the 14th of July, on the
principles both of humanity and of commerce. I
have sufficiently declared myself a friend to humanity in the hand-bill that preceded the dinner.
It did not seem politic to give the commercial reasons to the public. But I now state, that, as a
friend to the town, I thought myself particularly
called upon to promote the dinner, because I well
knew that the trade it enjoyed with France, which
was one of its most valuable branches, was in danger
of suffering very materially from the spirit of discontent which the commercial treaty had very generally occasioned in France. And because I well
knew that the patriotic popular party there were so
much affected by this spirit of dissatisfaction, that
they were forming associations, and by their example promoting the disuse of English manufactures.

I also knew that this circumstance had alarmed
K 4   some

ſome of the firſt commercial characters in Birmingham. I thought nothing ſo likely to do away this
threatening evil as to teſtify, in a ſeaſon of conviviality, a friendly diſpoſition towards this, the firſt nation
in Europe, by rejoicing in its emancipation from
deſpotiſm, and in its reſolutions to live in peace with
all mankind. I thought nothing more likely to
promote a ſpirit of concord than applauding their
declaration, that they would never go to war any
more for the ſake of conqueſt. I have always
thought peace and commerce very cloſely connected, and therefore conceived it my duty, as a ſincere
friend to both, and as a good citizen, to rejoice
publicly in this ſolemn harbinger of both to this
country. But when it appeared that my views and
thoſe of my friends were miſrepreſented by ſome of
our neighbours, and miſconceived by others, we
who were concerned in promoting the dinner joined
in publiſhing an advertiſement which ought to have
ſatisfied every reaſonable perſon of our attachment
to our preſent conſtitution at home; and which
would no doubt have done it, had not many calumnies been circulated, and much exertion been made
to prevent it by thoſe who are the real authors and
abettors of this miſchief*.

Had

---

* *Birmingham Commemoration of the French Revolution.*

Several handbills having been circulated in the town which
can only be intended to create diſtruſt concerning the intentions of
the meeting, to diſturb its harmony, and inflame the minds of the
people,

Had there not been particular meafures ufed at Birmingham, the dinner there would no doubt have paffed over in peace, as it did in every other place in the kingdom where they were held. In no place whatever was the commercial part of the community fo much interefted in celebrating this feftival as at Birmingham. The value of the commerce of France with this town and neighbourhood fhould not be publicly eftimated. When the late commercial treaty was pending, the minifter was particularly folicited to prevent any calculation of its value being made, left its magnitude fhould be communicated to the French, and impede the treaty. I can affert, however, from the beft authority, that one houfe alone (which was among thofe that were moft defirous of promoting the dinner) has exported to France to the amount of fome millions of the manufactures of the town and neighbourhood of Birmingham. Yet, extraordinary as it may feem, in a town thus interefted has the only difturbance of the feftivity of this memorable day been found. Through the whole kingdom befides all was peace: and yet that it

people, the gentlemen who propofed it think it neceffary to declare their entire difapprobation of all fuch handbills, and their ignorance of the authors. Senfible themfelves of the advantages of a free government, they rejoice in the extenfion of liberty to their neighbours, at the fame time avowing, in the moft explicit manner, their firm attachment to the conftitution of their own country, as vefted in the three eftates of King, Lords, and Commons: furely no *free-born Englifhman* can refrain from exulting in this addition to the general mafs of human happinefs.—It is the caufe of *humanity*;—it is the caufe of the people.

Birmingham, July, 13, 1791.

would

would not be fo here, feveral perfons befides the gentleman Mr. Dadley mentioned, it now appears, ventured to foretel before the day arrived. The induftrious circulation of Dr. Tatham's inflammatory letter, which was diftributed gratis in the public houfes of the town, the advertifement which was publifhed with the words " Incen-" diary refuted" at the head of it, the impertinent infult of an anonymous bigot who advertifed, that he would publifh a lift of the names of thofe who dined at the hotel upon a black page in white letters, though all of them were meafures manifeftly calculated to promote a difturbance, they would, I believe, have been ineffectual, if the magiftrates had not continued in town, and feen without refifting fome among the mob infult the gentlemen as they came to the hotel to the dinner; and if other principal gentlemen too, who placed themfelves upon the fteps of Mr. Brooke's houfe, the very next to the hotel, had not been feen to encourage rather than difcountenance the people. Without fome extraordinary exertions to miflead the people they could not poffibly have taken offence at any thing that was faid or done by the parties who met and dined.

The advertifements that preceded the dinner were as explicit as could be penned. The toafts and the fongs, too, were fuch as the people would, I am perfuaded, have moft cheerfully encored, had they

been

been left to follow the dictates of their own honest hearts, and to confult their own feelings only. Nay, not a man among the High Church party itfelf, I fhould think, could have refufed to join in the clofing lines of the fong that was prepared for the occafion, which were:

" Let each loyal Briton then joyfully fing,
" The bleffings of freedom, and long live the king."

Is this language inconfiftent with the public profeffions of attachment to the conftitution held out in the advertifement? Is it not fufficiently declaratory to amount of itfelf to a full proof to every impartial perfon, that the meeting has been bafely calumniated, and that it has only been ufed as an oftenfible occafion of perfecuting and vilifying the Diffenters? And yet what is it that has been alleged againft them? Many indeed have been the frivolous charges againft yourfelf, who juftly ftand fo confpicuous among us; but againft the body of Diffenters what do all the charges that have been offered amount to?

Mr. Madan has feduloufly endeavoured to give a ferious alarm founded upon our proceedings to obtain a repeal of the teft laws. But that gentleman's apprehenfions were totally groundlefs. Had we entertained any unbecoming or illegal intentions, we fhould not have regularly publifhed our proceedings to the world; but this has been our practice. No
refolutions,

reſolutions, as far as I ever knew, or heard of, have been formed at any of thoſe meetings but what are before the public. I will venture to add, there are none paſſed upon the late attempt, but what are in every degree equalled in ſpirit and firmneſs by thoſe which were paſſed upon former occaſions, in proſecuting the attempt to obtain relief from the penalties to which Diſſenters were ſubject for keeping ſchools, in which, though repeatedly unſucceſsful at firſt, we were at laſt happy enough to be redreſſed.

If Mr. Burn and his brethren have any inſtances of diſloyalty to charge us with, any acts of diſaffection to the ſtate to accuſe us of, let them bring them forth ; let the charge be made. When the advertiſement expreſſing our loyalty and attachment to the government of this kingdom was publiſhed on the 14th of July, what was further neceſſary to prove us good citizens ? Was it becoming us, who were conſcious of none but upright motives, and undiſguiſed actions, to be deterred from an innocent purpoſe by a dread of the machinations of thoſe who we were told had been ſecretly plotting miſchief againſt us ? Surely not.

After expreſſing myſelf thus unreſervedly upon real facts, you will eaſily imagine with what feelings I read Mr. Burn's modeſt inſinuation of the activity of the magiſtrates. He ſays, p. 44, " They " ſtaid

" ſtaid in town for the expreſs purpoſe of interpoſ-
" ing their authority, *ſhould any attempt be made to*
" *break the peace.*" If it was ſo, why did they not
interfere when they both heard and ſaw the notorious inſults offered to ſome of the gentlemen as
they went into the hotel? What did they do in this,
the ſuppoſed origin of the buſineſs? What did they,
when in the evening they ſaw the two meeting-
houſes and your houſe deſtroyed? Did they make
any extraordinary conſtables, or enter upon any
other ſpirited oppoſition? No: while the meeting
houſes were ſtill burning, and the mob deſtroying
your furniture and your houſe, they both returned
home, and went very peaceably to bed; and when
two reſpectable gentlemen went over to them at my
requeſt early the next morning, one of them expreſſed much anger at being called out of his bed.
And yet the " diffident" Mr. Burn very modeſtly
repreſents the merit of the magiſtrates as approved
and ſanctioned by one of the moſt numerous and reſpectable town meetings that was ever convened in
Birmingham, and ſays the only proof of delinquency
on the part of the magiſtrates was their want of ſucceſs*. A ſtriking proof, indeed, this ſcene affords of
the *faithful diſcharge of their duty!* as Mr. Burn declares
it; and, that he may not loſe the full emphaſis of the
words, he prints them in italics. I confeſs, however,

---

* Will Mr. Burn ſay that the magiſtrates were neither of them
intoxicated with liquor, in the courſe of the firſt evening of this
intereſting and diſgraceful event?

that, before this scene of outrage, I never heard of
an instance wherein a magistrate " *faithfully dif-*
" *charging his duty,*" in quelling a mob, when addressing the rioters, whom he found in the very
act of pulling down a house, should desire them to
" *take care not to hurt one another.*" And yet this is
one among many other proofs furnished upon the
present occasion. I think it renders all others su-
perfluous. Otherwise many more equally in point
might be mentioned, as well as the following singular
fact, viz. that throughout the whole of the late scene,
though the justices personally attended at your
house, and at several other houses, whilst the rioters
were destroying and burning them, the Riot Act was
never once read, or even attempted to be read *.

But probably you may have already been informed of this through another channel. I will not
therefore detain you any longer, for I fear you must
already have thought this letter too long. But as in
writing it I have not been actuated by any desire of
criminating others, or retorting their malevolent
calumnies, I hope you will excuse its prolixity, or
any little degree of warmth that may appear in
this artempt in justification of myself, to which
I have steadily endeavoured to confine my remarks. For after all that I have suffered, and am
still suffering, I can truly say that I am more dif-

---

* A striking contrast this to the repeated readings of this
Act when the brothels were in danger.

posed

pofed to pity, than to criminate the authors and abettors of it. Their feafon of reflection, I hope, is approaching, and I would by no means retard it by any irritating reflections. I therefore moft cheerfully clofe this letter with my beft wifhes for the reftoration of that peace and good neighbourhood which reigned amongft us at Birmingham previous to this truly unexpected and cruel interruption of it; and I am confident nothing will be wanting to promote it that can *confiftently* be required at the hands of the Diffenters.

Believe me, with more refpect, gratitude, and affection, than I can exprefs,

Dear Sir,

Moft fincerely and truly yours,

Birmingham,   WILLIAM RUSSELL.
Aug. 20, 1792.

APPENDIX.

APPENDIX.

No. I.

The Rev. Mr. Scholefield's Advertisement relating to the Sunday Schools at Birmingham.

TO THE EDITOR OF THE BIRMINGHAM GAZETTE.

SIR,

AS Mr. Burn, in his reply to Dr. Priestley's Appeal, hath, in the moſt confident and even exulting manner, charged the Doctor with a groſs and culpable miſ-ſtatement of facts, in relation to the Sunday Schools in this town, and aſſerts, that the reſolution of allowing the children of Diſſenters to attend their own places of worſhip never was reſcinded; you will be doing an act of juſtice by inſerting the following paragraph, copied from the Birmingham Gazette, dated October 2, 1786, and greatly oblige,

Your humble ſervant,

RADCLIFFE SCHOLEFIELD.

" Public Office, Sept. 26, 1786.
" *At a General Meeting of the Subſcribers to the Sun-*
" *day Schools in Birmingham, held here this Evening,*

" REV. MR. CURTIS IN THE CHAIR.

" IT being repreſented to this meeting, that ſeve-
" ral gentlemen have threatened to withdraw their ſub-
" ſcriptions to the Sunday Schools, in conſequence of an

L   " alteration

" alteration of the general rules made at the request of the
" Diffenters, on Friday, the 10th of March, 1786: Re-
" folved, that the refolution granting that request (which
" the Diffenters themfelves have not availed themfelves of,
" and adhered to as they engaged) be refcinded; and that
" in future the rules, as they originally ftood, be fteadily
" attended to."

Who ought not to have been ignorant now?

See Burn's Pamphlet, p. 11.

P. S. As you, fir, frequently admit original effays, or extracts from other authors, you will probably indulge me
with room for a few reflections upon the foregoing extract, and Mr. Burn's extreme negligence and inattention
in refpect to it.—What was meant in the refolution, by
the Diffenters having not availed themfelves of it, or attended to it, as they engaged? I believe they are wholly
uninformed to this day. Perfectly fatisfied with having
removed fo illiberal a reftriction (a reftriction unknown in
any place I have heard of, where the Eftablifhment and
Diffenters had united in fupport of Sunday Schools, and a
confirmation of what Dr. Prieftley has obferved concerning the unhappy fpirit prevailing in this town), I never
heard of their giving themfelves any farther concern about
it. I much queftion whether a Diffenter ever recommended an object, much lefs infifted upon their attending a place of worfhip among the Diffenters; if they did, I
have no doubt of their being attended to by their patron.
Of this I am firmly perfuaded, that the refcinding of the refolution was the primary caufe of fetting up Sunday Schools
amongft themfelves, as feparate from the Eftablifhment.
In Sheffield, I am informed, the fubfcriptions go all into
one ftock, from whence the mafters and miftreffes of the
diftinct focieties are regularly paid, and why the fame

plan

plan could not have been adopted here (except the fpirit had prevailed which Mr. Burn fo confidently denies to have an exiftence) I leave the public to form their opinion and judgment.—How Mr. Burn could have been ignorant of a fact fo eafy to be proved muft be left to him, and he can beft explain. From his ignorance however in this in-ftance the public will be ready to infer that his coadjutors (in whofe defence he writes) have left him, as we fay, in the lurch, or that, however he blames Dr. Prieftley, as a falfe accufer of the brethren, he is the firft perfon upon whom (from a certain undeniable fact) the character can at prefent reft. They will likewife be enabled to judge what degree of credit is to be given to the other parts of his performance, which, I have no doubt, are either in whole, or in part, capable of the fame refutation; but, as Mr. Burn calls upon Dr. Prieftley himfelf, to him I fhall refer the farther part of the bufinefs, only obferving, that even Mr. Burn's friends may now be ready to exclaim, and he himfelf feel in part the force of the exclamation in the words of Juvenal:

> *Seu tu magno difcrimine caufam,*
> *Protegere affectas, te confule, dic tibi quis fis.*

Ere thou attempt weak caufes to fupport,
Be fure, be very fure, thou'rt able for't.

Creech's Tranflation.

No. II.

No. II.

Extract from the original Advertisement relating to the
Public Library at Birmingham.

Birmingham Library, Dec. 9, 1789.

LEST any perfon fhould miftake the nature of
this library, it is thought proper to give the following general account of it.——This library is formed on the plan
of one that was firft eftablifhed at Liverpool, and which
has been fince adopted at Manchefter, Leeds, and many
other confiderable towns in the kingdom. The books are
never to be fold; and, from the nature of the inftitution,
the library muft increafe till it contains all the moft valuable publications in the Englifh language; and from the
eafy terms of admiffion, it will be a treafure of knowledge
both to the prefent and all fucceeding ages.

As all the books are bought by a committee of perfons
annually chofen by a majority of the fubfcribers, and every
vote is by ballot, this inftitution can never anfwer the purpofe of any party, civil or religious; but, on the contrary,
may be expected to promote a fpirit of liberality and friendfhip among all claffes of men without diftinction.

No. III.

No. III.

An Addrefs to the Subfcribers to the Birmingham Library on the Subject of Mr. Cooke's Motion, to reftrict the Committee in the Choice of Books, with a View to exclude Controverfial Divinity.

Mr. COOKE's MOTION.

MANY of the Subfcribers to this very ufeful inftitution are much concerned to fee a fpirit of controverfy creeping into the library, by the purchafe of fo many books in religious difputes; books of no real ufe, and after the prefent moment mere lumber: they are read but by a particular few, and do not anfwer the purpofe of the original intention, which was to collect a body of ufeful and inftructive literature for the ufe of pofterity, as well as the prefent time.

Doctor Prieftley, the learned author of many of the books, is of that fpirited and generous turn of mind, and has the fuccefs of this library fo much at heart, that, if he thought them neceffary or proper, he, as the writer, would prefent them.

It is requefted that the committee will at prefent order no more of thofe books until the fenfe of the whole fubfcribers fhall be known at the next general annual meeting.

It is likewife propofed to the next general annual meeting to make a motion* for a law to exclude in future all books of *controverfial divinity.*

To the Subscribers to the Birmingham Library.

GENTLEMEN,

AS this motion (which I have not been albe to prevent being brought before you, at your next general meeting) appears to me to be of considerable consequence, affecting one of the first principles of the constitution of our library, viz. restricting the committee in their choice of books, and I am particularly appealed to in it, I take the liberty to address you on the subject, and to give you my reasons why I think it highly improper that it should pass into a law. I choose to do it in this manner, because it is well known, that on several accounts, nothing can be discussed with advantage in a large assembly; and by this means you will have an opportunity of considering the matter coolly, and of being better qualified to vote with judgment on the question.

When you have attended to my reasons, be assured, that I shall acquiesce in your determination, whatever it may be. The library, injured as I cannot help thinking it will be, by the proposed change in its constitution, will still be of great value to the town and neighbourhood, and deserving of the encouragement of all the friends of literature. And, though overruled, I shall not even be out of humour with any of the subscribers, and least of all with the institution itself. For the greater distinctness, I shall digest what I have to propose to your consideration under separate heads, and I beg your dispassionate attention to each of them.

I. The object of the institution is to provide a stock of such books as any of the subscribers may wish to read, or to consult. All other libraries of this kind throughout Eng-

land

land are, I believe, upon the fame liberal and extenfive plan, no fubjects whatever being excluded.

It has, indeed, been faid, that it is contrary to the original defign of the inftitution to admit books of *religious controverfy*. But I defire to fee the evidence of this. Your printed *laws*, and alfo your *periodical advertifements*, which were all drawn up by myfelf, fay nothing on the fubject. If we look back to the hiftory of the library, we fhall find two epochas, viz. the firft inftitution, in the year before I came to Birmingham, and in the year after, the new modelling of its conftitution according to the plan of that of Leeds. Thofe who were concerned in the firft plan fay, that when it was propofed by fome perfon to exclude books relating to the three profeffions, the motion was abfolutely rejected. The new modelling of the conftitution was, in a great meafure, made by myfelf; and I am fure it was not my intention, or that of any who acted with me, to exclude interefting publications of any defcription whatever.

II. The propofed regulation is unneceffary. For if any evil whatever exift in the conduct of the library, the conftitution of it is fuch, as that a fufficient remedy is always provided in the method of choofing the committee, fince they are annually chofen by the fubfcribers at large. Nothing, therefore, can be wanted but more *attention* in the fubfcribers in choofing the committee, and in the committee when they are chofen. It is always deemed wrong to alter a regulation that is generally ufeful for the fake of a particular inconvenience. The time may come when the fubfcribers in general fhall change their opinion, and then they will wifh for an adminiftration, like the prefent, which will always change with themfelves.

III. The committee fhould confider themfelves as reprefenting the fubfcribers at large, and, without confulting their own inclination, endeavour to oblige as many of them

L 4

as

as they can, and *all* if poffible.   It has been the cuftom to
order books which it was well known could intereft only a
few of the body.   But it was thought that even a few had
a right to be gratified, if it could be done without a difpro-
portionate expence.

IV. The readers of theology among the fubfcribers to
this library are more numerous, and more refpectable, than
the author of the motion imagines, and they think they
have a right to be gratified even to a greater extent than
they hitherto have been ; confidering that, of perhaps feven
or eight hundred pounds that have been expended in the
purchafe of books, the price of all the publications objected to
has not been five pounds.   As far as I can judge, the principal controverfy to which thofe books relate is not likely
to produce many more expenfive publications, and another
controverfy, equally interefting, may not arife in many
years.

V. It has been faid that, by the introduction of books of
controverfy, the Diffenters only will be gratified.   This is
by no means true; many members of the church of England being as much friends to free enquiry (and wifhing to
have the means of promoting it in this library) as any Diffenters.   But admitting this to be the cafe, it fhould be
confidered that the founders of the inftitution were all Diffenters; as they have been, I believe, of almoft every inftitution of the fame nature through the kingdom.   Some refpect is, therefore due to them, and to their liberality, in
purpofely conftituting the library in fuch a manner, as
that their particular influence muft neceffarily be excluded,
whenever they fhould be, as they now are, a minority.

VI. Books of controverfy have, farther, been objected
to, as being of a *temporary* nature.   But it has been the
conftant cuftom to buy any books, or pamphlets, on interefting fubjects, however *temporary*.   And it is defirable
that

that this library fhould be a repofitory for things of this kind, as they are often curious, and perfons have occafion fometimes to look back to them.

VII. The controverfy that I am now carrying on with the learned defenders of the doctrine of the Trinity, grows every day more interefting, efpecially as it has gained the attention of the two univerfities. The publications relating to it are, I believe, in moft, if not *all*, the libraries of the fame nature with this; and it would be very extraordinary indeed, if they fhould be excluded from this of Birmingham only, where it may well be fuppofed that more attention will be drawn to them. My controverfy with the Jews alfo promifes to be highly interefting, as it actually engages the attention of the Jewifh nation in all parts of Europe, and is the only one that ever has done it.

VIII. The works that have been chiefly complained of, viz. the *Hiftory of the Corruptions of Chriftianity*, and that of *Early Opinions concerning Chrift*, are not of a *temporary* nature, but a collection of materials, which will be ufeful in future time, if they be of any ufe at prefent. In the former of them, there are not more than *two* articles, out of a great number, that can give the leaft offence to any Proteftant who is not a Calvinift. And one part of it is a defence of Chriftianity, in anfwer to Mr. Gibbon, whofe hiftory is in the library.

IX. It is obferved in the propofed motion, that if I had thought my own controverfial writings proper for the library, I would have prefented them to it. In anfwer to this I muft fay, that I fhould very readily have made a prefent of them, but that I thought it would be objected to, as a method of obtruding them upon the library. I alfo imagined that it was not the *price* of the books, but the *books* themfelves, that were objected to.

So far, however, have I been from being forward to introduce

troduce books of religious controverſy, that for two years I prevented the introduction of my *Hiſtory of the Corruptions of Chriſtianity* into the library. This at that time gave offence to many, and it was ſaid, that my motive for it was to promote the ſale of the work in the town. At the ſame time I repeatedly ſaid in the committee, that, whenever the funds of the ſociety ſhould be ſufficiently ample (as they now certainly are) I ſhould have no objection to publications in any intereſting controverſy, provided the choice was impartial, ſo that no favour was ſhewn to any one party more than to another.

When the above mentioned work was ordered, it was entirely unknown to me, and much againſt my will, by members of the church of England. A particular friend of mine (Mr. Ruſſell) being preſent, and knowing my wiſhes, voted againſt it. I will add that it is very poſſible I might have uſed my endeavours much longer to keep out of the library every book of this nature, if it had not been for the unreaſonable offence that was taken at the ordering of that work, by ſeveral of the clergy, their intemperate, and, I will take the liberty to ſay, their childiſh behaviour, on the occaſion. Whether this change of my conduct, in theſe circumſtances, was natural or juſtifiable, I appeal to the feelings of any man. I never took any meaſure to introduce any publication of mine except the *Letters to Dr. Horne*, &c. when they had been rejected, and the anſwer to them admitted, which I thought an uncandid and unfair proceeding. I alſo recommended the *Theological Repoſitory*, of which I am the publiſher. But this was neceſſary to the controverſies already introduced. It is, beſides, a work open to all parties It contains ſeveral articles againſt Socinianiſm, and many others that muſt give the greateſt ſatisfaction to all the friends of Chriſtianity, of every denomination.

When

When my work, contrary to my wishes, was introduced, I proposed *Dr. Horsley's Answers*; and I have constantly voted for every thing written against myself.

X. They who have objected the most to the introduction of books of controversy are the *clergy*, no doubt thinking such books improper for the perusal of the subscribers to this library. But they distributed a pamphlet, entitled, *A Preservative against Socinianism*, to all who were confirmed at the late visitation. And, if controversial treatises be proper for the perusal of boys and girls, or of their parents, they certainly cannot be improper for the subscribers to this library. This conduct looks as if they were not controversial treatises in general that they objected to, but those only in which their peculiar opinions were opposed; and that they could not decently decide against those on one side of the question without rejecting *all*. I would not be uncandid; but I appeal to all that are candid, whether this be not the most natural construction of their conduct, and whether it does not betray a suspicion of the influence of reason and argument, and a dread of free inquiry.

XI. Others hate *religious controversy* because they hate *religion*, having no belief in Christianity. These will vote with the friends of the established church, whatever it be, in all such questions as these, but on very different principles. If there be any such among us, they ought, in decency, to decline giving any vote at all. Otherwise their conduct will be the same with that of the dog in the manger. They will neither read any books relating to religion themselves, nor suffer others to read them.

XII. No objection was made to several books of controversy before my *History of the Corruptions of Christianity* was voted into the library, such as *Mr. White's Sermons*, and *Mr. Howes's Observations on Books*, which are all controversial.

troverſial.   And both theſe writers are among my anta-
tagoniſts.

XIII. The committee will be unſpeakably embarraſſed
by diſtinguiſhing books of controverſy from others, and
many works, highly valuable on other accounts, are in part
ſo.   If controverſy be *wholly* excluded, we muſt even have
no Reviews, and no Gentleman's Magazine.

Under the deſcription of *religious controverſy* may fall many publications which the ſubſcribers in general would
wiſh to ſee.   If, for inſtance, Mr Gibbon ſhould reſume
his attack on the evidences of Chriſtianity, and an Engliſh
biſhop, as has been the caſe, ſhould undertake the defence
of it, muſt ſuch intereſting publications be excluded from
ſuch a library as ours, becauſe they are *religious controverſy?*
In ſuch a caſe as this (and many other ſuch might be mentioned) the law would either be repealed, or, which is always a bad thing, would be explained away, and evaded.

This is a *ſuppoſed* caſe, but I ſhall mention two *real*
ones, to ſhew how improper, if not impoſſible, it will be
for any committee to act as the friends of the motion
would have them.   At one of our late meetings a clergyman whom I truly reſpect propoſed to us *Father Courayer's
Declaration of his laſt Sentiments concerning Religion*; and
certainly a publication of ſo much curioſity, and ſo much
talked of, was highly proper for our library.   Accordingly
it was voted unanimouſly.   But it is, in fact, a book of *controverſial divinity* (which is ſo much the bugbear at preſent), for the author gives his reaſons for all his opinions,
eſpecially on the ſubject of the *Trinity*, and appears to have
died an Unitarian.

On the other hand, at our laſt meeting, the ſecond part
of my *Letters to a Philoſophical Unbeliever*, which I ſcruple
not to ſay is one of the moſt valuable of all my publica-
                                                        tions,

tions, and the moft proper for the library, was rejected, though it is a cuftom (and I believe was never departed from before) to admit all *continuations* of works once voted in without any balloting at all, not to fay, that, in other fimilar inftitutions, it is a rule to receive any publication of a fubfcriber, whatever it be. I was prefent, and declined giving any vote on the occafion; only obferving, that the book did not relate to the doctrine of the Trinity, and therefore that they did not need to be afraid of it. Fear, however, the fear of fome lurking mifchief, prevailed. No *reafons* were given, but a fufficient number of filent and decifive *votes*.

XIV. Some perfons are, or affect to be, alarmed left this difpute fhould break up the library. I have no fuch apprehenfions. It is fo well conftituted as to be able to bear much more than this. Should the fubfcribers at large, after mature confideration, not only admit the motion, but repeal the moft fundamental law of the conftitution, by throwing out of the library any of the books that were regularly voted into it, I fhall acquiefce; trufting that in due time good temper, and good fenfe, will refume their natural influence. For, though *prejudice* may have more apparent ftrength, and act with more violence, *reafon* has better ftamina, and will outlive it.

As fome things are beft illuftrated by comparifons, I hope no offence will be taken at the following. Suppofe a number of gentlemen agree to have an annual public dinner, and appoint ftewards to conduct the entertainment. Thefe officers, confidering the number, and confequently the different taftes, of thofe for whom they have to provide, befides fuch fubftantial boiled and roafted meat as fuit every body, and alfo fifh, venifon, and turtle, which many like, but feldom fee, may think proper to add a deffert, confifting of ices, fyllabubs, fweetmeats, &c. and likewife think

think it not amiſs, on ſuch an occaſion, to introduce ſuch things as *olives*, &c. which, though not generally reliſhed, *ſome* fancy.

If, on ſeeing this deſſert, any of the company ſhould ſay, " I diſlike theſe olives, and wiſh they might not be intro- " duced;" would he not be thought very unreaſonable. If he ſhould ſay, he was confident that not one tenth part of the company would taſte them; might it not be ſaid, that even a tenth, or a much ſmaller proportion, of the company, had a right to be obliged in ſuch a trifle. He might ſay, that olives were unwholeſome, and unfit for any body to eat. But might it not be replied, that neither himſelf, nor any body elſe, was obliged to eat of them, and that others ought to judge for themſelves. If he ſhould ſay, " But my money is expended on this abſurd article, which " I think a great hardſhip;" it might be replied, that the money of the reſt of the company was expended on things that were agreeable to himſelf, and, perhaps, only a few others.

He might add, " olives will do my wife, or my children, " hurt, and I would not bring them into temptation." But it might be replied, " Sir, you muſt take the beſt care " you can of your wife and children. This is not the only " place in which they will be in danger of ſeeing olives, " or hearing of them." Perhaps, heated by the alterca- tion, he might add, " If theſe abominable olives be ad- " mitted, though they ſhould not coſt a groat, I and my " friends will abſolutely kick down the table, demoliſh " the furniture of the room, and prevent any body from " dining here any more;" would not a ſenſible friend tell him, that if this was a point on which he laid ſo much ſtreſs, he would do well to decline being of the party, and avoid all public dinners, where he would always be in dan- ger of meeting with theſe offenſive olives.

I would

I would be far from infinuating by this compar.fon, that books of religious controverfy refemble fuch a trifle as *olives* in a deffert, except with refpect to the fmall *expence* attending them. Religious truth is, in itfelf, invaluable; and that the inveftigation of it is as pleafing to an ingenious mind as that of any philofophical truth, I appeal to thofe who are acquainted with both. Others cannot be competent judges in the cafe. They defpife what they do not underftand.

I fhall conclude this addrefs with obferving, that it is merely as a friend to the library, and the reputation of it (which I really think will be materially affected by any meafure that would reftrict the committee in the choice of books) that I wifh to prevent the motion from paffing into a law. As the author of the publications principally objected to, I fhould be moft gratified by their being excluded altogether, as this circumftance would draw much more attention upon them, and make them more generally read than they would otherwife be.

Submitting thefe obfervations to your candid attention,

I am, Gentlemen,

Your humble fervant,

Birmingham,   J. PRIESTLEY.
Aug. 14, 1787.

———*Si quid novifti rectius iftis*
Candidus imperti.

No. IV.

No. IV.

*Extract from the free Address to Protestant Dissenters;
as such.*

IT is also natural for the Dissenters to wish well
to every mild administration, which secures to them their
privileges, and opposes the attempts of a bigoted and head-
strong multitude, of clergy or laity, to oppress them.   For
the same reason, too, when the country, by its established
laws, favours the interest of the Dissenters, so that they
have a *legal right* to their privileges, they naturally consider
their country, and *its laws*, as their guardians, and will stre-
nuously oppose all the encroachments of the prerogative on
the constitution, and on the rights of the subjects in general.
For they must be sensible, that the established laws of a free
community must be a better security for their privileges than
the will of any single man whatever.   They have too much
at stake to be willing to hold it on so precarious a tenure.

It also clearly follows, from the same principle of *self-in-
terest*, independent of gratitude, that the more indulgence
Dissenters meet with from the government, the stronger
will be their attachment to it.   Though, therefore, it should
seem proper to the legislature to give a preference to one
mode of religion, by a legal provision for the maintenance
of its ministers, it is clearly for its interest to attach all
Dissenters to it, as much as possible, by a participation of
civil privileges; and it is both injustice, and bad policy, in
civil governors, to debar themselves from the service of men
of ability and integrity, and, at the same time, to alienate
their affections, by such an *opprobrious exclusion* from civil
honours.

Yet, though I think it right that these things should be
publicly

publicly faid, that they may have weight with thofe whom it may concern, far would I be from encouraging the leaft tendency towards difaffection in the Diffenters to the prefent conftitution of England.   Imperfect as it is, and hard as the prefent laws bear upon us Diffenters in fome refpects, our fituation in England is, upon the whole, fuch as we have great reafon to be thankful to divine providence for, being abundantly more eligible than it would be in any other country in the world; and it is not fo defirable to obtain even a juft right by clamour and contention, as by the continuance of a prudent and peaceable behaviour.

This may convince our legiflators, that we are deferving of their indulgence.   Men who harbour no refentment, though under a reftraint, of the injuftice and unreafonablenefs of which they are fully fenfible, muft be poffeffed of generofity enough to be capable of the moft grateful and firm attachment to the hand that frees them from the reftraint.   If a man have magnanimity enough not to bear malice againft an enemy, much more will he be fufceptible of a generous zeal for his friend.

Befides, though, from a regard to the honour and intereft of our country, it is to be wifhed that Diffenters might be admitted to all civil offices of honour and truft, in common with others, their fellow-fubjects, who have no better title to them in other refpects: yet a perfon who fhould confult the intereft of the Diffenters only, as a body of men who feparate themfelves from a principle of *religion*, without regard to the intereft of the community at large, might, perhaps, hefitate about taking any fteps to procure an enlargement of their privileges.

Profeffing a religion which inculcates upon us that we are *not of this world*, but only in a courfe of difcipline, to train us up for a better, it is worth confidering, whether a

M   fituation,

fituation, in which more fcope would be given to ambition, and other paffions, the tendency of which is to attach us to this world, is to be wifhed for by us. Should not a Chriftian, as fuch (though he fhould by no means fecrete himfelf from fociety, or decline any opportunity of ferving his friend, or his country, when divine Providence feems to call him out to the fphere of active life) be content to pafs unmolefted in the private walks of life, rejoicing, as his mafter did, in doing all kind offices to his fellow-creatures, without afpiring at civil power, and thofe honorary diftinctions, with which the hearts of the men of this world are fo much captivated, and, very often, fo fatally infnared.

As our Lord warned his difciples, that *the world would love its own*, and would hate them, becaufe they were not of the world; and that he who would follow him, muft *take up his crofs* to do it; is it not, *cæteris paribus*, more probable that we are thefe difciples, when we fuffer fome degree of perfecution, and are rather frowned upon by the powers of this world, than if we had free accefs to all the emoluments of it? Certainly fuch a fituation is far more favourable to our gaining that fuperiority of mind to the world, which is required of all Chriftians, whatever be their ftation in it. We know that, *if perfecution fhould arife on account of the word*, we muft be ready to forfake houfes, lands, relations, and all the endearments of life, rather than make fhipwreck of faith and of a good confcience; and that, in thofe trying times, if we deny Chrift, he will alfo deny us. Then he that would fave his life fhall lofe it, and he only that is willing to lofe his life, fhall fave it to life eternal. This, Chriftians, is the tenure on which we hold all the bleffings of the gofpel.

Now, if this be the temper to which we are to be formed, whether perfecution fhould actually arife, or not, what

kind

kind of a fituation fhould we (from the knowledge we have of human nature) prefcribe, as the moft favourable for the purpofe? Certainly, not one in which we fhould have nothing to bear or to fuffer, and where every thing fhould be juft as we could wifh it. A mind accuftomed to this treatment would be ill prepared for encountering the various hardfhips of the Chriftian warfare, in a time of perfecution. In a fituation in every refpect favourable to the purfuits and enjoyments of this life, it would not be eafy for a man to attain to any thing like a fatisfactory conviction, that he had the proper temper and difpofition of a Chriftian. Habits of mind are not acquired by *putting cafes* (which, however, perfons would little think of doing, when the cafes were not likely to occur) but by actual experience and feeling. A habit of caution can never be given to a child by admonition only. It is by frequent hurts that he learns to take care of himfelf. So likewife courage and fortitude are acquired by being frequently expofed to pains and hardfhips, by exerting our powers, and feeling the benefit of fuch exertion.

All thefe things duly confidered, a man who entertains the truly enlarged fentiments of Chriftianity, and is fenfible how momentary and infignificant are all the things of this world, in comparifon with thofe of a future, will, in proportion to the influence of thefe views, be lefs impatient of the difficulties and reftraints he may lie under in a civil capacity. He will more eafily acquiefce in a fituation not perfectly eligible, when he is prepared even to bear the greateft fufferings that can befall him in this life with Chriftian fortitude, patience, and refignation; at the fame time that the benevolence of his heart is always ready to take the form of the moft generous patriotifm, whenever there occurs a clear and great caufe to exert it. If a true

M 2 Chriftian

Chriftian be confcious that he is engaged in a good caufe, he, of all men, has the leaft reafon to fear *what man can do unto him*, and therefore he is more to be depended upon, in any critical emergence, than any other perfon whatever.

A Diffen·er, then, who is fo *upon principle*, who has, confequently, the jufteft notions of the nature and importance of civil and religious liberty; who is, on many accounts, thoroughly fenfible of the bleffings of a mild and equal government, and, therefore, heartily attached to the intereft of that conftitution which allows him the rights which he values fo highly; whofe mind is prepared to bear *irremediable* hardfhips with patience, but whofe active courage, in cafes in which the great interefts of his country call him to exert himfelf, may be depended upon, is a very valuable member of civil fociety. Such a man will fcorn the mean arts of court intrigue. If he can gain his laudable ends, and be admitted to his natural rights, as a loyal Britifh fubject, by fair and open means, he will not defpife it; but he will rather continue to fuffer unjuftly, than proftitute his intereft to a corrupt, profligate, and oppreffive adminiftration.

No. V.

Copy of the Forged Letter found at my Houfe,
16th July, 1791.

DEAR DOCTOR,

I AM now provided with every thing neceffary, and will be ready at the time appointed to affift in endeavouring to attain that long looked for by us, and root out the conftitutional men who have wielded the fhield againft our rights as free-men, and truft you will alfo exert yourfelf,

felf, and get all our friends to be ready at the fame time, to make the grand pufh. In expectation of that and fuccefs, I am, dear Doctor,

Your true friend,

London,
May 2, 1791.

WILLIAM RUSSELL.

No. VI.

Mr. Abel Humphrys's Advertifement relating to the Calumny of Mr. William Gem.

TO THE PUBLIC.

Mr. WILLIAM GEM, refident with his father in New Street, in this town, having had the effrontery to affert fome time ago in public company, at the Dog Inn, in Spiceal Street, that—" *meeting at Lady Well Baths the* " *young Meffrs. Humphryfes, one of them had, in his pre-* " *fence, expreffed a wifh to wade up to his chin in churchmen's* " *blood, and that he, irritated at fuch an expreffion, inftantly* " *knocked him into the water,*" together with other parti-culars, equally unfounded, but tending to give an air of plaufibility to his tale, they find it neceffary thus publicly to expofe his character, that they may defend their own.

Upon the earlieft intimation of the exiftence of the re-port, having traced it through its various channels, and found Mr. Gem its fole author, one of them waited upon that gentleman, and demanded an explanation. He with-out hefitation confeffed himfelf the fabricator of the ca-lumny, begged pardon, and pleaded intoxication. This at that time they deemed fufficient; but on perceiving the prevalence of the report, that it had even become the topic of converfation in alchoufes, and in manufactories, they found it neceſſary again to wait upon that gentleman, in company with a very reſpectable attorney, and to require that his apology ſhould be public. This reaſonable requeſt, though he again acknowledged the criminality of his conduct, he refuſed to comply with, and it is this refuſal which now conſtrains them to proclaim him to the world an unprincipled calumniator.

So cruel and unmerited an attack upon the characters of young men would, at all times, be infamous; but when made upon the characters of thoſe with whom he was totally unacquainted, in whoſe company he had never been, and the ſons of a man already the victim of popular deluſion, its infamy is extreme.

Inhuman muſt be the heart that could conceive the idea; but what language can define the man that could premeditately aſcribe it to the innocent?

At another time they had perhaps truſted to their known characters to repel the charge; but in the preſent ſeaſon of alarm, when party ſpirit eagerly nurtures every wicked defamation, in juſtice to themſelves, and to the body to which they belong, they are bound to expoſe the defamer who can thus wantonly worry their innocent reputation.

For ſelf and brothers,

Birmingham,   ABEL HUMPHRYS.
June 19, 1792.

No. VII.

Copy of a Letter intended to be addreſſed to the Clergy of the Town of Birmingham.

GENTLEMEN,

I WOULD addreſs you by the title of *my brethren in the Chriſtian miniſtry*, if I did not think it might offend you, and the object of this addreſs is not irritation,

but

but peace. As you, and the moft zealous friends of the eftablifhed church, now fee the fatal confequences of harfh language, and harfh meafures with us, I am willing to think you will have no objection to trying a different conduct. The dreadful effects of *violence* fhould teach you *moderation*, and urge you to exprefs this moderation in the cleareft and leaft equivocal manner. Then a lafting peace may be eftablifhed, and from this your caufe will be a greater gainer than ours.

In the laft eleven years, in which you have fhewn a difpofition peculiarly hoftile to the Diffenters, they have increafed in an unprecedented proportion. Not lefs than ten new congregations of Diffenters, or Methodifts, have been formed in that time. Two places of worfhip are at this time building, and another is intended. We are only looking out for a proper fituation. In the mean time, though your places of worfhip are but five, thofe who attend public worfhip in them are little, if at all, increafed.

But let hoftilities ceafe, though we are gainers by them. It is for your advantage that they fhould; and as a fure pledge of reconciliation, good will, and friendfhip, generoufly allow us the ufe of your churches, till our meetinghoufes can be rebuilt. We contribute to the fupport and repairs of them as much as yourfelves, and this is but a fmall advantage in return. It has been long ago dearly purchafed by us. We fhall not interfere with your hours of worfhip. We fhall not profane or defile them. We will preach in *them the gofpel of peace*, and we will blefs and pray for you in them. If any thing can enfure the continuance of your church, it will be fuch lenient meafures as thefe.

The thing that I propofe is far from being new in the Chriftian world. There are churches in feveral parts of Germany alternately occupied by Catholics and Proteftants, ever fince the Reformation, and no inconvenience what-

M 4 ever,

.ever, but much good, has arifen from it. When one of your churches was rebuilding, the Diffenters of the place lately offered the members of the eftablifhment the ufe of their meeting-houfe, and the various denominations of Diffenters, who differ from one another in fentiment as much as they do from you, make no difficulty of accommodating one another on fuch occafions. The ufe of the new meeting-houfe, now in ruins, was given to the Independents when, on a particular occafion, they wanted a place larger than their own; and whenever it fhall be rebuilt, I will anfwer for its being at your fervice, or that of any other denomination of Chriftians whatever.

Believe me, that this or fome other meafure, that fhall fhew the decreafe of bigotry, is abfolutely neceffary for the peace of the town, and the good of the country. It is neceffary on the part of the clergy in general, and of the court too. By the manner in which our late applications for the repeal of the teft laws were rejected, more than the rejection itfelf, the country at large has taken up the idea, that the Diffenters, and efpecially the Prefbyterians, and Unitarian Diffenters, are odious to government, and that all connexion with them is to be fhunned by the friends of the church and of the king; an idea which may have the moft fatal confequences.

What muft be the feelings of a fet of men, confcious of no crime, but who confider themfelves as the beft citizens, and when induftry, peaceable behaviour, and loyalty, have been approved at all times, but efpecially fince the abdication of their enemies the Stuarts, and who were always deemed the beft friends of the family on the throne, finding themfelves now regarded in a different light, and as it were *profcribed* by the government under which they live? And what muft be the fentiments of others towards perfons in this fituation? It is like fetting a price upon our heads, and

inviting

inviting the mob to infult us, as of late they have done in almoft all parts of England.

It is highly neceffary, therefore, for the peace of the country, (which, as its burdens and difficulties increafe, requires the united ftrength of the whole, to enable it to bear them) that the bifhops, and the court itfelf, fhould take fome meafures to convince the public that they con-fider us as worthy not only of protection, but of confidence. The late riots will give them a good opportunity of doing fomething that fhall have this tendency, and their concur-rence in the repeal of all penal laws in matters of religion would not hurt, but greatly ftrengthen, the eftablifhment, and abate the animofity of all fects; who would, with infi-nitely lefs reluctance, contribute to the fupport of a religious fyftem which left them accefs to all civil privileges, and did not fet a mark upon them, as people *not truft worthy.*

By all means, let the prefent opportunity, in fome way or other, be improved in favour of future peace and har-mony. Such another will never, I hope, be given us. Otherwife, no man can tell what may be the effect of the animofity which through all England will be increafed by it. Our difcuffion of particular doctrines may go on as before. Inquiries into religious truth have no tendency to break the peace of fociety, even though writers fhould not always conduct themfelves as becomes fcholars and gentle-men. Do you, the clergy of the eftablifhed church, do your part in this *work of peace, and labour of love,* and our governors will be more ready to do theirs. For it can only be to oblige the church, that the Diffenters have been frowned upon as they have been. Let us, mutually weep-ing over the difmal fcene that is now before us, embrace as brothers, whofe eyes are opened, and who will not again fuffer them to be blinded by our common enemy, *party fpirit, spirit.* I call this a common enemy, becaufe it is hoftile to our common Chriftianity, and is too apt to affect us all.

My own principles and conduct, though they are confpi-cuous enough in my writings, have been induftrioufly mifreprefented. But without looking back to the paft, let us mutually fign an *act of oblivion*, and hope for better times in future. I love my country, notwithftanding all the defects in its conftitution, which I therefore earneftly wifh may be removed. And fuch reforms as are eafily practicable, and by which all parties would be gainers, would for ever remove the neceffity, and with that the prefent dread, of any great *revolution*. While this country is tenable for me, I fhall think myfelf happy to ftay in it. When it is untenable, I thank God that others, and thofe not undefirable ones, are ready to receive me, and efpe-cially I truft a country more diftant, but infinitely pre-ferable to them all. Hoping to meet you there, notwith-ftanding we may now and then *fall out by the way*, I am, from my heart,

Gentlemen,

Your well wifher, and

A friend of peace,

London,   J. PRIESTLEY.
July 20, 1791.

No. VIII,

Extract from a Letter inferted in the Shrewfbury Chro-nicle, Sept. 14, 1791.

For the *Shrewfbury* Chronicle.

MR. PRINTER,

SINCE Dr. Prieftley continues to breath out his threatenings againft the eftablifhment of this country, and to diffufe his prognoftications of the fpeedy downfall of

what

what he has blafphemoufly called, "The idolatrous Wor-
"fhip of JESUS CHRIST;" and fince long experience
evinces that arguments the moft demonftrative, drawn from
the only fource whence man can derive any knowledge of
Divine things, are all thrown away upon him: I fubmit it
to the confideration of thofe whofe immediate duty it is to
watch over the Chriftian religion, as part of the fundamental law of this realm, Whether it be not incumbent on
them to put the ftatutes in force againft him as a Blaf-
phemer of GOD, and a difturber of the peace? Had this
been done a few years ago, it is plain from the declarations
of the rioters lately executed at Warwick, that the depredations, which they fo outrageoufly, unlawfully, and
wickedly committed, had never taken place. Can any
time be better for the Attorney General to take fuch a notorious delinquent in hand, than the prefent; when it is
evident that a *legal* profecution for his repeated blafphemies
againft GOD, and threats againft the eftablifhment, would
be grateful to an undoubted majority of all ranks of people,
notwithftanding his vain boafts to the contrary?

" Sedition, which ufed formerly to hide its trains of mif-
" chief in caverns, under ground, now brandifhes its torch
" in broad day-light: and the policy of the age (too deep
" for *me* to underftand) leaves it to itfelf, and waits to fee ·
" what it will do; and when the ftreets are in flames, tries
" to put out the fire as well as it can ; and difperfes a law-
" lefs multitude with blood and flaughter; which might
" have been reftrained and faved by a timely execution of
" the laws."—*Jones's Sermon, at Bury St. Edmunds, May*
31, 1791, *p.* 10, 11.

There is fcarce one publication of Dr. Prieftley's, either
on a *theological* or *political* fubject, that will not furnifh co-
pious matter whereon to ground an information; or in-
dictment.

Sept. 14, 1791. ΟΥΔΕΙΣ ΔΕΥΤΕΡΟΣ.

No. IX.

An Epitaph written for me by some Person in the West of England.

Near this Place lies the BODY of

JOSEPH FUNGUS, LL. D. F. R. S.

And, strange as it may appear,

This FLAMING INCENDIARY,

Owing to the Clemency of a mild Government,

DIED A NATURAL DEATH.

In him *Sedition* hath lost its most *zealous* and *indefatigable* Friend; the *World*, an *imperious* and *turbulent* Member of Society; and the *Diſſenters from the Eſtabliſhed Church*, a *furious* and *indiscreet* Advocate, who did irreparable Injury to their common Cauſe. He was a profeſſed *Enemy* of every *Syſtem of Government*, and an *avowed Friend to Anarchy* and *Confuſion*. Led by extreme Vanity, and the Imbecility of abstract Reaſoning, to think he was capable of raiſing a *Storm violent enough to tear up the Eſtabliſhment of his Country by the Roots*; he wanted Penetration to diſcover that the *ſame Hurricane*, by taking a contrary Direction, might ſweep away his own " *baſeleſs Fabrick, and leave not a Wreck behind.*" His Publications were numerous, among which, his Treatiſes on Natural and Experimental Philoſophy diſcover conſiderable Abilities and great Application ; but his *religious*, or rather *irreligious Tracts*, abound with ſuch *Arrogance, Egotiſms*, and *unpardonable Indecencies*, that Charity will not ſuffer the candid Part of Mankind to ſuppoſe that any Chriſtian Society will ever ſanction them,

them. He was altogether a man of fuch an *ambitious* and *reftlefs* Difpofition, that *Heaven* and *Earth*, beholding his Prefumption in endeavouring to unite in his own Perfon the Characters of *Lucifer* and *Cromwell*, difclaimed him; which coming to the ears of *his black Friends* on the other Side of the *Stygian Lake*, they unanimoufly elected him HIGH PRIEST in the Temple of their GREAT MASTER.

THIS MONUMENT was ERECTED

By a confiderable Number of *principled* and difpaffionate DISSENTERS, who, preferring the peaceable Enjoyment of *real Property*, to the infamous Idea *of living on Plunder*, or the *chimerical one of equalizing all Ranks and Orders* of Men, thought it *their Duty* to publifh and perpetuate their entire Difapprobation of

GUNPOWDER JOE's Political Conduct,

And their utter Abhorrence of his

UNCHRISTIAN DOCTRINES.

No. X.

A Letter addreffed to the People of England in the Public Advertizer for Saturday, Aug. 18, 1792.

Quos JUPITER *vult perdere, prius dementat.*

WHOLE nations may become infane, planetftruck, as well as individuals. God Almighty often delivers up whole nations, as well as individuals, to the depravity

vity and flagitioufnefs of their own vitiated feelings, the greateft calamity that can poffibly befal them. Had the French exhibited on the ftage of the world no other proof of their having loft their fenfes, and of their being under the immediate flagillation of Heaven, (*'tis God, not man alone*, that *precipitates* the *torrent* of *difafters over France* at the *prefent tremendous moment)*; had they given no other proof of their infanity but the late public deification of that abandoned fyftematical profeffional infidel, Voltaire, and their more *recent panegyric* on Dr. Prieftley, of prophane and blafphemous memory, the ftupendous magnitude of this folly would have demonftrated and juftified the propriety of taking out the ftatute againft the whole body of the nation. Whoever made a panegyric on Judas, but Lucifer the father of darknefs? What Roman ever praifed Catiline, but his colleagues Lentulus and Cethegus? Who ever called the two incendiaries, Tyler and Straw, honeft patriots, but Thomas Paine? Who ever thought John the painter a worthy candidate for fame, but an Englifh Jacobine? Doubtlefs there is fuch a thing as decency, as propriety, as confiftency of conduct: was it decent, was it acting like rational beings, to hold up two fuch callous dogmatical *profligates* in *opinion*, as Voltaire and Prieftley, as examples of excellence, as models of wifdom, as patterns to be followed? Why call the one Socrates, and the other Fenelon? Was not this moft egregious proftitution of language, moft flagrant abufe of words? Socrates and Fenelon were the fhining ornaments, the bright luminaries of the age they lived in; they were public bleffings; they were the great apoftles of virtue, delegated by heaven to inftruct and meliorate the world with the falubrious doctrines of truth. They preached nothing but goodnefs, and univerfal philanthropy; and were themfelves illuftrious examples of the important leffons they taught. But what doctrines

do

do our modern philofophers preach? Why, they very gravely tell us, and with a confidence as if they really believed it, that revelation is nothing but a folemn impofture, that the gofpel is a fable of the firft magnitude, the Saviour a fantaftic idol, a phantom of imagination; they maintain and prove it as clear as any propofition in Euclid, (if you will believe them) that the *foul is mortal*, that the golden promifes of religion are idle dreams, fantaftick delufions, to catch weak unenlightened minds.

Thefe fanguine and laborious emiffaries of darknefs preach the black creed of infidelity with as much zeal, and affiduity, as the apoftles preached the creed of falvation. The apoftles were not more ardent to propagate and difseminate the great truths of Chriftianity, than thefe men are ftrenuous and indefatigable in their endeavours to abolifh them. But with this fignal difference, reader, God evidently co-operated with the apoftles in the firft promulgation of the gofpel, and demonftrated their divine miffion by figns, wonders, and fplendid miracles; but who co-operates with Voltaire and Prieftley in their indefatigable efforts to abolifh the gofpel? Beyond a doubt the great enemy of mankind, the father of fin, is with them tooth and nail. They have likewife moft ftrenuoufly combating in their caufe the whole tribe of ancient and modern unbelievers, the great mafs of atheifts, freethinkers, and libertines, exifting in the world, the vaft herd of recently corrupted and adulterated Socinians; add to thefe the whole crew of modern philofophers and metaphyficians, (the tarantulated Humes and Rouffeaus of the day); all thefe militate againft revelation, litigate the great truths of Chriftianity, with as much rancour and acrimony as Voltaire and Prieftley. They have, moreover, moft ftrenuoufly combating in their caufe vain prefumption, impudent affertion, dogmatical opinion, licentious affumption, un-

S   blufhing

blufhing mifquotation, wilful mifreprefentations of authors; all thefe co-operate with Voltaire and Prieftley in
propagating the black creed of infidelity.   Will you praife
thefe men then? Did they make a proper ufe of the talents
God had fo pre-eminently gifted them with? No, they
proftituted their abilities to the moft depraved and moft fla-
gitious purpofes.   They pointed, emuloufly pointed the
great gun of their intellect, the whole artillery, the whole
battery of their faculties *againft the very God who gave it.
them*.   They ftretched every nerve of their fouls to degrade
and extirpate the great fundamental truths of religion;
they laboured morning, noon, and night, moft anxioufly to
perfuade the *world* to *ceafe to be Chriftian*, and once more
to *become Pagan*, to relinquifh revelation, and once more
adopt the religion of nature.   This *par nobile fratrum*, this
indefatigable yoke of infidels have practifed every logical
knavery, manoeuvred every fubtle literary fraud.   They
have exhaufted the whole proteuifm (if we may fo fpeak)
of chicane and fineffe, in endeavouring to explode and abolifh the foothing doctrine of redemption, the grand panacea
of the gofpel, the only infallible antidote againft the common unavoidable ills of life, the *nobleft cordial* in the gift
of heaven.   This golden noftrum, my countrymen, revealed to you by our Saviour, thefe lettered bravos, thefe
fierce infulting Goliaths of argument, thefe wilful mur-
derers of the repofe of the world, want to rob you of.   In
order to accomplifh their infernal purpofe, they put the
gofpel upon the bed of Procruftes; if the text is too *fhort*,
they *lengthen* it, if too *long*, they curtail it; if neither will
anfwer the point, they boldly *amputate*, totally *annihilate*,
and fwear it is fpurious.   Are *thefe men* then *bleffings* to the
world? Are they of benefit to mankind? No! they are
curfes of the firft magnitude; they are great national calamities, calamities more dreadful than nature's worft cala-
                                                     mities,

mities, far worfe than plague or earthquake; thefe only
kill the body, the perifhable part of man, but the doctrines of thofe men infallibly kill the foul, the immortal part of man, that is, they poifon it, and prepare
it for everlafting perdition. Drink one drop of the
Lethe of their creed, and you are loft for ever. You
are tranfmuted—you are changed—you inftantly forget your God—you forget you are a man—you *materialife*
the God, and you *brutalife* the man—you are loft to every .
honeft glow of the heart, dead to every generous manly
fenfation; in fhort, you are as *literally* a *beaft* as if *really
touched* with the *wand Circean*. To lump, accumulate,
and concentre every curfe in one, you are a Painift in your
political, and a Prieftleyan in your religious creed. Could
heaven, in the plenitude of its ire, inflict a heavier punifhment on you?

You, my countrymen, have avoided the rock the French
have fo miferably fplit on; you are fo far from confecrat-
ing and embalming books of blafphemy and treafon, as the
French have done, that you have moft fignally, and moft
pointedly, expreffed your abhorrence and deteftation of
both, in reprobating in the moft public manner the works
of the Paines and Prieftleys of the age.—You have demonftrated to all Europe, with a blaze of loyalty almoft unex-
ampled in the annals of hiftory, your love and attachment
to your king and country. You have ftood boldly forward
in the face of the day, the ftrenuous champions of the nobleft caufe that ever warmed and animated the heart of
man. You have demonftrated to all the world, in the moft
fplendid manner, with an effufion of honeft zeal that will
do honour to your feelings to the lateft pofterity, that *you
will* no longer *fuffer your conftitution* to be *defamed,* your
religion to be *blafphemed,* nor your *king* to be *calumniated* by
a gang of impoftors, who impudently prefume to call

N   themfelves

themfelves Englifhmen. Can that man be an Englifhman who labours inceffantly to deftroy the civil and
ecclefiaftical eftablifhment of the country? It is true,
you have fhewn moft noble, moft manly refentment,
againft the turbulent incendiaries of the times. But remember, my countrymen, Paine and Prieftley ftill live;
their works are not yet buried:—one rotten fheep, they
fay, will pollute a whole flock; a little leaven will agitate
and ferment a large mafs; two turbulent haranguing foldiers have been known to make a whole army mutiny.
Beware of thefe men, my countrymen! One of them, in
fpite of the penal ftatute, will fell you blafphemy enough
for two-pence to contaminate and blaft a whole county,
and the other treafon enough for fixpence to convulfe and
difmember a whole kingdom. What then is to be done
with thefe callous, hardened delinquents? What further
marks of public deteftation would you wifh to fix on them?
The grand jury of Middlefex (as was obferved in the letter
preceding this) prefented the pofthumous works of Boling-
broke as public nuifances. Why not then, my countrymen, prefent the works of Paine and Prieftley as
public nuifances? Are they not nuifances of the firft
magnitude, of the moft dangerous tendency? Contain they
not doctrines declaredly inimical to church and ftate? declaredly fubverfive of both? Prefent them, then, at the
next grand inqueft of the nation, at every county affize in
the kingdom, and infift on their being burnt by the hands
of the common hangman, in token of your abhorrence—
boldly declaring to the world, as hath been obferved before,
—that *you will no longer fuffer* your *conftitution* to be
blackened and reviled, your *God* to be *blafphemed*, nor your
King to be *calumniated* with impunity.

Cirencefter.

CAUSIDICUS.

It

It is reported in Eufebius, " that the apoftle St. John going
" one day into a public bath, faw Cerinthus there, one
" of the firft oppofers of the Divinity of the Saviour,
" and depravers of the gofpel.   The apoftle inftantly
" retreated at the fight of fo abandoned an infidel, with
" the ftrongeft marks of abhorrence and indignation in
" his countenance."   Dr. Johnfon being on a vifit to
Pembroke College, Prieftley's arrival was announced;
the moment Johnfon faw him enter, he retired with the
greateft precipitation, impreffed, no doubt, with the fame
ideas as the apoftle at the fight of Cerinthus.   On the
above anecdotes the following lines are built.

    JOHN faw Cerinthus in the bath; he faw
    The monfter, and lo! inftant did withdraw,
    Dreading left heaven fhould fudden vengeance fend,
    To crufh the wretch who durft the Chrift offend;
    To crufh the wretch who durft the *Chrift deny*,
    And God the *Father* in the *Son* defy.
    Johnfon *faw* Prieftley, *faw*, and big with ire,
    Behold! the good old man with fpeed retire;
    Fearing, no doubt, fome fad tremendous doom,
    With fuch a rank blafphemer in the room.
    Th' apoftle and the fage both felt the fame;
    What honeft Chriftian can their conduct blame?

                              CAUSIDICUS.

No. XI.

*Copy of an Advertisement in the Birmingham News-
paper, relating to the Address to me from the Philosophical Society at Derby.*

ADVERTISEMENT.

Derby, Oct. 3, 1791.

AN address to Dr. Priestley having been inserted
in Mr. Pearson's paper, as agreed upon at a meeting of the
Philosophical Society in Derby, Sept. 3, 1791; it is
thought expedient by some of the members, who were not
privy to the address, who cannot approve of it, and who
think it improper a few individuals should publish their
own sentiments as those of the society at large, to inform
the public, that the same was agreed to, and fabricated by
only five members of the society out of thirty-seven; and
that in consequence thereof, at the General Annual Meeting, on Saturday, October first, the following resolution
was agreed to: That in future no act of publicity shall
be carried into effect, except at an annual meeting, or
at a monthly one, a fortnight's previous notice being
given of the business to every member of the society.

No. XII.

An Answer to the preceding by the Society.

SIR,

AN advertisement, misrepresenting a transac-
tion of the Philosophical Society at Derby, having been
inserted in a late newspaper, it is judged proper to refute it
by a statement of the following circumstances.

I. That

I. That all bufinefs of the fociety, viz. the electing members, ordering in books, and enacting new laws and regulations, has been conftantly, fince the firft inftitution of the fociety, tranfacted at the monthly meetings.

II. That of thirty-feven members, thirteen only are refident in the town, and that the addrefs to Dr. Prieftley was voted unanimoufly at a regular monthly meeting, at which was prefent the ufual number of attending members, and that as it contained no reference to the doctor's *political opinions*, and even recommended to him to decline thofe theological controverfies which feem to have provoked the vengeance of his adverfaries, it was conceived that no man of a liberal mind would object to the congratulating him on his efcape from the violence of an enraged mob; and that there could be no member of a *philofophical* fociety who did not regret the demolition of his valuable laboratory and manufcripts; and on that prefumption they judged it unneceffary to delay till another month, a meafure which, from the relation in which Dr. Prieftley ftands to all philofophical focieties, feemed peculiarly and immediately proper on the prefent occafion.

III. That at the half-yearly meeting on the firft of October, Mr. Hope was the only perfon who exprefled a difapprobation of the addrefs, declaring that his reafon for doing it was his differing from Dr. Prieftley in political fentiments, adding, that no man could refpect the doctor's religious and philofophical opinions more highly than himfelf.

IV. That, when the late propofition was made for giving a fortnight's notice previous to all public tranfactions of the fociety, fo far from its being underftood to be a cenfure on the addrefs, (as is very difingenuoufly infinuated in the advertifement referred to) the gentleman who moved the propofition, prefaced it by declaring that he intended

nothing

nothing lefs than a difapprobation of the meafure; for fo defirous was he of expreffing his refpect to Dr. Prieftley as a philofopher, and his abhorrence of all perfecution as a man, that he felt a fingular mortification at having been precluded from figning the addrefs, by not having received previous information of fuch a circumftance being intended; and that on that account alone he was induced to propofe a regulation for fimilar occafions which might occur in future.

The members of the philofophical fociety, refident in and near Derby, having been fummoned to an extraordinary meeting, *exprefsly* to take into confideration the advertifement in the Derby newfpaper, of which the Rev. Mr. Hope avowed himfelf to be the author,

It was refolved unanimoufly, by ballot,

That the Rev. Mr. Hope having, in defiance of the refolution made at the laft general meeting, committed an act of publicity, by printing in the Derby newfpaper the refolution of the fociety without its knowledge or confent, and having in his advertifement infidioufly mifreprefented an act of the fociety, and Mr. Hope having been this day fully heard upon the fubject, and not having explained his conduct to the fatisfaction of the meeting, It is the opinion of this meeting, that he be defired to withdraw his name from the lift of the fociety.

Derby,
Oct. 10, 1791.

R. ROE, Secretary.

No. XIII.

No. XIII.

A Defcription of an Allegorical Medal publifhed at Birmingham fince the Riot.

This Day is publifhed,

DEDICATED TO ALL REVOLUTIONISTS IN THE BRITISH DOMINIONS,

AN ALLEGORICAL MEDAL!

1791-2.

OBVERSE.

THE demon or evil genius of the 14th of July, is difplaying her democratic ftandard; the flag contains a king's crown, furrounded with drops of blood, alluding to the regicide of the laft century. On the top is a cap of liberty, the miftaken idea of which is the fource of all her enormities. The young fiends fhe cherifhes proves her prolific wickednefs, which illuftrates this motto:

" OUR FOOD IS SEDITION."

REVERSE.

A Viper in the grafs;—this character cannot be better illuftrated than where hiftory proves that his fubtilty brought mifery on all mankind. He here partakes of the bleffings of heaven and earth, at the fame time, in fecret covert, is premeditating deftruction againft the very caufe of his comfort. The motto,

" NOURISHED TO TORMENT,"

fhews the reftlefs ingratitude of a corrupt and difloyal heart.

N 4 No. XIV.

No. XIV.

' *An Account of the Clergy of Birmingham refusing to walk in funeral Processions with Dissenting Members since the Riot.*

IN this present month of October 1792, the Rev. Mr. Scholefield was requested by the surviving relatives of one of his hearers (of the name of Thomson) to attend at the funeral, to which he readily assented, but enquired at which of the churches the corpse was to be interred, and whether the clergyman had been apprized of the intention of the family respecting the invitation given to himself. These questions were put to the daughter of the deceased, and before she had replied to them, the son came in, who had just then been to the Rev. Mr. Young, lecturer of St. Paul's Chapel, (where it was intended to inter the corpse) and his report was, that when he gave Mr. Young an invitation to attend the funeral from the house of the deceased, he very readily assented; but, upon being told that Mr. Scholefield was expected there, and that it was hoped he would have no objection to going in the same coach with him, he said, at first, that he did not know, but after a very short pause, added, " the clergy of the town had " come in general to a resolution not to ride or walk with " any Dissenting Minister at a funeral."

This declaration from Mr. Young is the more remarkable, as he has rode in the same coach with Mr. Scholefield upon a former similar occasion.

No. XV.

Extract of a Letter written to me by a Person who was in my Library during the Demolition of the House, in Answer to one in which I had requested his Evidence concerning it.

Birmingham, March 5, 1791.

DEAR SIR,

I DEEM it right thus immediately to inform you, that I did not arrive at your house till after the destruction of the library. The road for half a mile of my approach was strewed with your books, the mob were carrying others away, and there was not above twelve octavos on the shelves when I entered the room, the floor of which was totally covered, two or three inches deep, with torn leaves, chiefly manuscript. The books that I saw collected at the top of the field behind the house with part of the furniture, were those, I presume, which were the only ones saved.

No. XVI.

An Address of the Dissenters and Delegates of the Dissenters in England, to the Sufferers in the Riot at Birmingham.

To the Protestant Dissenters of the Town and Neighbourhood of Birmingham, who suffered from the Riots which happened in the month of July last.

WE, the assembled deputies and delegates of the Protestant Dissenters of England, in the name of the numerous and respectable body of our constituents, feel it

incumbent

incumbent on us thus publicly to teſtify our aſtoniſhment and horror at the outrages which you have experienced from an ignorant and miſguided multitude, and our reſpect for that manly fortitude with which you have ſupported theſe unmerited ſufferings.

While however, as ſuſtaining one common character, we are anxious to pay this ſincere tribute of affectionate and fraternal ſympathy to all our injured brethren, we are perſuaded that we ſhall gratify alike your feelings and our own, when, waving our various ſpeculative and eſpecially our theological differences, we deſire to expreſs our peculiar concern on the account of that diſtinguiſhed individual, whom the rancour of this cruel perſecution ſelected as the firſt victim of its rage.—Deeply convinced of the importance of truth, we unite in admiring the ardour which he has ever diſcovered in the purſuit of it; as freemen, we applaud his unremitted exertions in the great cauſe of civil and religious liberty; as friends to literature, we are proud of our alliance with a name ſo juſtly celebrated as that of Dr. Prieſtley; and we pray the Almighty Diſpoſer of events long to continue to us and to the world, a life which ſcience and virtue have contributed to render illuſtrious.

We rejoice in the thought, that, though loaded with calumny and overwhelmed by violence, you have not yet been diſgraced by one ſerious imputation of a crime; and it is therefore reaſonable to confide in the juſtice of your country for an ample reparation of the wrongs you have ſuſtained.—But, in proportion to your innocence, the infamy of theſe proceedings falls with accumulated weight on the authors and the perpetrators of ſuch miſchief; nor can we avoid obſerving in the circumſtances of this tranſaction evident ſymptoms either of ſome groſs defect in our general ſyſtem of police, or of the moſt ſupine and culpable negligence in thoſe whoſe immediate duty it was to have pro-

tected

tected the places of public worſhip, as well as the lives and property, of their fellow-citizens; and we truſt that the executive government, which exerted ſo much laudable activity to repreſs the diſorders on the firſt notice, will proceed more fully to vindicate its own dignity and the national honour, by ſeriouſly inquiring how it came to paſs that they were permitted to riſe unchecked to ſuch a height of deſtructive fury.

Whatever may be the event, we deſire to aſſure you of our warmeſt affection, of our ſteadieſt ſupport. Although in this inſtance the ſtorm has fallen on you alone, we all feel ourſelves to have been equally within the aim of the ſpirit which directed it; nor ſhall we ever attempt to elude ſimilar violence by meanly abandoning the common cauſe, or deſerting our brethren in the hour of diſtreſs.

Our adverſaries betray little acquaintance with the character and principles of the men whom they preſume to inſult and vilify, if they imagine that the ſpirit of the Diſſenters is to be ſubdued and broken by the means which have been employed at Birmingham. Such meaſures can only tend to cement more cloſely our bond of union, and to invigorate our efforts to procure the repeal of thoſe invidious and injurious laws, by which we are held forth as the proper objects of ſuſpicion and inſult to the unthinking vulgar.

Perſuaded that we have never merited thoſe abſurd and malicious imputations by which ignorance and bigotry have always attempted to excuſe illegal violence, we boldly appeal for our juſtification to our general conduct, whenever on great national emergencies we have been drawn forth to action. We cannot point out any other criterion of our principles as a body, than the uniform tenor of our public conduct. We know that on ſuch occaſions we ſhall be found ever to have ſhewn the moſt affectionate and invariable

riable attachment to the conftitution of this kingdom, as fettled on the principles of the glorious revolution, on which alone depends the title of the prefent auguft family to the Britifh throne; and on this fair and open ground we challenge any clafs of our enemies to a comparifon.

But although we have no wifh to conceal our fentiments, yet maintaining, as we fhall never ceafe to do, the equal right of every citizen to all the common benefits of fociety, we apprehend that to call on us to purchafe protection, fafety, or even the good opinion of our fellow-fubjects, by any avowal which the law does not require of all, or by any filence which it does not univerfally enjoin; is an affumption of fuperiority, which liberal minds will difclaim, and to which, confcious of no inferiority but in numbers, of no guilt but the love of liberty and of our country, we fee not the fmalleft reafon to fubmit.

We truft that our countrymen will at length difcover that it is not our fault if fome degree of difcontent be ever the effect of oppreffion. We fhall not relinquifh the attempt to convince them, that civil diftinctions founded on religious differences, are the real fource of the difturbances which have fo frequently arifen among contending fects in the fame community; and we flatter ourfelves that Britain, which formerly took the lead in religious toleration, will not be the laft nation in the world to acknowledge the juft claims of religious liberty; but that the day will arrive much fooner than thofe imagine, who reflect not on the prefent afpect and tendencies of human affairs, when the good fenfe of our country will admit us to that equal rank for which we contend, and when all fhall cordially concur to efface the ftain which the late outrages have fixed on our national character.

Signed by the unanimous order of the meeting,

King's Head, Poultry,   EDW. JEFFRIES, Chairman.
London, February 1, 1792.
8

No. XVII.

The Answer by the Sufferers.

To the Deputies and Delegates of the Proteftant Diffenters of England, affembled in London.

Birmingham, April 22, 1792.

GENTLEMEN,

WE the fufferers by the late riots in the town and neighbourhood of Birmingham, were highly gratified by the reception of your affectionate addrefs, and though local circumftances and confiderations have retarded our acknowledgment of it, we have not been the lefs fenfible of its value, or unmindful of the return it fo forcibly demands from us. Though we were never fo fenfible of the value of our common faith as at this trying period, though its invigorating principles were not before this æra either juftly known, or fully experienced; though we have derived continual fupport, as well as unfpeakable fatisfaction and comfort from them, yet we confefs they receive frefh energy from the friendly fympathy, and the truly Chriftian fpirit, which you have manifefted upon this trying occafion.

We rejoice that, notwithftanding all the opprobrium our malicious adverfaries are endeavouring to caft upon us, you have the firmnefs and generofity to ftep forth and acknowledge us as brethren. We rejoice that at the very inftant in which our common principles are made the fubject of general cenfure and ridicule, your truly refpectable body has given public teftimony to their efficacy, and generoufly acted upon them, by thus holding out to us the right hand of fellowfhip. Perfecuted, and injured as we have been, and ftill are, an addrefs of fympathy and condolence from fo

refpectable

respectable a body as the assembled deputies and delegates of the Proteftant Diffenters of England, fent in the name of your numerous conftituents, gives us a fatisfaction we cannot defcribe, and affords a profpect which reanimates our fpirits and revives our beft hopes. Fully perfuaded of the truth of our principles, of the juftice of our caufe, and confcious of none but benevolent views in our public efforts, we are determined to perfevere in fupport of thofe great truths which have been too long concealed from the world.

The honourable mention you make of that noble individual who has done fo much to enlighten the minds of his countrymen, as well as to extend fcience, was by no means the leaft pleafing part of your addrefs. Nothing but the perfonal fafety and happinefs of him, at whofe praife even the tongue of fcandal is forced to be filent, could have in any degree reconciled us to his lofs. We efteem him as the friend of the whole human race, and as an honour to his country; but the world knows not his value; his country is infenfible of his worth. The full effect of his ftrenuous exertions in his paftoral duty alone cannot at prefent be computed. It will be more and more felt, and acknowledged. In the fpace of eleven years he has erected a monument more fubftantially founded than the pyramids of the Eaft, and infcribed it with characters which fhall furvive the wreck of nature; we mean in the minds of youth enlightened and improved by his inftructions.

There is a time coming, and we truft it is at no great diftance, when the foolifh and ignorant perfons who perpetrated thofe difmal acts which you lament, and which we cannot think upon without horror, will be fenfible of their folly. Pofterity will ftamp an anathema on them. The broad blot of this infamy muft alfo remain to tarnifh the annals of our country. Hiftory muft relate, that

at

at the clofe of the eighteenth century fhe moft virtuous and ufeful members of the community of Great Britain, were oppreffed and perfecuted without fympathy from the multitude, and that a meft diftinguifhed individual met with opprobrium and infolence from a country which he had endeavoured through life to ferve in every way that benevolence, fcience, and uprightnefs, could point out. To have our names tranfmitted to pofterity with his, as thofe who have incurred reproach for their firm adherence to the principles of civil and religious liberty, is an honour which we did not anticipate, but of which we would not be deprived.

Be affured, Gentlemen, that we fhall cheerfully concur with you in your endeavours to obtain the repeal of all penal ftatutes in matters of religion, hoping that unanimity in the grand principles of liberty and truth will unite the common body of Diffenters, and that they will perfevere in their endeavours till thofe intolerant and unchriftian ftatutes, which have fo long been a difgrace to our code, fhall be expunged from it.

We remain,

Gentlemen, &c.

Signed in the name, and with the unanimous concurrence of a general meeting of fufferers,

WILLIAM RUSSELL.

No. XVIII.

An Account of the Alarm and Loſs of Mr. Carpenter of Woodrow, in a Letter from his Brother.

W. RUSSELL, ESQ. DIGBETH, BIRMINGHAM.

Woodrow, near Bromſgrove, May 9, 1792.

SIR,

THE firſt intelligence we had of the riots in Birmingham, was on the 15th of July, but being extremely buſy in haymaking, we paid but little attention to it, thinking the civil power would ſoon reſtore every thing to peace and order again. However, on the following evening ſeveral of our neighbours who had been at Bromſgrove, came to inform us that the Woodrow was in the liſt of proſcribed houſes, and that my eldeſt brother's life was threatened. This alarmed us; but my brother, not chooſing to truſt to theſe reports, went to Bromſgrove to gain more authentic information. He returned about eleven o'clock, and informed us that the reports ſeemed but too true, that many of the lower claſs of people in Bromſgrove ſeemed very much diſpoſed to rioting, ſome of them calling after him as he rode along the ſtreet, ſaying, that the meeting-houſes ſhould come down the next day, and curſing the Preſbyterians with the utmoſt bitterneſs.

At twelve o'clock we were ſurpriſed by a poſt-chaiſe driving to the door; it contained Mr. and Mrs. Benton, the nurſe maid, and ſeveral children: they came to beg a night's lodging, as they durſt not ſtop any longer ſo near Birmingham, either in their own houſe or with their friends; and ſo precipitate was their flight, that they were obliged to bring

the

the children out of bed with only their night clothes on—
Poor little innocents! it was a diftreffing fight to fee them,
and ftill more diftreffing not to be able to afford them a fafe
afylum : for, on hearing our dangerous fituation, Mrs. Benton
thought it moft prudent to go farther on. Brother Thomas, myfelf, and a neighbour, then went to the top of the
Lickey, from whence we could plainly fee a large houfe in
flames towards Birmingham ; this proved but a poor confolation, and we returned home with heavy hearts. At fix
o'clock on Sunday morning we difpatched two meffengers,
one to Bromfgrove, the other to Birmingham. The latter
returned about eleven o'clock with an account that a large
party of the rioters were gone to burn Kingfwood Meeting,
and from thence they would proceed to the Woodrow.
My brother alfo returned from Bromfgrove with fimilar
information. I immediately took our moft valuable papers
and writings, and buried them in a neighbour's garden. It
was alfo thought moft prudent to remove part of our furniture ; but where to take them was the queftion, as our
neighbours, though many of them were willing, durft not
take them in, for fear of bringing a mob after them, and
thereby endangering their property. After a fhort conful-
tation it was thought moft advifable to fend it to Kidderminfter. We immediately packed up our plate, linen, beds,
books, &c. &c. and fent off three waggon loads (including
a quantity of wool) in the afternoon. At the fame time
my mother, fifter, and youngeft nephew, went to Boar-
cote, where they found an afylum at the houfe of Mr. Cox,
who treated them with the utmoft kindnefs. We fat up
all night, (indeed we had never a bed left in the houfe, had
any of us been difpofed for one) and kept a ftrong guard
both in and around the houfe.

On Monday morning we had information that the rioters
were difperfed in parties around the country, committing

O   various

various depredations; and that the soldiers were too few in number to leave Birmingham in pursuit of them.

Parties of people from Bromsgrove and its vicinity went to join the rioters; and about one or two o'clock a number of people from this neighbourhood collected together upon Round Hill, half a mile from the Woodrow, to be ready in all appearance to join the rioters when they came   In this party were several who had been heard to threaten brother John in the most violent manner. Things wearing such a serious aspect at this time, we thought proper to remove the remainder of our houshold effects, which we conveyed into the fields, and hid among the corn, or buried in the earth. Brother Thomas and myself also removed our wheat and flour from the mill. A very violent shower happily dispersed the people on Round Hill, and also prevented the Birmingham rioters from coming forwards.

About nine o'clock in the evening a gentleman rode to the Woodrow, and said he had left a body of the rioters on the top of the Lickey marching towards the Woodrow, their number uncertain. Brother John then determined to defend his house, and desired his men to prepare for action; but at length, from the excessive importunity of those about him, he gave it up, and left his house for the first time, with the melancholy prospect of never seeing it again. He had not rode more than a mile before he fell in with fifteen or sixteen rioters with blue cockades in their hats, and armed with bludgeons. On my brother's inquiring where they were going, several of them answered, *to burn Mr. Carpenter's house, according to orders from justice Carles*. My brother perceiving they did not know him, said, Why, I thought Mr. Carpenter was a good sort of a man, why should you wish to burn his house? The answer was, he may be a very good sort of a man for all we

know,

know, but *we have juſtice Carles's orders*, and down it ſhall come. On being aſked for what reaſon, they ſaid, *for being at the hotel.* My brother then told them they had better go to Bromſgrove, and get ſomething to drink, and ſome more gentlemen coming up, and giving the ſame advice, they thought beſt to follow it.

The next morning (Tueſday), on their return from Bromſgrove, they called at the Woodrow to beg ſomething to drink, and, while brother Thomas went to draw ſome beer, they attempted to go into the houſe, but our men prevented them. After pillaging ſeveral of the poor people's houſes as they went along, they ſtopped at a public houſe about two miles from the Woodrow. Brother John returned home about half an hour after the rioters went away; and, as ſoon as he heard where they were, ſet off to Birmingham to procure ſome ſoldiers, and take them priſoners. In the mean time a Mr. Lane, who ſaid he was a conſtable from Birmingham (and who, as I am ſince informed, died through exceſſive fatigue in the zealous performance of his duty), called at the Woodrow, and, on my informing him where the rioters were, ſaid he would go and take them if I could get ſome reſolute people we could depend upon to go with us. I immediately rode to Bromſgrove, and called ſeveral of my friends together, whom I found willing to join us; but as no member of the eſtabliſhed church would go with us, it was given up for fear of giving offence. My brother returned from Birmingham in the evening, and gave the following account of his interview with the juſtices. On his introduction he informed them that a party of the rioters had been at his houſe that morning, and came, as they informed him, the preceding evening, by the order of juſtice Carles, to burn his houſe down; and, as he knew where they were, begged the favour of half a dozen light horſe to ſecure them: but

O 2

this requeſt not being granted, my brother offered to take
them without the aſſiſtance of the military, if it met with
their approbation: but their approbation was not given.
Mr. Carles aſked my brother if he knew ever an honeſt
Preſbyterian about the Lickey? My brother ſaid he did not
come there to talk about religion, he wiſhed to prove himſelf a good citizen, and thought he was doing his duty by
endeavouring to ſecure a ſet of lawleſs villains who were
plundering the innocent inhabitants of the country. My
brother was aſked if he was at the hotel on the 14th of
July?—Yes. What toaſts did you drink?—Several; the
king, for one. We don't believe it.—It is true. Will you
ſwear it?—Yes. Dr. Spencer then offered him a bible for
that purpoſe: my brother was going to take it, when the
Doctor changed his mind, and put the book down.

It is inconceivable the fatigue we underwent, and the
anxiety we felt during the riots. On the Monday I was
on horſeback, reconnoitring, &c. near fifteen hours, and
wet to the ſkin through two great coats, and was at laſt ſo
overcome with fatigue that I could ſcarcely ſit on my
horſe. Brother Thomas put on his boots on Sunday morning, and did not pull them off till Wedneſday night. My
mother and ſiſter were in continual fear left brother John
ſhould loſe his life, as it was ſo repeatedly threatened. We
eſtimate our loſs in damage, loſs of poperty, expences, &c.
at near 60l.

I am, ſir,

Your moſt obedient ſervant,

Wм. CARPENTER.

P. S. A man whom we ſent to gain intelligence on the
Sunday, fell in with the rioters at Mr. Wakeman's houſe
near Kingſwood: he ſaw the general, as he was ſtyled,
pull

pull a paper out of his pocket, which feemed to be a lift of houfes, and, on looking over it, faid, " that houfe was to " come down; but, as Mr. Wakeman had behaved fo " well, it fhould ftop a little longer, but that they would " come back, and pull it down before the next morning."

No. XIX.

An Account of the High Church Spirit which has long prevailed at Stourbridge.

AS the violent High Church fpirit which produced the riot at Birmingham has been generally afcribed to *me*, I have taken fome pains to inquire into the ftate of fome of the neighbouring places in that refpect; and thinking that from *Stourbridge* (which it is fomething remarkable I never was at except in once riding through it) to be as much to my purpofe as any, I fhall give it, as collected from different perfons, whofe accounts, I have no doubt, may be depended upon.

The Prefbyterian church at Stourbridge was founded by Mr. Foley, an anceftor of the prefent Lord Foley, the members of which church firft affembled in his houfe for public worfhip. This houfe has fince been converted to an inn, and the room now called the Old Affembly Room was the room ufed for that purpofe. Mr. Foley's domeftic chaplain (a Mr. Flower) was their paftor

O 3   for

for many years. About this time the faid Mr. Foley erected a large building for the reception of fixty poor boys, whom he directed fhould be clothed in a blue uniform, lodged and boarded in the houfe, and taught reading, writing, and merchants' accounts; and that afterwards they fhould be placed out with a fmall premium to fuch trades, and to fuch mafters, as the boys and their parents fhould approve of. This good man lived to fee his benevolent defign carried into execution; and, having amply endowed the charity with confiderable eftates, it has continued to this day to anfwer the ends for which it was intended, as many opulent tradefmen now living, who were educated there, can with gratitude teftify. For feveral years laft paft the feoffees of this inftitution have not permitted any Diffenter to take a boy from the fchool as an apprentice.

A Diffenting tradefman now living, who had an apprentice from thence about thirty years fince, applied for one fome years afterwards, and was told by the feoffees, that his requeft could not be complied with, as it was their determination that no Diffenter fhould have a boy from that fchool.

A gentleman of Bewdley, now living, applied about ten years fince for an apprentice: the firft queftion the feoffees afked him was, whether he was a Diffenter, and, upon replying in the affirmative, he received the fame anfwer *. Knowing that the founder of the inftitution was a Diffenter, one would have thought that the principles of common integrity would have prevented them from fuch a fhameful perverfion of the intention of the donor: but, where bigotry fupplies the place of charity and candour, fhame is

---

* I have frequently heard that the feoffees are equally careful in preventing the children of poor Diffenters from gaining an admittance into the faid School.

generally

generally difcarded, and every profeffion of virtue is little more than a tinkling cymbal.

Owing to the mifmanagement of a former fteward, the feoffees were fome years back much involved in debt, and were obliged to take long credit with goods bought for the ufe of the houfe, fo that nothing induced many tradefmen to continue to fupply them but the expectation of their being better cuftomers in future, which the ftewards always affured them would be the cafe in a few years. A Diffenting tradefman of Stourbridge, who had fupplied them for many years, and with whom they ufually took a credit of two or three years, was informed about eight or ten years fince by the then fteward, who called to difcharge the account with the faid tradefman, that he had orders from the feoffees to go elfewhere for the goods in future. The tradefman being naturally defirous of knowing the reafon of their leaving him, after having done bufinefs with him for fo many years, was importunate with the fteward to be fatisfied on that head, to which (after much hefitation) he replied, that they did not wifh to do bufinefs with Diffenters. Upon this the tradefman defired to know how this objection never occurred to them before, which was fully explained by the fteward, who faid, that formerly they were obliged to get goods where they could, but that now, as feveral leafes of eftates had dropped, their finances were in fuch a ftate that the feoffees were enabled to pay ready money for all the goods they bought, and, therefore, were determined now to buy of no Diffenter.

It is worthy of remark that one of the prefent feoffees has, or formerly had, in his poffeffion a buft of the late pretender; and that his father was one of a party, whofe ufual practice it was at their convivial meetings to fall upon their knees before the faid buft, and drink each of them

their

their firſt glaſs to the reſtoration of the Stuart family to the throne of theſe kingdoms. Theſe are the men who, with matchleſs effrontery, would now perſuade the nation that they are the only true friends of the conſtitution *.

After the death of Mr. Foley, the congregation of Diſſenters met for public worſhip in a meeting houſe in the Coventry ſtreet; and about the year   , the High Church party aſſembled, and by violence tore up the pews and pulpit, which they burnt with the miniſter's bible, in the midſt of the market. This atrocity the court very properly noticed, brought the perpetrators thereof to puniſhment, and ordered the place to be new pewed, the expence of which was paid out of the treaſury. I have heard of no abſolute violence exerciſed againſt the Diſſenters of that town ſince that period; but, until the preſent rector of the pariſh, of which Stourbridge is a part, came to reſide there, a ſtiffneſs and unkindneſs on the part of the Epiſcopalians was obſervable towards them. Two circumſtances which happened in one family will tend to ſatisfy any perſon of the truth of this remark.

A clergyman of the pariſh having been invited to the funeral of a Diſſenter, and obſerving, upon his being introduced into the room where the bearers were aſſembled, that Mr. Edge, the Diſſenting miniſter, was one of the party, left the houſe in anger, and ſent his clerk to apologize for his conduct by ſaying that, " as he could not ride " with Mr. Edge, if they would ſend his hatband and

* The enmity of this gentleman to the Diſſenters may in ſome meaſure be accounted for. An anceſtor of his having by will left a large ſum of money to the father of the ſaid gentleman, IN TRUST, to be divided among the indigent Diſſenting miniſters of the midland counties; and he having thought fit to apply the ſame to his own uſe, the aſſociated body of miniſters in London undertook the cauſe, which was at length brought before the Lord Chancellor King, who awarded the money to be applied as the teſtator directed, and the whole of the coſts (which were conſiderable) to be paid by the truſtee.

" ſcarf,

" fcarf, he would meet the corpfe at the church." The hatband and fcarf were very properly refufed, and he was obliged to bury the corpfe without them.

Another clergyman of the parifh being invited to a funeral in the fame family, and having an equal diflike to ride with the Diffenting minifter, had the art to difguife that diflike until he had procured his hatband and fcarf, and till the proceffion was ready to move, when he galloped through the town before the hearfe to the aftonifhment of the fpectators. The names of thefe clergymen were Brown and Male, and the facts are perfectly in the remembrance of many perfons now living: but it is juftice due to Mr. Male to fay that he lived to fee the folly of his conduct, and afterwards became a very liberal man.

As was hinted before, the intercourfe between the people of the Eftablifhment and the Diffenters of Stourbridge was much increafed by the prefent rector fettling among them. Soon after he came he requefted to be admitted a member of a reading fociety belonging to the Diffenters, which had been eftablifhed near forty years, and of which the Diffenting minifter was the prefident; his admiffion was followed by that of many gentlemen of the church, and the frequent meetings to tranfact the bufinefs of the fociety tended very much to rub off that ftiffnefs which had before been obfervable in their conduct towards each other. Upon the refignation of the Diffenting minifter another Diffenter was chofen prefident; and the fame unanimity continued to prevail until the fociety was diffolved for the purpofe of forming a different inftitution.

The Diffenters were thus led to fuppofe that the former hatred of them by the Church was done away, and they were pleafing themfelves with the perfuafion, until the breaking out of the riots at Birmingham completely con-

vince

vince them of their miftake. For no fooner did the news reach Stourbridge, but the moft violent invectives were poured forth againft the Diffenters by the fame perfons who had before profeffed fo much liberality and kindnefs towards them. Every thing was faid which could tend to ftir up the minds of the people; the circulation of the handbill was charged upon a Diffenter, the report was propagated with great induftry, and they heard from all quarters that their meeting houfe, and the houfes of the Diffenters, would be levelled with the ground. The public houfes were feveral of them filled with men who were ready to embark in the diabolical bufinefs; and, had it not been for the vigilance of an active magiftrate, God only knows what would have been the confequence.

Thus difappointed, they evinced their determination to injure their Diffenting brethren, by withdrawing their cuftom from the fhops of Diffenters, fome of whom find their bufinefs much decreafed. One tradefman, who had been in the habit of fupplying many of the firft families in the neighbourhood with goods, loft, immediately after the riots, thirty families who had for years had ledger accounts with him, befides many other ready money cuftomers, and yet could never hear of the leaft charge which they had againft him, except that of his being a Diffenter.

Some time before the Birmingham riots, the minifter of a congregation of Diffenters at Cradley, near Stourbridge, interefted himfelf in procuring a fubfcription for building a meeting houfe at a place called the Lye-wafte, about a mile and a half from Stourbridge, a very populous neighbourhood, where the people are extremely ignorant, and where there is no place of worfhip of any denomination. The faid minifter, and the minifter of the congregation at

Stourbridge,

Stourbridge, had engaged to preach alternately when the place fhould be erected, without any falary, actuated by no other motive than the defire of doing good.   Having procured a fufficient fubfcription for the purpofe, they applied to a gentleman of Stourbridge for land to erect the building upon, who readily told them they might have which ever part of his eftate they chofe ; in confequence of which the land was meafured out, and a price was fixed on it by an appraifer, which price was agreed to by both parties; an attorney was fent for, who received inftructions in the prefence of both to prepare articles of conveyance; and bricks were drawn upon the fpot for the building: yet, notwithftanding all this, he afterwards refufed to let them have any part of it.   After the Birmingham riots, other gentlemen who had land at the Lye-wafte were applied to, but they all refufed to fell their land for fuch a purpofe. After this the minifter of Cradley waited upon the rector of the parifh, and affured him that he had no intention of diffeminating any peculiar doctrines, that his only motive was to ferve the beft interefts of his neighbours, and that, if the people of the eftablifhment would fubfcribe towards building a church, he would abandon his defign, and affift them in theirs : but this good young man has been unable to accomplifh either; and the money now lies unemployed, and the poor of that diftrict uninftructed.

Some months previous to the Birmingham riots, the Stourbridge Diffenters had engaged a London minifter to preach a charity fermon at their meeting houfe, on the fecond Sunday in Auguft (which was foon after the riots happened) ; and it is a little remarkable that the rector of the parifh advertifed a charity fermon to be preached by himfelf in his own church, *on the fame day*, though no charity fermon had been preached in that
church

church for fome years before. As the notice was fhort, the fermon was advertifed by handbills diftributed through the parifh, in confequence of which the church was extremely crowded; and, though it was profeffedly a *charity* fermon, the greateft part thercof confifted of invectives againft the Diffenters of Stourbridge and Cradley, and of charges againft the managers of their Sunday Schools which had no foundation in fact. The Diffenters not being prefent, could only hear this account from thofe liberal churchmen who heard the fermon, and who were much difgufted with the virulence of the preacher. Some Diffenters of both congregations waited upon the rector to deny the charges, and to fatisfy him of their untruth— this they were enabled to do; upon which he acknowledged that he had made them upon the teftimony of a woman of diffipated character. However he promifed to contradict what he found he had afferted without good foundation, and to do it in every company where he had an opportunity; but whether he has performed his promife or not, has not yet come to the knowledge of the Diffenters. However the Diffenters have it now in their power to bring ferious charges, and to eftablifh them as facts, againft the managers of the Church Schools. They can prove that a minifter refiding in the parifh threatened a poor wafherwoman with the lofs of her employment in his family, if fhe did not take her child from the Prefbyterian School. And yet it is well known in the parifh that the Diffenters inftruct the children of their fchools in no other than the common doctrines of Chriftianity, in which all Chriftians agree. Thefe are fome of the fcandalous proceedings of thofe who call themfelves the difciples of him who went about doing good.

The intereft of feveral fums of money is annually diftributed

tributed to the poor of the parifh in bread and cloathing, and lately the rector of the parifh, and the minifter of the chapel, have been accuftomed to interrogate the paupers who apply for the faid donations, refpecting the church to which they belong; and thofe who are found to attend the Prefbyterian meeting-houfe lofe the benefit of the faid charities.

ADDITIONS AND CORRECTIONS.

After p. 52, add—The behaviour of one of my maid fervants affords a pretty ftrong prefumption that fome mifchief was defigned me on the fourteenth of July, and that fhe was apprized of it. She afked leave to go and fee her friends fome days before, and defired to ftay a few days after that time. When fhe went, fhe defired the fervant boy to write to her " if any thing happened." She not only was not folicitous about the clothes fhe loft, but evidently dreaded being obliged to attend the affizes. When fhe was fubpœnaed, though on the part of our opponents, fhe endeavoured to evade it, by denying her name; and fhe either actually went to Ireland, or her friends pretended that fhe did, fo that fhe could not be found at the time. Some of her connections were with the High Church party, and from fome of them it is not improbable fhe received a hint that it would be better for her to be out of the way. Many other perfons in the lower clafs appear now to have had the fame apprehenfions of a riot. Nothing of this, however, came to my knowledge, and I had no more apprehenfion of any fuch thing than I had at any other time in my life.

P. 52. l. 16. Read—and it *does not appear that he had any proper authority.*

P. 55. l. 2. Read—*thou wilt make a damned good cock.*

P. 59. l. 16. Read—*on Sunday the other magiftrate.*

P. 72.

P. 72. l. 2. from the bottom.   He has alſo been made ſteward of the manor.

P. 82. l. 7, (b.)   Whatever elſe may be objeſted to my conduſt, it cannot be ſaid that, after the example of my adverſaries, I ever ſhrunk from an inveſtigation into the part I had aſted.   The day that I arrived in London I deſired Mr. Ruſſell, who had to wait on the King's miniſters, to inform them that I was in town, and ready to anſwer any queſtions they might chooſe to put to me relating to the riot; and when the inquiry into the cauſe of it was propoſed in the Houſe of Commons, my friends were authorized by me to ſay, that I wiſhed to be examined on the ſubjeſt at the bar of the Houſe.   But in neither of the caſes were my wiſhes gratified.

P. 83. l. 6. (b.)   Beſides, this was not the only faſt of which he was conviſted.   He was ſeen knocking out the window frames, and beating things to pieces, and he made a fire of the boards he had pulled up.   See the Trial, p. 146, &c.

P. 92. l. 6. (b.)   This, however, was only with reſpeſt to that part of his loſs which Mr. Ruſſell claimed in court. In reality he was probably a loſer to a greater amount.

P. 100.   *At the cloſe of the ſecond paragraph add—* This Mr. Allen was the clergyman who fought a duel with a Mr. Delaney, and killed him.   He may perhaps ſend *me* a challenge; but Diſſenting miniſters do not fight duels.

P. 121.   To the note add—Will he do us the favour to ſay what ſum was ſubſcribed by this moſt reſpeſtable meeting

ing to pay for the prefents they fo generoufly voted, and
will he have the goodnefs to tell us how foon afterwards a
fufficient addition was made to it to defray the coft of them,
and when the plate was prefented to thefe worthy magiftrates?

P. 127. l. 4. (b.) dele, *and that of all who were prefent at
the time he refers to.*

P. 132. l. 5. (b.) dele, *and I believe even afterwards followed by fome of the mob.*

P. 142. Note, read, when the brothels, and Mr. Brooks's
houfe, were in danger in May laft.

P. 143. l. 7. Read—*which, notwithftanding the party
fpirit which has fo long governed fome bigots among us.*

Till the whole of this part of my *Appeal* was printed off,
I never read the *Letter* addreffed to me on my *Addrefs to
the fubfcribers to the Birmingham library,* No. III. of this
Appendix, by SOMEBODY M. S. printed in 1787, and generally afcribed to Mr. Clutton, a clergyman in Birmingham, whofe fermon on the fubject of the Teft Laws Mr.
Madan laments was not publifhed. Having had a copy
of this Letter fent me, I have had the curiofity to read
it through, and have been not a little amufed with the
fcurrility with which it abounds; and for the amufement
of my readers, as well as to give them a fpecimen of the
fpirit which actuated the Birmingham clergy, and to enable them to judge of the tendency of their writing, and
no doubt of their preaching and daily converfation, to
inflame the minds of the common people againft me, I
fhall quote fome paffages from it. But I wifh that my

                                                    readers

readers would firſt peruſe the *Addreſs* which occaſioned this extraordinary Letter, and alſo my *Appeal to the Profeſſors of Chriſtianity*, to which it alludes.

According to this Mr. Clutton, I am, p. 25, " a de- " luded viſionary;" " a proud and haughty ſcorner," p. 4; and " a ſecret aſſaſſin," p. 19. He accuſes me both of " daring oppoſition, and ſubtle ſtratagem," p. 21; of " covered artifices to deceive the unwary," p. 1; and like- wiſe of " outrageous bellowing," p. 25.

My *Appeal to the Profeſſors of Chriſtianity*, he calls " poiſon, and an engine of ſedition," p. 5; conſiſting of " plauſible, but treacherous reaſoning, ſubtle ſophiſtry, nay, " a murderous pamphlet," p. 17.

With reſpect to my general character, I am " a pub- " lic nuiſance," p. 38. and " muſt not expect to go un- " horſewhipped." I have " forfeited all indulgence, and " muſt expect every ſpecies of deſerved retaliation, that " thoſe who have been injured by me, their friends, and " allies, can inflict," p. 44.

My " attachment to Chriſtianity," he ſays, p. 13, is " ideal;" for I am " ſunk into the gulph of deiſm," p. 36. He adviſes me to " go to a free country," (meaning, I ſup- poſe, either France or America) " which has no laws, no " rulers, no religion." " There," ſays he, p. 40, " you " may give the reins to your reaſon, gratify your appetites, " and let looſe all your luſts." But whether I go to this country or not, " a hideous gulph," (by which he evi- dently means hell) " is gaping for me, and my fol- " lowers," p. 39.

Beſides

Besides more such language as this, which, as coming from a clergyman, must not be termed *abuse*, he introduces a long epitaph for me, p. 13, of which the following is an extract.

" The assumed meekness and simplicity of the dove,
" hiding the guile and subtlety of the serpent, smoothed his
" wrinkled front. The honey dew of rhetoric flowed from
" his tongue, and became the unsuspected vehicle of the
" poison of asps. Reason, he said, would teach us how to
" weaken the authority and force of scripture, &c. He
" beseeched us, for the credit of the human race, for the
" sake of truth, of conscience, and our immortal souls, to
" pay divine honours to his goddess, &c. &c. &c."

It is some consolation to think, that whether I be able to find a grave or not, my enemies have already taken care to provide me with a sufficient number of epitaphs.

THE END.

www.ingramcontent.com/pod-product-compliance
Lightning Source LLC
Chambersburg PA
CBHW022012110726
47901CB00006B/1498